Cren

Jesus is Lord

THE
GOSPEL OF
John

ROUSAS JOHN
RUSHDOONY

VALLECITO, CALIFORNIA

Library of Congress Catalog Card Number: 00-090839
ISBN:1-879998-16-5

Printed in the United States of America

Other books by
Rousas John Rushdoony

The Institutes of Biblical Law, Vol. I
The Institutes of Biblical Law, Vol. II, Law & Society
The Institutes of Biblical Law, Vol. III, The Intent of the Law
Systematic Theology (2 volumes)
The Biblical Philosophy of History
Foundations of Social Order
The Messianic Character of American Education
The Philosophy of the Christian Curriculum
Christianity and the State
Salvation and Godly Rule
Romans & Galatians
God's Plan for Victory
Politics of Guilt and Pity
Roots of Reconstruction
The One and the Many
Revolt Against Maturity
By What Standard?
Law & Liberty

For a complete listing of available books
by Rousas John Rushdoony and other
Christian reconstructionists, contact:

ROSS HOUSE BOOKS
PO Box 67
Vallecito, CA 95251

Table of Contents

Chapter One
"The Word Was Made Flesh"
(John 1:1-14)

1. In the beginning was the Word, and the Word was with God, and the Word was God.
2. The same was in the beginning with God.
3. All things were made by him; and without him was not anything made that was made.
4. In him was life; and the life was the light of men.
5. And the light shineth in darkness; and the darkness comprehended it not.
6. There was a man sent from God, whose name was John.
7. The same came for a witness, to bear witness of the Light, that all men through him might believe.
8. He was not that Light, but was sent to bear witness of that Light.
9. That was the true Light, which lighteth every man that cometh into the world.
10. He was in the world, and the world was made by him, and the world knew him not.
11. He came unto his own, and his own received him not.
12. But as many as received him, to them gave he the power to become the sons of God, even to them that believe on his name.
13. Which were born, not of blood, not of the will of the flesh, nor of the will of man, but of God.
14. And the Word was made flesh, and dwelt among us (and we beheld his glory, the glory as of the only begotten of the Father), full of grace and truth. (John 1:1-14)

The Gospel of John begins with the same two Greek words, as does Genesis in the Septuagint, the Greek translation of the Old Testament which was in common use in our Lord's day. These two Greek words are translated as "in the beginning" in English. John deliberately chose the opening words of the creation account because he gives us a summary of the history of creation and proceeds to the great work of re-creation, the regeneration of all things. There is also and echo of Proverbs 8:22-31, which begins:

> 22. The LORD possessed me in the beginning of his way, before his works of old.
> 23. I was set up from everlasting, from the beginning, or ever the earth was. (Proverbs 8:22-23).

The great miracle and mystery of the incarnation, of God the Son made flesh, is predicted and previsioned in the Old Testament and celebrated in the New. Paul in Colossians 1:17 declares of Christ, "And he is before all things, and by him all things consist." *Consist* means that all things stand together and are constituted in their nature and being by Him. As they reflected on this great miracle of God made flesh, the apostles were awed in retrospect at what had occurred. The last men and women who had physically seen, heard, and touched Christ, in their old age greeted one another joyfully with the words, "Have you seen?" *"We have seen."* "Have you heard?" *"We have heard."* "Have you touched?" *"We have touched."* John speaks of this in his first letter: "That which was from the beginning, which we have heard, which we have seen with our eyes, which we have looked upon, and our hands have handled, of the Word of life...That which we have seen and heard declare we unto you" (1 John 1:1, 3).

John declares that Jesus Christ is God the Word, the Son by whom all things were made *and* by whom all this shall be remade.

In v. 1, John begins by declaring Jesus Christ to be the Word of God, God Himself. The Greek word is *Logos*, word or speech, the creative, declarative, and binding Word of God who is God the Son. He is eternal and preexistent; it was He who spoke in the Law and the Prophets in that the Old Testament is as much Christ's word as the Sermon on the Mountain. The word is identical with all that God is and has done. Jesus Christ is the incarnation of the Wisdom or Word of God; in Him, deity and humanity are in perfect union and peace, but without confusion.

"In the beginning" means before creation existed or was made. Thus we are told that first, before creation, the Word eternally was. *Second*, we are told that when nothing save God existed, "the Word was made with God," because, *third*, "the Word was God." In Genesis 1:1-3, we are told that the Holy Spirit was with God when creation began; in John 1:1-3, we are told that the Word was there before creation and active in creation.

Because we are created in the image of God, we are speaking, communicating beings. By identifying Jesus Christ as the Word of God, John tells us that through Him, God is communicating to us, and revealing Himself to us, in order to re-establish communion with fallen mankind. Because God made all things, all things are revelational of God: they witness to the triune God. "The heavens declare the glory of God; and the firmament showeth his handyworks" (Ps. 19:1). It is blasphemous to try to "prove" that God is: nothing can exist apart from Him, and all things derive their meaning and proof from Him.

God in His grace and mercy chose Christ to reveal Himself to the human race (Gen. 3:15) in order to destroy the work of the Destroyer. *Second*, He chose a family and a people, Shem and Israel (Gen. 9:26). *Third*, He later narrowed this to the tribe of Judah (Gen. 49:8-12). *Fourth*, God chose a royal line as the line of promise, the House of David (2 Sam. 7:14-16). *Fifth*, the chosen person was declared and predicted (Ps. 2; Isa. 9).

Some theologians speak of three creations: the *first* is described in Genesis 1; the *second* takes place when we are born again in Christ; the *third* is the creation of the new heavens and the new earth, the culmination of the renewal of all things begun in Christ. Others have called attention to the fact that "in (the) beginning" can mean also, "at the root of the universe."

In v. 2, we are told that God the Word "was in the beginning (or, at the root of the universe, i.e., its creator along with God) with God." We are not told that God was the Word, but that the Word was God and *with* God; this makes it clear that, while we have one God, we have here two different Persons of the Godhead described. John here combines the first two clauses of v. 1 to prepare us for the great creative and regenerative word of God the Son. Nothing in creation is to be understood apart from Christ as Creator, and also therefore as Lord and King.

This means that God is not "the unknown God" (Acts 17:23), but the fully expressed God in the Word, Jesus Christ — not exhaustively expressed but truly expressed *to us*. When we know the Son, we know the Father: "He that hath seen me hath seen the Father" (John 14:9). Our Lord speaks of His identity with the Father, and yet His separate Person in these words, among others: "all men should honour the Son, even as they honour the Father" (John 5:23).

John Calvin translated *Word* as *Speech*. God was always totally self-conscious, for the Word was in the beginning with God. There is not, nor ever has been, an unconscious or subconscious aspect to God's being. Psalm 121:3-4 tells us, "He that keepeth thee will not slumber. Behold, he that keepeth Israel shall neither slumber nor sleep." Because Greek philosophy had an evolutionary doctrine of being and of God, John uses the term *Word* or *Speech* to tell us that God, who never changes (Malachi 3:6), is eternally the same, as is God the Word: "Jesus Christ, the same yesterday, and today, and forever" (Heb. 13:8).

"In (the) beginning" is repeated in v. 2. John requires us to remember Genesis 1:1-2 and the creation of all things by God the Father and God the Spirit. In John 1:1, he tells us that God the Word was equally fully present and active at the root of all things, in their creation, so that we are told that all three persons of the Godhead are distinct yet in perfect harmony in their work of creation and re-creation. As the Spirit moved over the face of the waters in the first creation, so too, the Spirit will move over the face of the of the deep in man's being to make us a new creation, and Christ's death and resurrection are the means whereby we have atonement and regeneration.

In v. 3, we are told of the Word, "All things were made by Him; and without Him was not anything made that was made." The Word as Creator is again declared in v. 10. There is a reference to Psalm 33:6, "By the word of the LORD were the heavens made; and all the most of them by the breath of his mouth." Thus, we have already been told in vv. 1-3 that the

Word is God; He was active in creation; the whole of the Law and the Prophets is His self-revelation as well as the words of the Father; and, finally, that all things were made by His fiat word, "by the breath of his mouth."

We are told that "all things were made by Him," and then this is qualified with the statement, "and without Him was not anything made that was made." All things were made by the Father. All things, the whole universe, was created by the triune God; there was no matter before God created it.

The New Testament celebrates this greatness of God the Son, the Word and revelation of God the Father. Some of the central verses setting this forth are the following:

> And to make all men see what is the fellowship of the mystery, which from the beginning of the world hath been hid in God, who created all things by Jesus Christ. (Eph. 3:9)

> For by him were all things created, that are in heaven, and that are in earth, visible and invisible, whether they be thrones, or dominions, or principalities, or powers: all things were created by him and for him. (Col. 1:16)

> (God) hath in these last days spoken unto us by his Son, whom he hath appointed heir of all things, by whom also he made the worlds. (Heb. 1:2)

> Thou are worthy, O LORD, to receive glory and honour and power: for thou hast created all things, and for thy pleasure they are and were created. (Rev. 4:11)

We are told, among other things, in these verses that, *first*, the mystery and meaning of life is set forth by God through Jesus Christ, who created all things. *Second*, all things were "created by him and for him," for His purposes. *Third*, Christ is also the heir of all creation, and we are a part of His inheritance from the Father. *Fourth*, we are here not only to serve God, but also for His "pleasure." In the Greek, the word *thelema*, translates as desire, pleasure, or will. It means here that God created us simply because He willed it; creation itself is an act of grace. Peter speaks of life as grace from God (1 Peter 3:7).

In vv. 1-2, the relationship of the Word to the Father is declared; in v. 3, His relationship to creation is set forth. The word *by* ("all things were made *by* Him") is more accurately *through*: "all things were made *through* Him." In Exodus 3:14, God identifies Himself as "He Who Is," or "I AM THAT I AM."

In the Gospel of John, Jesus makes it clear that He and the Father are one, that He is very God of very God. He therefore declares: "I am the bread of life (John 6:35); I am the light of the world (John 8:12; 9:5); I am the door (John 10:7, 9); I am the good shepherd (John 10:14); I am the resurrection and the life (John 11:25); I am the way, the truth, and the life (John 14:6); I and the true vine (John 15:1)."

Of the Word, John next tells us in v. 4, "In him was life; and the life was the light of men." The Creator, the Word, the eternal God the Son, is the creator and source of life. In creating man, God created mankind in His image, which Scripture tells us is knowledge (Col. 3:10), righteousness, and holiness (Eph. 4:24), having the law of God written in our hearts (Rom. 2:14-15), and dominion (Gen. 1:28).

When men sin, they thus sin against God their maker and against their own nature as an image bearer of God. While creation was *through* the Word, life is *in* the Word, because He is God. When men turn from Christ, they turn from the light and from life. Life is a light in us because our life as God's image bearers requires us to exercise knowledge, righteousness, holiness, law-keeping, and dominion, and we sin against the Word and life when we turn from these things.

John is again echoing the Old Testament. According to Genesis 1:3, God's first creating words were, "Let there be light, and there was light." Psalm 36:9 declares, "For with thee is the fountain of life: in the light shall we see light." God having made us, we malfunction apart from Him, and to deny Him is to love death (Prov. 8:36).

In v. 5, the focus shifts to man's history. In vv. 1 and 2, we have the Word before creation; in v. 3, creation through the Word is declared; in v. 4, man before the Fall is described in terms of the Word; in v. 5, we see man after the Fall: "And the light shineth in the darkness; and the darkness comprehended it not." The darkness is sin, and its consequence, death. Our Lord repeatedly declares Himself to be the light of the world:

> Then spake Jesus again unto them, saying, I am the light of the world: he that followeth me shall not walk in darkness, but shall have the light of life. (John 8:12)

> As long as I am in the world, I am the light of the world. (John 9:5)

> Then Jesus said unto them, yet a little while is the light with you. Walk while ye have the light, lest darkness come upon you: for he that walketh in darkness knoweth not whither he goeth. (John 12:35)

> I am come a light into the world, that whosoever believeth on me should not abide in darkness. (John 12:46)

> And this is the condemnation, that light is come into the world, and men loved darkness rather than the light, because their deeds were evil. (John 3:19)

Jesus Christ, as the Word incarnate, reveals what men are to be in Him. He is the Light of the world; apart from Him, we walk in darkness. Evil men, however, hate the light and love darkness. Light and life are as closely connected as death and darkness. The darkness could not "comprehend" the Word incarnate. The Greek word translated as "comprehended" is *katelambanem*; it means apprehend and comprehend, so that John, who may be using it in both senses, says that the world of darkness, fallen men, could neither understand the Word nor seize and take possession of Him. By His resurrection, Christ destroyed the power of sin and death: they could not take possession of Him. He who created all things came to restore and reconstruct all things; the powers of darkness sought to prevent this and failed. The world of darkness hates the light and seeks vainly to put it out, but the Light is now shining because it cannot be put out.

In vv. 6-8, John the Baptist is introduced, of whom more is said later. These verses witness the greatness of John. *First*, John "was a man sent from God." *Second*, he was sent to bear witness to the Light, but he was not himself that Light. This statement should wake us up to a significant fact, the greatness of John's impact. Men asked John if he were the Christ (John 1:19-20). For us, because of Christ, John is over-shadowed, but we must recognize the greatness of his presence in his day. *Third*, John's purpose was that men *believe* in the coming Christ. It was the testimony of John that brought Jesus His first disciples (John 1:35-37). The purpose of John the Baptist, that men might *believe* in Jesus Christ, is also the apostle John's purpose in his gospel. The word b*elieve* in the Greek is a form of the verb *pisteno*, which John uses ninety-nine times. Its meaning in English falsifies John's meaning. For us, it means mere credence, agreeing that something is true. In the New Testament, it means a trust which places our life on the line. To illustrate, forty years ago, on an isolated Indian reservation, I was with a fine old Indian. As our wagon and horses came to a river, I wondered if the ice in early fall could hold us. To go through and get wet would mean freezing before we could get to a house and stove. The old Indian said, given the heavy freezes of late, the ice would be thick enough to support us. I could have said, I "believe" you, but, no thanks, I'll cross some other way. However, by agreeing to go with him, I showed faith in his judgment. Biblical believing means putting our life on the line, putting our lives in the Lord's hands in total faith. The Gospel of John summons us to place our lives totally in Christ's hands: this is believing; this is faith.

In John 1:1, we are told, "In the beginning *was* the Word;" the word *was* in the Greek is *en*; in John 1:6, we are told, "There *was* a man sent from God," and *was* here translates *egeneto*, the same word used in John 1:3, to mark a difference between the eternal Word and creation. In John 5:35, Jesus calls John the Baptist "a burning and a shining *light*," but the word *light* here is literally *lamp*. Jesus alone is the Light (John 3:19; 8:12; 9:5).

John the Baptist's ministry was that "all men...might believe," so that in John the world mission of the Old Testament is again set forth (Ps. 87; 2 Chron. 6:32-33).

In vv. 9-11, John again turns to the Word, "the true Light which lighteth every man that cometh into the world." Jesus is the *true* or original Light, the source of all life. All men are created in God's image; in trying to define and order their lives without the triune God, they are denying their light and life and choosing death.

This Word or Light came into the world; the Creator came into creation to save all men and nations (Isa. 49:6). More than that, He came to "his own," to Israel; "the world knew him not," and "his own received him not." Men, blinded by the Fall, refused to see the Light. Our Lord knew this would be the case (Luke 19:14). His atonement was necessary for men's salvation.

The rejection of the Word, of "the way, the truth, and the life" (John 14:6) was the acceptance of death. Christ, crucified, arose from the dead, but His accusers were destroyed by the Jewish-Roman War, A.D. 66-70. The rejection of Christ, of the Light, meant that men chose death and destruction.

In vv. 12-13, we have a plain reference to the virgin birth. The birth of Jesus was not of blood, i.e., a human act; nor of the will of the flesh, by man's choice; nor of the will of man, man's determination, but by God's supernatural act. The rebirth of all believers is compared to the virgin birth: there is now a new life in us, and the source of this new life is supernatural. Our conversion is a miracle patterned after the virgin birth. Adam was born entirely by God's miraculous act. Jesus, the last Adam, was a member of Adam's race, of all of us, in His mother Mary. He was a man, very man of very man. But he was conceived of the Holy Ghost (Luke 1:31, 35), and in His parentage was thus very God of very God. We too, while not at all divine by being born again, are reborn supernaturally by the work of the triune God in us, so that we belong to two realms. Until heaven and our perfect sanctification, we are still members of the old humanity of the first Adam; by our regeneration in Christ, we are also members of the new humanity of Jesus Christ, the new human race for a new creation.

Our growth in this new humanity is possible because all who are Christ's are given "power" to become the sons of God by adoption. Thus the Christian is not an impotent person but a man of power.

In v. 14, John sums up the glory of the incarnation: God the Word was made flesh; He dwelt among us, and His glory, the glory of God the Son, was manifest. In Him was the fullness of grace and truth. God the Son became *man*, the new man at the head of a new creation. Because He is the fullness of grace and truth, there can be no truth apart from the Word, nor any grace from any other man, gods, or religion.

The word "dwelt" is literally tabernacled or tented. For a lifetime, 33 years, God the Son was on earth. His stay was temporary, but His incarnation is an eternal reality.

John, in telling us that Jesus is the glory, or *Shekinah*, has in mind the Presence of God in the Holy of Holies. That Presence is now made flesh in Jesus. The words *"made* flesh" are literally *"became* flesh." The Word did not temporarily inhabit or possess a child; He became one. He is truly man, and He is the Adam or Head of God's new human race; it is in Him and into this new humanity that we are born again.

Turning again to Calvin's rendering of *Logos* as *Speech*, we can see the cultural implications of his translation. *Speech* means communication and community. We have today what is called a "communications gap" between generations, classes, and races. Because of the Fall of man, man is accursed in every area of life and thought. There is no true communication in hell because it is total separation from the *Logos*, *Speech*; in the sense of any community of meaning, hell is a speechless place. God the Son is the *Logos*, the Word, Speech, and apart from Him men move into ultimate speechlessness and meaninglessness. In Christ, we find our voice. He is the life-giving Word, the *Logos*, who enables us in Him to become the expression of God's creating purpose.

Chapter Two

"A Man Sent from God"
(John 1:15-34)

15. John bare witness of him, and cried, saying, This was he of whom I spake, He that cometh after me is preferred before me: for he was before me.
16. And of his fulness have all we received, and grace for grace.
17. For the law was given by Moses, but grace and truth came by Jesus Christ.
18. No man hath seen God at any time; the only begotten Son, which is in the bosom of the Father, he hath declared him.
19. And this is the record of John, when the Jews sent priests and Levites from Jerusalem to ask him, Who art thou?
20. And he confessed, and denied not; but confessed, I am not the Christ.
21. And they asked him, What then? Art thou Elias? And he saith, I am not. Art thou that prophet? And he answered, No.
22. Then said they unto him, Who art thou? that we may give an answer to them that sent us. What sayest thou of thyself?
23. He said, I am the voice of one crying in the wilderness, Make straight the way of the Lord, as said the prophet Esaias.
24. And they which were sent were of the Pharisees.
25. And they asked him, and said unto him, Why baptizest thou then, if thou be not that Christ, nor Elias, neither that prophet?
26. John answered them, saying, I baptize with water: but there standeth one among you, whom ye know not;
27. He it is, who coming after me is preferred before me, whose shoe's latchet I am not worthy to unloose.
28. These things were done in Bethabara beyond Jordan, where John was baptizing.
29. The next day John seeth Jesus coming unto him, and saith, Behold the Lamb of God, which taketh away the sin of the world.
30. This is he of whom I said, After me cometh a man which is preferred before me: for he was before me.
31. And I knew him not: but that he should be made manifest to Israel, therefore am I come baptizing with water.
32. And John bare record, saying, I saw the Spirit descending from heaven like a dove, and it abode upon him.
33. And I knew him not: but he that sent me to baptize with water, the same said unto me, Upon whom thou shalt see the Spirit descending, and remaining on him, the same is he which baptizeth with the Holy Ghost.
34. And I saw, and bare record that this is the Son of God.
(John 1:15-34)

The credentials of John are very strongly stressed in the New Testament: they are from God. Malachi 3:1 speaks of John's coming as God's messenger. John denies that he is Elijah come back to earth, but our Lord says, "if ye will receive it, this is Elias, which was for to come" (Matt. 11:14).

Moreover, our Lord says of John that he is "a prophet...and more than a prophet" (Matt. 11:9). But this is not all. Our Lord declares that John the Baptist is the greatest man of the entire world's history before Himself; at the same time, "he that is least in the kingdom of heaven is greater than he" (Matt. 11:11). Furthermore, all who believe in Christ will not only do His work, "but greater works than these shall he do" (John 14:12). The believer is called to a dominion work, to bring all the world and the things in it into captivity to Christ. Great as John the Baptist was, we are all created to greater works. Notice that our Lord's emphasis is on *works*; this is because faith without works is dead (James 2:17-26). Our works reveal our faith; a bad faith manifests bad works (Matt. 7:16-20).

In belief, John is important, and Christ says he is; at the same time, our Lord says that greater *works* are required of us. We must not construe works as miracles; John was not a miracle worker; he did summon men to a living, *working* faith (Luke 3:1-18).

John's witness (v. 15) of Jesus begins with a threefold emphasis. *First*, the coming one is the man of whom the prophets spoke, and of whom John speaks: "this was he of whom I spake." He cites Isaiah as a prophet of Christ's coming (v. 23). *Second*, the coming one is greater than John, and He is the focus of John's preaching and work. *Third*, the coming one is not only greater, but also pre-existent: "he was before me," a fact stressed repeatedly by John (vv. 18, 30).

In vv. 16-17, the apostle John again speaks, revealing John the Baptist's testimony as the witness of all believers. All of us have received Christ's *fullness*, i.e., His "grace and truth" (v. 14). The fullness of the Godhead is in Christ, Paul tells us (Col. 1:19; 2:9), and from Him, among other things, we receive life (John 10:28), peace (John 14:27), and joy (John 15:11), and also the gift of the Holy Spirit (John 20:22). We also receive "grace for grace"; grace is ever added to grace. We receive grace because He gives it, not because we merit it. All this is possible only because He is God incarnate; because of His fullness, we are inexhaustively supplied. His *fullness* means *that which fills*, and God alone can so supply man's needs.

"The law was given by Moses," i.e., it came through Moses. Moses gives us God's very words; we are told over and over again "the LORD spake unto Moses," or "God spake all these words." But "grace and truth come by Jesus Christ": He is the incarnation of grace and truth because He is God the Son. Grace and truth cannot exist in abstraction from God: He is their only source. Hence, in Christ the fullness of grace and truth walked on earth. The Greek word "truth" is *aletheia*, and it can also be translated as "reality." Truth and reality are not abstractions in the Bible; in modern man's thinking, truth and reality can be two different things. The truth can be an ideal, and the real something bad. For Scripture neither can be defined apart from God: He is the truth, and He is reality. Hence, it is truth, it is reality which we see in Jesus Christ; anything separate from Him is a lie. The law given by means of Moses was an expression of God's grace and truth to covenant man; now the reality of this grace and truth comes into the world in all His fullness.

In v. 18, John sums up all that is said in vv. 1-17 and prepares us for all that is to follow. The invisible God is incarnated in Jesus Christ, who is the declaration of God. The word "declared" in present English is *exegesis*: to bring out the meaning of Scripture, to make known. Jesus Christ is the one true exegesis of God; He makes God known to us. "He that hath seen me hath seen the Father" (John 14:9). We do not speculate about God; we know Him in Jesus Christ. Man's ability to know God is limited, although very real. By the incarnation, we are delivered from our speculation into God's sure revelation and declaration. Therefore, we must not rely on our thinking nor on our own ideas about God, because our thinking reflects still the willful blindness of man's sin. Rather, our total dependence must be on God's revelation and declaration of Himself. In Jesus Christ, God Himself fully answers the question: Who and what is God? We dare not have a speculative or false opinion, because the true revelation and exegesis has been given to us in Jesus Christ. This is why John says that grace and truth came to us in the person of Jesus Christ; neither can be separated from Him.

In v. 19, we return to John the Baptist, the man sent from God. Here we have his record, or witness, again. "The Jews" sent priests and Levites from Jerusalem to ask, "Who art thou?" The reference to "the Jews" is a usage limited in the Gospels to the apostle John. John was an Israelite, or Galilean, from the northern tribes, but he did have close connections to highly placed Jews, including the high priest (John 18:15). In his Gospel, John separates himself from the Judeans by this term. As perhaps the closest in many ways to the Jerusalem leadership, he most stresses his separation from them. By the term "the Jews," he means the ruling elite of the nation. A deputation of these men now come to John the Baptist; they are disturbed by the prophetic and messianic character of John's ministry, and so they ask: who are you? In a sense, John the Baptist was taken more seriously than Jesus Christ as no deputation ever called on Jesus, only hostile critics from the elite. John was not respected for this ministry, but for his lineage as the son of a priest, and an important one, Zechariah (Luke 1:5-22). As priests, the leaders were respectful of priestly blood.

In v. 20 and 21, John the Baptist begins his testimony to these leaders: he was not the Christ. It was this which was on the minds of the deputation members: was John the messiah? Three questions are asked of John, all messianic in their concern, and all three titles are denied by John. *First*, he is not the Christ. *Second*, he is not Elijah physically returned to earth. *Third*, he is not the Prophet of Deuteronomy 18:15, 18, where Moses refers to the Messiah, but rabbinic thought separated this great Prophet from the Messiah as another person. John's answers are brief. These men have no desire to believe; thus, he neither wastes time on them, nor seeks to please or offend them.

In vv. 22-25, the interrogation of John the Baptist continues. We are also told that these men were "of the Pharisees." The ruling priests were Sadducees and were not likely to be as concerned about the Messiah; hence, the deputation was made up of Pharisees, men to whom the matter was of greater concern. The Sadducees were politically and socially "liberal," in that they were ready to work with Rome; religiously, they saw themselves as "conservatives," because of their strict adherence to the Law. They rejected the resurrection of the body, and they saw the law as a means of government. As an elite group of the prominent and the wealthy, they conceived of themselves as the governing class.

The Pharisees were anti-Roman, or anti-foreign. Socially and politically, they were intensely "conservative," but religiously, they were regarded as "liberals" by the Sadducees, because they added tradition to the Law and sometimes gave it greater weight.

These Pharisees, come now to see John the Baptist, asked: who then are you? We are required as an investigating committee to make a report. How would you identify yourself?

The questions asked of John had reference to his *person*. Was he the Christ, Elijah, or the Prophet of Deuteronomy 18:15, 18? John answers by referring them to his *calling*. He shifts attention from himself to God's mandate: "I am the voice of one crying in the wilderness, make straight the way of the Lord, as said the prophet Elias. I am only a voice," John says. It is the word of God, and His coming Messiah, that is everything.

The investigators then asked a key question. If you are not the Messiah, nor Elijah, nor the Prophet, why are you baptizing Jews? Such baptism is a sign of the coming of the Messiah. Passages like Ezekiel 36:25 and 37:23 (also Zech. 13:1; Isa. 52:15) identified it as such. There was to be a general purification at the coming of the Messiah. All Gentile converts were baptized on becoming converted, and the baptism signified the calling of all peoples in the Messiah. Unless the Messiah had come, such baptism placed Jews on the same level as Gentiles, as defiled and in need of cleansing.

We can see why John is called "the Baptist." What he was doing was summoning all the people to the Lord, and in so doing, he was not only acting in obedience to his calling, but also making clear the lost condition of the Jews, God's chosen people.

In vv. 26-27, we see John's brief answer. Indeed, he is baptizing, but there is a great difference between his preparatory baptism and that which is to come. John's baptism is with water; the Messiah's is with power.

Moreover, the Messiah is here; He is of this generation, but you do not know Him; the implication is, you will refuse to acknowledge Him.

This Coming One, John adds, is greater by far than I; I am not worthy to tie the thongs of His shoes, i.e., to do even a slave's task, tying shoe-thongs, is a greater honor than I deserve.

The locale of this meeting of John the Baptist and the deputation was Bethabara, or, another Bethany beyond Jordan, where John was baptizing.

The next day (v. 29), John sees Jesus coming to him, and he declares, "Behold the Lamb of God, which taketh away the sin of the world." Here, John refers to Isaiah 53:7, the prophecy concerning God's plan for the atonement of sin by the Redeemer-Servant. "The iniquity of all" is laid upon Him by the Lord (Isa. 53:8), and He atones for "the sin of the world." By "the world," John means that Christ is the Savior for all peoples, all nations and races, not every man individually. Every morning and every evening, a lamb was sacrificed in the temple to atone for sin (Ex. 29:38-42). Now God's Lamb had come for the efficacious atonement.

The Pharisees were looking for a savior-king; John says that a savior-priest is coming. We are later told that Jesus is also the prophet and the king, but He must first be our savior-priest. It was this fact which the Pharisees and others chose to ignore. Moreover, Isaiah 53:8 reads, "for the transgression *of my people* was he stricken." The Pharisees read "my people" to mean Israel; John reveals that it means all the called and redeemed of God in all the world.

Then, in v. 30, John the Baptist spells out for those near him that Jesus is the Messiah, the one of whom he spoke and for whose coming his work was a preparation. "He was before me," says John, i.e., He is the preexistent one. In other words, He is not only man, but also the eternal God. Here, John the Baptist says essentially the same thing as in v. 15; in both instances he declares, This is the One of whom I have been speaking. In other words, the coming of Christ had been the subject of much of John's preaching, so that his hearers were familiar with his teachings concerning the Coming One. John, as the son of a priest, stresses Jesus as the Lamb of God, not only because it was his calling to do so, but because his family background made him realize the centrality of atonement.

Then, in John's next sentence (v. 31), he says, "I knew him not." John was a relative of Jesus (Luke 1:36), and they were thus doubtlessly acquainted. John no doubt knew from his mother of Jesus' miraculous birth. However, John's own birth had been miraculous (Luke 1:5-25). He may have regarded Jesus as, like himself, another prophet sent by God to prepare the way for the Messiah. He had come baptizing with water to prepare the way for the Christ.

By this baptism, those of Israel who received it acknowledged that, like all other peoples, i.e., the Gentiles, they were under sentence of death. In the words of Arthur W. Pink, "they acknowledged that *death was their due.*" In this, John's baptism differs from Christian baptism. In Christian baptism, the believer does not confess that death is his due, but he shows forth the fact that he *has already* died to sin, died *with Christ* (Rom. 6:3-4). Christian baptism marks the fact that we are now members of the new creation and of Christ's new humanity.

According to an early church father, Justin Martyr, in his *Dialogue with Trypho* (ch. viii), the Jewish belief was that the Messiah would be unknown "and has no power until Elias come to anoint Him, and to make Him manifest to all." Justin's Jewish friend felt that, because Elijah had not come literally, Jesus therefore was not the Messiah. Now John the Baptist declares that the Messiah is manifest, and he is Jesus.

After baptizing Jesus, John declares, "I saw the Spirit descending from heaven like a dove, and it abode upon him (John 1:32; Matt. 3:16; Mark 1:10; Luke 3:22). All four Gospels speak of this remarkable event. "It abode upon Him," can be rendered as, "It *remained* upon Him," i.e., the Presence of the Spirit now became part of Jesus' life and person. This was in fulfillment of Isaiah 11:2, "And the spirit of the LORD shall dwell upon him." The Gospels tell us that this descent of the Spirit was in bodily form, "*like* a dove," not something to speculate about. What we do know is that this was the anointing of Jesus as the great priest, prophet, and king. His baptism is an anointing in which the Old Testament takes a part in the person of the last prophet, John the Baptist, and in which God the Father and God the Spirit take part. Jesus replaces Adam as the head of a new humanity and a new creation (1 Cor. 15:45-49).

In v. 33, John the Baptist again says, "I knew him not." His recognition of Jesus as the Messiah is supernatural. God who sent him had declared that the Messiah would be anointed and confirmed by the descent of the Spirit. This man, God's Messiah, would baptize with the Holy Spirit: He would make men a new creation and endow them with power. A new world was now in the making to replace the fallen world and its sin.

In v. 34, John concludes his testimony by witnessing to the fact that Jesus is "the Son of God." John has said that he can only administer the sign of the new creation, water baptism; the Messiah will administer its power and its regenerating life. Since God is the creator, God the Son is the re-creator, together with the Father and the Spirit. The Son comes as the great high *Priest*, to make atonement to God and to remove sin. He comes as the great *Prophet*, to speak God's authoritative and final word of revelation. He comes as the *King*, to rule the new humanity and the new creation. In Christ, we are citizens and members of God's new and eternal world.

Chapter Three

"Behold, the Lamb of God!"
(*John 1:35-51*)

35. Again the next day after John stood, and two of his disciples;
36. And looking upon Jesus as he walked, he saith, Behold the Lamb of God!
37. And the two disciples heard him speak, and they followed Jesus.
38. Then Jesus turned, and saw them following, and saith unto them, What seek ye? They said unto him, Rabbi, being interpreted, Master, where dwellest thou?
39. He saith unto them, Come and see. They came and saw where he dwelt, and abode with him that day: for it was about the tenth hour.
40. One of the two which heard John speak, and followed him, was Andrew, Simon Peter's brother.
41. He first findeth his own brother Simon, and saith unto him, We have found the Messias, which is, being interpreted, the Christ.
42. And he brought him to Jesus. And when Jesus beheld him, he said, Thou art Simon the son of Jona: thou shalt be called Cephas, which is by interpretation, A stone.
43. The day following Jesus would go forth into Galilee, and findeth Philip, and saith unto him, Follow me.
44. Now Philip was of Bethsaida, the city of Andrew and Peter.
45. Philip findeth Nathanael, and saith unto him, We have found him, of whom Moses in the law, and the prophets, did write, Jesus of Nazareth, the son of Joseph.
46. And Nathanael said unto him, Can there any good thing come out of Nazareth? Philip saith unto him, Come and see.
47. Jesus saw Nathanael coming to him, and saith of him, Behold an Israelite indeed, in whom is no guile!
48. Nathanael saith unto him, Whence knowest thou me? Jesus answered and said unto him, Before that Philip called thee, when thou wast under the fig tree, I saw thee.
49. Nathanael answered and saith unto him, Rabbi, thou art the Son of God; thou art the King of Israel.
50. Jesus answered and said unto him, Because I said unto thee, I saw thee under the fig tree, believest thou? thou shalt see greater things than these.
51. And he saith unto him, Verily, verily, I say unto you, Hereafter ye shall see heaven open, and the angels of God ascending and descending upon the Son of man. (John 1:35-51)

Here, the apostle John uses a very ordinary episode to introduce a remarkable fact. John the Baptist declares Jesus to be "the Lamb of God," and John's two disciples, one of them being Andrew, immediately follow Jesus. The other was the author John himself, who remains unnamed. Andrew tells his brother Simon (Peter) that "We have found the Messiah." Later, Philip describes Jesus to Nathanael as the one whom the law and the prophets prophesied about. Nathanael declares Jesus to be the Son of God and the King of Israel. Thus John tells us that, from the very beginning, he and the other disciples followed Jesus because they believed Him to be the Messiah. Notice what these terms mean. "The Lamb of God" means the unblemished sacrifice for atonement; Jesus is thus recognized as the sin-bearer who makes atonement for the sins of His people. "The Messiah," or Christ, means the anointed one who comes to exercise dominion. "King of Israel" indicates that Jesus, as the promised Son of David, is the great restorer of the Kingdom of God, the one who brings it to its full power. "The Son of God" tells us that the disciples knew Him to be God in the flesh. These were men who had longed for Christ's coming and had been taught its meaning by John the Baptist.

The question then arises: why did John send two disciples later to ask Jesus, "Art thou he that should come, or do we look for another?" (Matt. 11:3). Why, too, did the disciples prove to be so uncomprehending when Christ spoke of His coming death in Jerusalem (Matt. 16:21-23)? The Gospels tell us plainly how well they were taught from the beginning. The answer to this question is important, not only to understand the disciples' problem, *but also our own.* Our Lord, in another context, describes the Kingdom of God thus: "first the blade, then the ear, after that the full corn in the ear" (Mark 4:28). We do not harvest corn immediately after planting the seed, nor the next day, nor the next week. False expectations lead to false actions, as well as misunderstanding. Over the centuries, the church's ministry has been warped because, with endless repetition, people have insisted that the end of the world has to be near, and that Christ will be here again any day. This has been done in spite of the warning against such things (Matt. 24:36). The disciples were not lacking in knowledge about Jesus; who could live with Him, hear Him, and see His miraculous works and be ignorant? Their problem was that they wanted all things fulfilled in their lifetime, a most common sin.

On the day before the incident of v. 35-39, John the Baptist spoke of Jesus in a like term, "Behold the Lamb of God, which taketh away the sin of the world" (John 1:29). E.C. Hoskyns said, "The place of sacrifice is the place where the glory and grace is made known (Ex. XXIX.43)." Jesus is the place, the glory, and the sacrifice. By this announcement, John the Baptist in effect concludes his ministry: the One whose coming he had proclaimed had arrived, and His ministry had begun. In these verses, 35-39, we hear the two men, Andrew and John, call Jesus "rabbi," which means "my great One or man," and to the Hebrews meant a teacher of God's Law-Word.

John gives us a sequence of three days up to this point. On the first day, the deputation of Jewish authorities came to John the Baptist. On the second day, John identifies Jesus as the Lamb of God. On this, the third day, he again so indentifies Jesus, and two men, Andrew and John, follow Jesus. John the Apostle, having been present, remembers these days vividly.

He and Andrew followed Jesus to the place where He was staying, and they remained until "about the tenth hour," four in the afternoon. The rest of the chapter illustrates Jesus' words, "Come and see." Of the two, it is said, "They followed Jesus."

But the day is not yet over. Andrew went after his brother, Simon, to bring him to Jesus (vv. 40-42). Jesus tells Simon that he will be called Cephas, stone, or in Latin, Peter, rock. The word "stone" is literally *petra*; Petros or Peter means that Peter belongs to the Rock, Jesus Christ. Because most people of the day spoke at least two languages, their own and that of their overlords, (and also the business language of the empire, Greek), they also often had names in two languages. The apostle *Thomas* (Aramaic) was also *Didymus*, the Greek work for *twin*. *Tabitha* (Aramaic) meant gazelle, as did her Greek name, *Dorcas*. At other times, a name sounding like one's original might be used, *Apelles* for *Abel*. Peter is given no introduction; he was so well known that none was necessary, whereas Andrew is identified as "Simon Peter's brother."

On the next and fourth day (vv. 43-51), Jesus took the initiative: He located Philip (a Greek name). Philip, in Matthew, Mark, and Luke, is only mentioned in the lists of apostles (Matt. 10:3; Mark 3:18; Luke 6:14). Eusebius tells us that Philip was important in Christ's work in Asia Minor (Hist. Eccl. iii, 31, 39; v.24). More important, Philip appears repeatedly in John's Gospel, here and in 6:5-7; 12:21-22; 14:8-9. Clearly, Christ had a particular fondness for Philip. Philip then brought Nathanael to Christ. Nathanael is from the Hebrew, meaning "gift of God," as do the Greek names Theodore and Dorothy.

Nathanael's response to Philip is skeptical. He was "under the fig tree," an Old Testament symbol for a place of peace (1 Kings 4:25; Micah 4:4; Zech. 3:10); when rabbis taught in the open air, it was often under a fig tree. Nathanael was a Galilean, and thus his remark about Nazareth, "Can there any good thing come out of Nazareth?," was not a Judean contempt for Galileans. Rather, to him Nazareth was not a part of Old Testament prophecy, and how would someone from Nazareth fulfill the law and the prophets as Philip claimed? His skepticism was based on a devout concern for Scripture; he was not aware of Jesus' birth in Bethlehem.

Our Lord, on seeing Nathanael, describes him as an "Israelite indeed," i.e., one from the heart as well as by birth, and a man without guile. Nathanael, whose other name was Bartholomew (son of Ptolmey), asked, how or from where do you know or have information of me? Like Philip, Nathanael receives particular attention from our Lord: "Before that Philip called thee, when thou was under the fig tree, I saw thee." Clearly, our Lord reveals His supernatural knowledge and sight. There is, however, more here as well. Our Lord chose something of significance. He was not merely demonstrating His supernatural power to Nathanael. It is reasonable to assume that, under the fig tree, Nathanael was studying Scripture and praying for the Messiah. His response to Jesus seems to indicate an answered prayer: "Rabbi, thou art the Son of God; thou art the King of Israel." By limiting the sway of the Son of God to Israel, Nathanael showed a limited awareness of Christ's world dominion and power. All the same, Jesus had, by His reference to the fig tree, spoken to Nathanael's hope, study, and prayer. Had it been simply an expression of supernatural power, Nathanael would have seen Jesus as a prophet; instead, he sees Jesus as exactly what he hoped and prayed for, and what Philip had declared Him to be.

Jesus then makes clear that Nathanael will see "greater things than these." This plural reference means that more is in mind than seeing Nathanael under a fig tree. What are these greater things? Our Lord refers to Genesis 28:10-22, Jacob's Ladder. In the Garden of Eden, there was communion between God and man. That communion, broken by the Fall, is restored by Christ's atonement; and the focal point of communion is "the Son of man." Hence, we pray "in Jesus' Name." He is our Jacob's Ladder. St. Bonaventura said, "The heavenly ladder was broken in Adam, and repaired in Christ."

Those who reject Christ as their Ladder, the sacrificial Lamb who restores communion by His atoning death, shall see Him as their Judge. As Jesus said to the high priest at His trial, "Hereafter shall ye see the Son of Man sitting on the right hand of power, and coming in the clouds of heaven" (Matt. 26:64).

There is an important fact in v. 51 as well as in Genesis 28:12: the angels are "ascending and descending," when our natural tendency would be to reverse that order, i.e., to have then come and go. We are thereby reminded that God's angels are already here. Psalm 34:7 tells us plainly, "The angel of the LORD encampeth round about them that fear him, and delivereth them." Our Lord speaks of the presence of angels in Matthew 18:10. *We are not alone.* We are never alone, and it is a sin to see ourselves as alone.

We saw how, at the beginning, the disciples knew Jesus to be the Lamb of God, the Son of God, and the Messiah. Remember, too, the committee of priests and Levites sent to meet with John the Baptist (1:19-28). They knew John the Baptist to be the son of an important priest, Zachariah, and thus himself entitled to priestly rank. John's miraculous birth was more a matter of public knowledge than was that of Jesus (Luke 1:5-25; 57-80). The facts were all there for men to see. The Pharisees wanted John and Jesus to conform to them and their world; otherwise, they would not believe in John and Jesus. The disciples believed, but they too wanted Jesus to meet their expectations, not themselves, His. Man seeks to make God over in man's own image and in terms of man's desires, and the result is always judgment and disaster.

Chapter Four
The "Beginning of Miracles"
(John 2:1-11)

1. And the third day there was a marriage in Cana of Galilee; and the mother of Jesus was there:
2. And both Jesus was called, and his disciples, to the marriage.
3. And when they wanted wine, the mother of Jesus saith unto him, They have no wine.
4. Jesus saith unto her, Woman, what have I to do with thee? mine hour is not yet come.
5. His mother saith unto the servants, Whatsoever he saith unto you, do it.
6. And there were set there six waterpots of stone, after the manner of the purifying of the Jews, containing two or three firkins apiece.
7. Jesus saith unto them, Fill the waterpots with water. And they filled them up to the brim.
8. And he saith unto them, Draw out now, and bear unto the governor of the feast. And they bare it.
9. When the ruler of the feast had tasted the water that was made wine, and knew not whence it was: (but the servants which drew the water knew;) the governor of the feast called the bridegroom,
10. And saith unto him, Every man at the beginning doth set forth good wine; and when men have well drunk, then that which is worse: but thou hast kept the good wine until now.
11. This beginning of miracles did Jesus in Cana of Galilee, and manifested forth his glory; and his disciples believed on him. (John 2:1-11)

The Gospel of John begins with a long introduction, chapter one, which declares Jesus to be, among other things, the Word of God, the Son of God, the Messiah, and grace and truth incarnate. John the Baptist declares Jesus to be "the Lamb of God, which taketh away the sin of the world" (1:29). Jesus is He who will destroy the power of sin and death and replace man's Fall with man's atonement and restoration. In the book of Revelation, John gives us the battle which ensues between Christ's Kingdom and the Kingdom of Man, and it culminates in the glory of the new creation. In his Gospel, John, having introduced Jesus as the great Redeemer who had come to remove sin from God's creation, goes on to tell us what life in that new creation means, beginning here and now, with our conversion. Because of this, John tells us of the visit with Nicodemus and of the necessity of being born again. All of our Lord's teachings in John focus on our lives as a new creation. We are also given a selected number of incidents and miracles which are called *signs*, because they tell us what life in Christ as a new creation means. The first of these signs occurs at the marriage in Cana of Galilee (2:1-11), and this is followed by the cleansing of the Temple (2:12-

19

22); the first was at a domestic, or family festival, the second at a religious festival.

In v. 1, we are told that, on "the third day, there was a marriage in Cana of Galilee;" this is the third day after Nathanael's conversion, or call, and it is the beginning of "the greater things" Nathanael shall see. By Jewish custom and law, the wedding of a virgin took place on a Wednesday. Weddings took place in the evening, after a feast. The guests then followed the couple to their home. The bride and groom held open house for three to seven days, providing hospitality for all.

We are also told that Mary was there. Since Mary knew at once (v. 3) that the wine had run out, she was obviously aware of the "kitchen secrets." Since family members assisted at wedding feasts and celebrations, and Mary was in a position to command "the servants," or helpers, to obey Jesus, she was apparently a close relative, and one with authority in the festivities. Jesus was accordingly also present as a kinsman.

In v. 2, we are told that both Jesus and His disciples were called or invited. Five are mentioned in the previous chapter: Andrew, Simon Peter, Philip, and Nathanael, with Jesus, making six in all.

Before long, the wedding party ran out of wine. Mary knew this, but the guests did not. She came at once to Jesus to say, "They have no wine." This was a serious matter, because a wedding was so important a Jewish festival. Edersheim tells us that the pious fasted before entering this holy estate, and confessed their sins. The relationship of husband and wife was a type of Jehovah and Israel. (In Ephesians 5:22-23, it is a type of Christ and His church.) On their wedding day, the bride and groom symbolized the covenant union of God and Israel. Marriage was thus seen as a holy institution and was to be honored by all. A wedding was therefore a joyful celebration. From the prayer for a boy at his circumcision on the eighth day on, marriage was the focus of life.

A wedding was thus a great religious and familial festival. A wedding procession took precedence over even a funeral. Every man who met such a procession had to rise and join it for a short distance. To honor marriage was to honor God.

Paul warned Timothy against heretics who forbade marriage (1 Tim. 4:1-3), and our Lord tells us that men who are physically incapable of marriage and those who are single for special purpose and called to service to God can alone remain single voluntarily (Matt. 19:10-12).

Mary, in telling Jesus, "They have no wine," was in effect saying, Do something about it. As the Messiah, as God incarnate, you can reveal yourself in a great miracle on a great occasion. As God's Bridegroom for the church or congregation, use this wedding to manifest your nature and being.

Verse 4 tells us that Jesus answered, "Woman, what have I to do with thee? Mine hour is not yet come." This answer sounds harsh in English, but it was not so. The word translated as *woman* is *Lady*, a term of respect and dignity; even queens were so addressed. Jesus did not say "Mother." That relationship did not extend to His ministry and messiahship, but He does treat her with respect. In His calling, and in His divine messianic function, Jesus acknowledged no earthly relatives, mother, brothers, or sisters, save the believing (Matt. 12:46-50).

"Mine hour is not yet come," i.e., the time for a full public revelation of Myself. Mary had asked for an open affirmation by Jesus of who He was. The occasion was right, and also the cause, a wedding and wine. Psalm 104:15 speaks of wine thus, "Wine that maketh glad the heart of man." Judges 9:13 says of wine that it "cheereth God and man."

"Mine hour is not yet come" means the great revelation of the beginning of His Kingdom, the cross and atonement for the sin of the world. Our Lord speaks repeatedly of that great coming hour, in John 5:25, 28; 7:30; 8:20; 12:23; 13:1; and 17:1.

Our Lord did not refuse Mary's request for a miracle to provide wine. It was His great work of atonement, His revelation as the Lamb of God that taketh away the sin of the world, of which the hour had not come. Mary recognized this, and so she told the servants, "Whatsoever he saith unto you, do it" (v. 5). The "servants" were not slaves, but probably friends who, like Mary, were helping at the wedding.

In v. 6, we are told of the six stone waterpots for purification, or cleansing. This was clean water drawn for washing before meals, or to provide water for the foot washing of guests. Each had a capacity of "two or three *firkins* a piece," or *measures*. A firkin, or measure, was 8 1/2 gallons; each jar could thus hold between 17 and 25 gallons of water. The six jars thus had a total capacity of between 100 and 150 gallons.

Jesus commanded that all six empty pots be filled to the brim with water (v. 7), and this was done. It was thus clearly visible that they contained *only* water. It was the custom in Judea to mix water and wine before serving; this purified the water, and also weakened it, since the mixture was 34-50% wine. In this instance, it was plain to all that the waterpots were totally water. The servitors thus could not assume that Jesus was simply cutting some wine with water. This custom of mixing wine and water is still practiced by many churches: the Jewish custom was carried into the preparation of the communion wine.

In v. 8, John tells us, and he was present, that Jesus then ordered the servants to draw out some of the contents and take it to "the governor of the feast," someone comparable to a master of ceremonies. The water had now miraculously become wine, the finest wine, and the governor of the feast called the bridegroom over to his side (v. 9). He commented in amazement that most men served their best wine first, and their poorest wine last, when palates and taste buds were hopefully dulled. Here, however, the last wine far excelled all else (v. 10).

John comments that this was the *beginning* of *miracles* by our Lord. This does not necessarily mean that it was the first; the word translated as "beginning" is *archen*, meaning "first in priority," as revealing the meaning of what follows. Our usage of another Greek word, *alpha*, carries the same sense of the beginning of meaning and understanding. "Miracles" translates *semlion*, signs or tokens. This miracle gives us the meaning of Christ's royal role and realm. It manifested His glory and purpose, and "his disciples believed on him" (v. 11).

Very simply, Jesus filled up what was lacking at a wedding celebration. By this, He set forth the meaning of life in Christ. He that takes away our sins also makes our life and joy in Him full.

Jesus honors the bond of marriage and our natural life. God created us and our world and life as "very good" (Gen. 1:31), and His purpose for us is a glorious one. Christ makes atonement for sin and then commissions us to remove sin and all its works from our lives and world so that His purpose for us in Eden may again prevail. Here, in this miracle, is set forth the purpose of Christ's atonement, to make a new creation of us and of our world, to bring about the regeneration of all things. Our Lord here blesses marriage also because it establishes His own relationship to His people.

The miracle, or sign, also reveals Jesus as the great Giver who gives lavishly, both of things spiritual and things material, both to fulfill our needs and to crown our joys. This is "the beginning of miracles" because it is a prophetic miracle.

Moreover, this sign tells us that Jesus Christ is the One whose infinite love is backed by infinite power, and that He is the One who is full of grace and glory and is the renewer of all things.

Here, too, we see the glorification of the world in His new creation, and of our lives here and now under His transforming power. This "beginning of miracles" sets forth all the miracles of Christ, culminating in the new creation, and it reveals our life to be one of *joy*. He tells us himself, "Ask, and ye shall receive, *that your joy may be full*" (John 16:24).

The Lord is interested, not merely in our bare needs, but in our joys. Ours is not a stingy God, and it is a sin to treat Him as such. John Newton expressed this well in the words of one of his great hymns:

> Thou art coming to a King;
> Large petitions with thee bring;
> For His grace and power are such,
> None can ever ask too much,
> None can ever ask too much.

Chapter Five

The Cleansing of the Temple
(John 2:12-25)

12. After this he went down to Capernaum, he, and his mother, and his brethren, and his disciples: and they continued there not many days.
13. And the Jews' passover was at hand, and Jesus went up to Jerusalem,
14. And found in the temple those that sold oxen and sheep and doves, and the changers of money sitting:
15. And when he had made a scourge of small cords, he drove them all out of the temple, and the sheep, and the oxen; and poured out the changers' money, and overthrew the tables;
16. And said unto them that sold doves, Take these things hence; make not my Father's house an house of merchandise.
17. And his disciples remembered that it was written, The zeal of thine house hath eaten me up.
18. Then answered the Jews and said unto him, What sign shewest thou unto us, seeing that thou doest these things?
19. Jesus answered and said unto them, Destroy this temple, and in three days I will raise it up.
20. Then said the Jews, Forty and six years was this temple in building, and wilt thou rear it up in three days?
21. But he spake of the temple of his body.
22. When therefore he was risen from the dead, his disciples remembered that he had said this unto them; and they believed the scripture, and the word which Jesus had said.
23. Now when he was in Jerusalem at the passover, in the feast day, many believed in his name, when they saw the miracles which he did.
24. But Jesus did not commit himself unto them, because he knew all men,
25. And needed not that any should testify of man: for he knew what was in man. (John 2:12-25)

The cleansing of the Temple was predicted in Malachi 3:1. The Temple was the *house of God*, His appointed dwelling place. God speaks throughout the Old Testament of the tabernacle and the Temple as "My house." Our Lord in Matthew 16:18 speaks of "My church." As against this, in Matthew 23:38, our Lord refers to the Temple as "your house." When the sanctuary or church becomes man's, it is doomed, because God will move against it. At the beginning and at the end of His ministry, our Lord cleansed the Temple (Matt. 21:12-13). He cleansed it because it was properly His house, required to serve Him and not itself. The Temple's rejection of an inner cleansing slated it for judgment.

The occasion was apparently the Passover, according to almost all scholars, a time when men made a pilgrimage to Jerusalem. Of course, John states it to be the Passover (v. 13), and the context indicates that our Lord's family went, as did His disciples (v. 12). It was necessary because the Passover's focus is on atonement, on the Lamb of God. John the Baptist portrayed Jesus as the Lamb of God, the sin-bearer (John 1:29). The cleansing of the Temple is essentially related to John the Baptist's proclamation and to the Passover as well.

The matter is also related to the validity of the sacraments, to baptism and to communion. The Donatist controversy was over the validity of the sacraments: could a faithless or immoral pastor or priest invalidate the sacraments? The church highly insisted, against the Donatists, that a faithless or immoral clergyman could not invalidate a sacrament if the form and words thereof remain Biblical and Trinitarian. A larger question remains: what if the church itself is faithless and apostate? Can the sacraments of a church which denies the Trinity and the atonement, for example, have any validity whatsoever?

Our Lord was not condemning the sacrificial system. He was not condemning circumcision, or the baptism of gentiles, nor the sacrifices of atonement, but rather the whole corrupt system which had made a lucrative merchandise of the sacrificial system. After the second cleansing, He declared the Temple and its worship null and void and said that their house would be made desolate.

Given this fact, we cannot assume the validity of the sacraments if the church be Christ's enemy. Our Lord, in fact, held that the religious leaders had in effect *destroyed* the Temple. They would soon seek to destroy the Lord of the Temple by crucifying Him.

Their response was, "What sign showest thou unto us, seeing that thou doest these things?" (v. 18). They demanded evidence that He had the authority to do such things, i.e., to cleanse the Temple. They did *not* contest the truth of our Lord's charge that the Lord's house had been debased into a money-making venture. Control of the sales of sacrificial animals and the money-charging was so profitable that the high priest would become immensely rich in a single year. As a result, the Romans insisted on an annual replacement of the high priest. The temple leaders did not contest the *validity* of our Lord's charge, only His *authority* or *right* to make it. The corrupt are often prone to legal technicalities as their defense. No attempt was made to justify their practices.

Our Lord's response is very pointed:

19. Jesus answered and said unto them, Destroy this temple, and in three days I will raise it up.
20. Then said the Jews, Forty and six years was this temple in building, and wilt thou rear it up in three days?
21. But he spake of the temple of his body. (John 2:19-21)

In Matthew 26:61 and Mark 14:58, we see that our Lord's statement was twisted at His trial into a subversive claim. What is apparent from its use in the trial is that the statement registered with His enemies. There were two Temples, the venerable building in Jerusalem and then Jesus Christ, His physical body. One had to be the false Temple, and for the leaders of the people it could not be the Temple which they controlled.

For them, the justification for the physical Temple was their control over it. We see this very clearly in John 11:47-53:

> 47. Then gathered the chief priests and the Pharisees a council, and said, What do we? for this man doeth many miracles.
> 48. If we let him thus alone, all men will believe on him: and the Romans shall come and take away both our place and nation.
> 49. And one of them, named Caiaphas, being the high priest that same year, said unto them, Ye know nothing at all,
> 50. Nor consider that it is expedient for us, that one man should die for the people, and that the whole nation perish not.
> 51. And this spake he not of himself: but being high priest that year, he prophesied that Jesus should die for that nation;
> 52. And not for that nation only, but that also he should gather together in one the children of God that were scattered abroad.
> 53. Then from that day forth they took counsel together for to put him to death.

Expediency ruled them. They recognized that Christ's focus was not national Israel, but the Kingdom of God, and this for them was intolerable. It was for them far better to kill the Christ than for the nation, meaning their rule over it, to perish. But, because God rules totally, the worst that men can do will only further His sovereign purposes.

During this Passover stay in Jerusalem, our Lord was active. In v. 23, we have a reference to "the miracles which he did." He was not merely a pilgrim and a spectator at the Passover, but, by His miracles, central to it. The first Passover in Egypt was the culmination of great miracles, the plagues against Egypt. That Passover made it clear that God's salvation of some means death to others, i.e., to the first-born of Egypt. Our Lord's miracles at this Passover had a like meaning. There was healing for some, implying death for others, for all who would reject the Lamb of God, the blood of the true Passover sacrifice. We are told, "many believed in his name, when they saw the miracles which he did" (v. 23). As Calvin noted, to believe "in his name" was to believe in His *authority*. The miracles were a sign of His authority, and many recognized it. We should remember that great numbers of Jews did become Christians after Pentecost, and, in Judea and abroad, the early church was for generations extensively a Jewish church.

But our Lord's trust or reliance was not on man, "for he knew what was in man" (v. 25). At the time of His trial, those closest to Him deserted Him.

The church does not rest on man's faithfulness nor obedience, but on Christ's saving grace. We are told that *"many* believed in his name" (v. 23), but the church does not rest on *the many*, but on Christ. The centrality of Christ is basic to our faith.

In the history of Israel, the Temple had to be cleansed by priests, prophets, and kings on many occasions before Christ brought desolation to it. The church also needs constant cleansing. It is a sign of serious danger when the church sees no need of cleansing and sees as enemies all who proclaim the need for continuing cleansing and purification.

In Jeremiah 7:11, we see that prophet's effort to cleanse the Temple; Jeremiah called the sanctuary "a den of thieves." In Zechariah 14:21, we have a vision of the Temple purged of its Canaanites or merchandisers. Micah 3:12 predicted judgment on the old Temple, whereas Haggai 2:7-9 looked ahead to the day of the Messiah.

There was thus no lack of warning of the meaning of substituting the worshipping institution for the Lord himself, of giving priority to the Temple or the church over the Messiah. The Jews were warned, and so too is the church.

Chapter Six

Nicodemus
(John 3:1-21)

1. There was a man of the Pharisees, named Nicodemus, a ruler of the Jews:
2. The same came to Jesus by night, and said unto him, Rabbi, we know that thou art a teacher come from God: for no man can do these miracles that thou doest, except God be with him.
3. Jesus answered and said unto him, Verily, verily, I say unto thee, Except a man be born again, he cannot see the kingdom of God.
4. Nicodemus saith unto him, How can a man be born when he is old? can he enter the second time into his mother's womb, and be born?
5. Jesus answered, Verily, verily, I say unto thee, Except a man be born of water and of the Spirit, he cannot enter into the kingdom of God.
6. That which is born of the flesh is flesh; and that which is born of the Spirit is spirit.
7. Marvel not that I said unto thee, Ye must be born again.
8. The wind bloweth where it listeth, and thou hearest the sound thereof, but canst not tell whence it cometh, and whither it goeth: so is every one that is born of the Spirit.
9. Nicodemus answered and said unto him, How can these things be?
10. Jesus answered and said unto him, Art thou a master of Israel, and knowest not these things?
11. Verily, verily, I say unto thee, We speak that we do know, and testify that we have seen; and ye receive not our witness.
12. If I have told you earthly things, and ye believe not, how shall ye believe, if I tell you of heavenly things?
13. And no man hath ascended up to heaven, but he that came down from heaven, even the Son of man which is in heaven.
14. And as Moses lifted up the serpent in the wilderness, even so must the Son of man be lifted up:
15. That whosoever believeth in him should not perish, but have eternal life.
16. For God so loved the world, that he gave his only begotten Son, that whosoever believeth in him should not perish, but have everlasting life.
17. For God sent not his Son into the world to condemn the world; but that the world through him might be saved.
18. He that believeth on him is not condemned: but he that believeth not is condemned already, because he hath not believed in the name of the only begotten Son of God.
19. And this is the condemnation, that light is come into the world, and men loved darkness rather than light, because their deeds were evil.
20. For every one that doeth evil hateth the light, neither cometh to the light, lest his deeds should be reproved.
21. But he that doeth truth cometh to the light, that his deeds may be made manifest, that they are wrought in God. (John 3:1-21)

We have in this text an encounter and conversation of very great importance. Nicodemus was "a ruler of the Jews" (v. 1); he came to see Jesus "by night" (v. 2). This night visit has often been described as a cowardly and covert one, but there is no truth to this. It was customary for rabbis to pay one another long visits by night, when interruptions were less likely. Nicodemus' statement in v. 2 is not flattery; he simply states that our Lord is obviously "come from God" because His miracles cannot be explained in any other way.

In vv. 1-15, we have a *summary* of their conversation. The details of an evening's discussion are not given, only the essentials. Our Lord's statement in v. 3, "Except a man be born again, he cannot see the Kingdom of God," is an answer to Nicodemus' central concern. Nicodemus begins by recognizing our Lord as at least a great prophet, if not the Messiah. Because our Lord, in vv. 5-15, does not evade the disclosure that He is the Messiah, and because Nicodemus does not contest it, Nicodemus' concern is not with Jesus Christ, but with *the people*, with the men of Israel who await the Messiah. *Nicodemus saw no hope in man.* As a ruler of the people, he knew that Judeans, representing in their time the world's best and most moral people, were still a fallen and depraved people. His familiarity with the best and the worst in Judea and Galilee had made clear to him that no Kingdom of God could be built on them. How then could there be a true Kingdom?

Our Lord's answer was a very brief one: "Except a man be born again, *he cannot* see the Kingdom of God" (v. 3). Nicodemus, discouraged by what he knows the best men to be, asks how, in effect, can any man reenter his mother's womb to be born again (v. 4)? Men are bundles of habits, and a fallen nature governs the formation of habits, so that a rigidity of self-will and egocentricity marks peoples. *They want changes in the world, not in themselves.* They long for a new world order, but not for a revolution in their lifestyles and habits. *How can a new world be built on fallen man?* The sons of Adam, the sons of man, do indeed want a new world order, but at no cost to their wants and desires.

Nicodemus began by confessing that our Lord's miracles "come from God" (v. 2). Now our Lord tells him that the regeneration of men comes from God also: *it is a miracle.*

A man's life is the sum of all his days, his inherited nature from his family, and his self-will. His nature is fixed *in a pattern*; he grows in terms of a self-determined direction. How can this be changed?

Our Lord was not a trained rabbi, but Nicodemus addresses Him as such because he recognized Him as the great and true teacher. His questions are thus intelligent and respectful.

In v. 5, our Lord states that rebirth means being "born of water and of the Spirit." B.F. Westcott tellingly said that "water" here means purification, and the Spirit supernatural quickening. The purification aspect is partially set forth in baptism; the Spirit points to a supernatural regeneration.

In v. 6, our Lord agrees with Nicodemus: "That which is born of the flesh is flesh." Generation simply reproduces man's fallen nature. It leads to no moral progression. Only "that which is born of the Spirit is spirit." A supernatural rebirth breaks the evil cycle of the Fall, the endless reproduction of sin and death. Apart from the Spirit, man's work is self-destructive. In the Spirit, man changes and grows.

Regeneration cannot be viewed as magical. It does not wipe out the past, but, in terms of Romans 8:28, it brings good out of the past. It is ironic that those who rail against predestination as though it makes puppets of men are also those who expect being born again to wipe out all their problems. *Regeneration does not eliminate our problems, but it does give us power to overcome them.* History is not canceled out by regeneration, nor is creation despised. God takes what we are and gives us power to become His children by the adoption of grace, and to become members of the new human race whose Adam is Jesus Christ.

Regeneration comes with the forgiveness of sins, a judicial act, and being made a new creation by the power of the triune God.

We meet with Nicodemus in John 7:42-52 and in John 19:39-42, and there is no reason to doubt his regeneration.

Our Lord tells Nicodemus (vv. 6-8) that we see the wind only in its effects as it blows things about. So, too, we can see the Spirit in its effects.

In vv. 11-15, our Lord speaks to Nicodemus' associates, those referred to in v. 2, "*we* know..." Their questions and unbelief are now dealt with plainly. Their concern has been with *historical* Israel, not *supernatural* Israel. Hence, they reject Christ's witness (v. 11). Because they have trouble accepting what He is doing before their eyes, in their time and history, how can they understand the supernatural dimension (vv. 12-13)? The reference to Moses and the serpent in the wilderness simply states the centrality of atonement as the necessary step towards the Kingdom of God (vv. 14-15).

In vv. 16-21, the apostle John spells out the meaning of this fact of atonement and its function as the entrance into the Kingdom of God. Our Lord's atonement is the expression of God's redeeming love (v. 16). Jesus Christ is the dividing factor in all human history. If men flee from Him, the light of the world, they shall perish. *Truth* is Christ; *evil* is the rejection of Christ. The dividing power in all history is Jesus Christ.

Men avoid Christ because as *truth* and *light* He *reproves* their deeds (v. 20). The word translated as "reproved" in v. 20 can also be rendered as "discovered." It also means in the Greek to *lay bare* or *expose*. The unpopularity of Jesus Christ with the ungodly rests on this fact. He is the light of the world who exposes ungodly men in their evil. He will always be hated by ungodly peoples, so that conflict is inevitable between Christians and a fallen world. To reject conflict is to deny the need for truth. Saint Paul did not say, "I have made a good compromise," but, "I have fought the good fight, I have finished my course, I have kept the faith" (2 Tim. 4:7). For this reason, he knew that "a crown of righteousness" (2 Tim. 4:8) awaited him, not for compromise, but for faithfulness to what must not be compromised.

Chapter Seven

"He Must Increase"
(*John 3:22-36*)

22. After these things came Jesus and his disciples into the land of Judaea; and there he tarried with them, and baptized.
23. And John also was baptizing in Aenon near to Salim, because there was much water there: and they came, and were baptized.
24. For John was not yet cast into prison.
25. Then there arose a question between some of John's disciples and the Jews about purifying.
26. And they came unto John, and said unto him, Rabbi, he that was with thee beyond Jordan, to whom thou barest witness, behold, the same baptizeth, and all men come to him.
27. John answered and said, A man can receive nothing, except it be given him from heaven.
28. Ye yourselves bear me witness, that I said, I am not the Christ, but that I am sent before him.
29. He that hath the bride is the bridegroom: but the friend of the bridegroom, which standeth and heareth him, rejoiceth greatly because of the bridegroom's voice: this my joy therefore is fulfilled.
30. He must increase, but I must decrease.
31. He that cometh from above is above all: he that is of the earth is earthly, and speaketh of the earth: he that cometh from heaven is above all.
32. And what he hath seen and heard, that he testifieth; and no man receiveth his testimony.
33. He that hath received his testimony hath set to his seal that God is true.
34. For he whom God hath sent speaketh the words of God: for God giveth not the Spirit by measure unto him.
35. The Father loveth the Son, and hath given all things into his hand.
36. He that believeth on the Son hath everlasting life: and he that believeth not the Son shall not see life; but the wrath of God abideth on him. (John 3:22-36)

This text is of interest because, among other things, we are told in v. 26 that our Lord authorized baptisms during His ministry. Thus, we have not only His authority for baptizing in Matthew 28:19, but also His practice thereof as indicated here.

John was also baptizing to prepare the people for Christ, for the Messiah.

In vv. 25 to 30, we have John the Baptist's testimony concerning Jesus. His disciples had reported that Jesus was baptizing in Judea. By what authority was Jesus baptizing? Since Jesus had been baptized of John the Baptist, had John given Him authority to do the same? These disciples were earnestly protective of John the Baptist's supposed priority.

In v. 25, we are told that an argument developed between some Jews and John the Baptist's disciples about baptism, and, implicitly, at least, the authority of Jesus in reference to John. What was the meaning of the rite? How did the two practices compare, or, how did their actions compare with Jewish purification rites?

In v. 27, we see the heart of the answer. John the Baptist said to his followers, "A man can receive nothing, except it be given him from heaven." His answer reverses our expectation that John would say that a man can *do* nothing unless God gives him the power. Instead, he says a man can *receive* nothing except from God. The word *receive* places the stress on God's gift, His sovereign grace. All good gifts come from heaven. In James 1:17 we are told:

> Every good and every perfect gift is from above, and cometh down from the Father of lights, with whom is no variableness, neither shadow of turning.

Total priority in all spheres rests in the triune God. John's emphasis on this is very strong, and this is also true of the apostle John. John the Baptist reminds his followers that he himself stressed the priority of Christ over himself (v. 28). In v. 29, John uses familiar Old Testament imagery of God and Israel, the bridegroom and the bride (Hosea 2:19; Ezekiel 16; Malachi 2:11). The "friend of the bridegroom" was what we now call "the best man." It was, in that era, his duty to prepare for the wedding reception and to bring forth the bride. John the Baptist tells his followers that he is such a one, the friend of the bridegroom, and this is his joy. He is not a competitor for the bride, but the friend of the bridegroom. The bridegroom's voice, his words to the bride, are therefore his joy and the evidence that his work is finished (v. 29). John's message to Jesus in Matthew 11:3, "Art thou he that should come, or do we look for another," is *not* treated by our Lord as doubt. John awaited death in prison; he was awaiting word of Christ's fulfillment of His mission and was impatient. Our Lord's answer to John is to cite His miraculous powers over sin and death (Matt.11:4-6): the new creation had begun.

Now John tells his disciples, "He must increase, but I must decrease" (v. 30). I am of the earth, born in the line of the old humanity of Adam, but Jesus is "He that cometh from above" and is therefore "above all." He stresses this again: "he that cometh from heaven is above all" (v. 31). Thus, He can be compared to no man of any era. He is above, or sovereign, and Lord over all. His testimony is in consequence the first-hand witness from heaven; it is a word unlike any other word. Men reject the testimony of the Christ, though they are receptive to His miracles, because it does not conform to their expectations and demands (v. 32).

All who then and now receive Christ's testimony and see Him as indeed God the Son incarnate, do thereby declare that "God is true" (v. 33), that every prophecy concerning the Christ in the Law and the Prophets is fulfilled in Jesus the Christ.

We know Christ to be *the truth*, "for he whom God hath sent speaketh the words of God: for God giveth not the Spirit by measure unto him" (v. 34). In Paul's words, "For in him dwelleth all the fullness of the Godhead bodily" (Col. 2:9). As the apostle John earlier wrote, "No man hath seen God at any time; the only begotten Son, which is in the bosom of the Father, he hath declared him" (John 1:18). Again, in Colossians 1:19, we are told, "For it pleased the Father that in him should all fullness dwell." This is at the heart of Christianity, that Christ is God incarnate. Our Lord tells Philip and all of us, "he that hath seen me hath seen the Father" (John 14:9).

"The Father loveth the Son, and hath given all things into his hand" (v. 35). Verses 31-36 are said by some scholars to be, not John the Baptist's words, but the added testimony of the apostle John; these verses are so close to those of John the Baptist that it is clear that a common inspiration marks them both.

The conclusion to all this is in v. 36: "He that believeth in the Son hath everlasting life: and he that believeth not the Son shall not see life; but the wrath of God abideth on him." Those who believe already have eternal life; those who disbelieve are the living dead who face eternal death. God is the Creator of life, and true life is only possible in Him; apart from God, existence is meaningless as is hell and judgment.

John the Baptist's word extended beyond Judea through his disciples. In Acts 18:24-28 and 19:1-5, we encounter some at Ephesus and others at Corinth. One notable follower of John the Baptist became an important Christian missionary, Apollos. The readiness of John the Baptist's followers to follow Christ and the apostles is a witness to their faith and the maturity and wisdom of John's ministry. Too often in history men have been ready to receive the truth but not to grow with it. Their mentality has been defined by a reluctance to move forward in terms of God's determination of all things. After a certain point, they say, in effect, as a 1970's phrase had it, "Stop the world; I want to get off!" This is to ask for hell. God, who ordains all things, makes all things work together for good for His people (Rom. 8:28). If we know Jesus Christ as Lord, we know that the present distress always leads towards His Kingdom and His reign over all things. "He must increase," *and He shall.* Unless we accept this fact, we do not know Jesus Christ. Until then, we are not even on the level of John the Baptist's disciples.

Chapter Eight
The Woman at the Well
(John 4:1-42)

1. When therefore the Lord knew how the Pharisees had heard that Jesus made and baptized more disciples than John,

2. (Though Jesus himself baptized not, but his disciples,)

3. He left Judaea, and departed again into Galilee.

4. And he must needs go through Samaria.

5. Then cometh he to a city of Samaria, which is called Sychar, near to the parcel of ground that Jacob gave to his son Joseph.

6. Now Jacob's well was there. Jesus therefore, being wearied with his journey, sat thus on the well: and it was about the sixth hour.

7. There cometh a woman of Samaria to draw water: Jesus saith unto her, Give me to drink.

8. (For his disciples were gone away unto the city to buy meat.)

9. Then saith the woman of Samaria unto him, How is it that thou, being a Jew, askest drink of me, which am a woman of Samaria? for the Jews have no dealings with the Samaritans.

10. Jesus answered and said unto her, If thou knewest the gift of God, and who it is that saith to thee, Give me to drink; thou wouldest have asked of him, and he would have given thee living water.

11. The woman saith unto him, Sir, thou hast nothing to draw with, and the well is deep: from whence then hast thou that living water?

12. Art thou greater than our father Jacob, which gave us the well, and drank thereof himself, and his children, and his cattle?

13. Jesus answered and said unto her, Whosoever drinketh of this water shall thirst again:

14. But whosoever drinketh of the water that I shall give him shall never thirst; but the water that I shall give him shall be in him a well of water springing up into everlasting life.

15. The woman saith unto him, Sir, give me this water, that I thirst not, neither come hither to draw.

16. Jesus saith unto her, Go, call thy husband, and come hither.

17. The woman answered and said, I have no husband. Jesus said unto her, Thou hast well said, I have no husband:

18. For thou hast had five husbands; and he whom thou now hast is not thy husband: in that saidst thou truly.

19. The woman saith unto him, Sir, I perceive that thou art a prophet.

20. Our fathers worshipped in this mountain; and ye say, that in Jerusalem is the place where men ought to worship.

21. Jesus saith unto her, Woman, believe me, the hour cometh, when ye shall neither in this mountain, nor yet at Jerusalem, worship the Father.

22. Ye worship ye know not what: we know what we worship: for salvation is of the Jews.

23. But the hour cometh, and now is, when the true worshippers shall worship the Father in spirit and in truth: for the Father seeketh such to worship him.

24. God is a Spirit: and they that worship him must worship him in spirit and in truth.
25. The woman saith unto him, I know that Messias cometh, which is called Christ: when he is come, he will tell us all things.
26. Jesus saith unto her, I that speak unto thee am he.
27. And upon this came his disciples, and marvelled that he talked with the woman: yet no man said, What seekest thou? or, Why talkest thou with her?
28. The woman then left her waterpot, and went her way into the city, and saith to the men,
29. Come, see a man, which told me all things that ever I did: is not this the Christ?
30. Then they went out of the city, and came unto him.
31. In the mean while his disciples prayed him, saying, Master, eat.
32. But he said unto them, I have meat to eat that ye know not of.
33. Therefore said the disciples one to another, Hath any man brought him ought to eat?
34. Jesus saith unto them, My meat is to do the will of him that sent me, and to finish his work.
35. Say not ye, There are yet four months, and then cometh harvest? behold, I say unto you, Lift up your eyes, and look on the fields; for they are white already to harvest.
36. And he that reapeth receiveth wages, and gathereth fruit unto life eternal: that both he that soweth and he that reapeth may rejoice together.
37. And herein is that saying true, One soweth, and another reapeth.
38. I sent you to reap that whereon ye bestowed no labour: other men laboured, and ye are entered into their labours.
39. And many of the Samaritans of that city believed on him for the saying of the woman, which testified, He told me all that ever I did.
40. So when the Samaritans were come unto him, they besought him that he would tarry with them: and he abode there two days.
41. And many more believed because of his own word;
42. And said unto the woman, Now we believe, not because of thy saying: for we have heard him ourselves, and know that this is indeed the Christ, the Saviour of the world. (John 4:1-42)

This episode with the Samaritan woman at the well confounds our normal expectation. We think of being born again as the simplest statement of the Gospel, but our Lord's conversation with Nicodemus shows us how far-reaching its implications are. We would have expected a statement on our Lord's messiahship in the meeting with Nicodemus, but we see it rather in our Lord's words to a Samaritan woman. She is a women five times married and divorced, and living at the moment with a man not her husband (vv. 16-18). Now, a married woman without a dowry was a concubine, a legal wife, but not an endowed wife. This was actually true of women whose social or economic status was low, and who would be ready to accept an unprotected status as a concubine. Divorcing a concubine was cheap; no financial loss ensued. It was thus no reflection on this Samaritan woman that she was five times divorced and her present man did not even bother to make her a concubine. She was obviously of a poor family, with no menfolk to demand a dowry and status for her.

The Pharisees were aware that Jesus was baptizing, or, rather, His disciples, under His direction, were baptizing more disciples than John the Baptist. Our Lord therefore withdrew from Judaea into Galilee. His route lay through Samaria (vv. 1-4). He came there near a city of Samaria called Sychar, close to the area given by Jacob to Joseph centuries earlier (Gen. 33:19; 48:22; Joshua 24:32; John 4:5).

At Jacob's well, they rested. Jesus, we are told, was *weary* (v. 6). This statement is an important one. John's Gospel strongly asserts the deity of Jesus, but, at the same time, His humanity also.

The disciples went into Sychar to buy food (v. 8). Jesus rested at the well, and the Samaritan woman came to draw water. Jesus said, "Give me to drink" (v. 7). The woman's reaction was one of honest surprise. Jews normally had no dealings with Samaritans (v. 9). The Samaritans were a mixed people, people who did not go into captivity, and who intermarried with other peoples. Jews and Samaritans each regarded themselves as the true heirs of God's promises.

Jesus made clear to the woman who He was, and how absurd her reaction was. She knew He was a Jew by His dress and by His speech, and her response was one of curiosity at His readiness to talk to her.

Our Lord's comment has been ably paraphrased by Plummer:

> 'Spiritually our positions are reversed. It is thou who art weary, and foot-sore, and parched, close to the well, yet unable to drink; it is I who can give thee water from the well, and quench thy thirst forever.'[1]

The gift of God is Jesus Christ: He is given to us as our great privilege and honor. The fallen world may regard Him with contempt and forever seek to crucify Him afresh with their venomous hatred, but He is our gift of freedom and salvation. Our Lord offers "living water," forever fresh and life-giving.

In vv. 11-12, the woman responds literally; she insists on a literal meaning because this rabbi's religious emphasis might embarrass her. Our forefather Jacob gave us this many centuries-old well, she says. Can you do better?

In vv. 13-14, our Lord, disregarding the woman's comment and yet answering her thinking, tells her that Jacob's well can only satisfy a temporary thirst, but the living water He provides shall have everlasting consequences.

[1.] A. Plummer, *The Gospel According to St. John* (Cambridge, England: Cambridge University Press, 1880, 1906), 108.

In v. 15, the woman continues her literal emphasis. "Provide me," she says, "with your water so that I will not need to return to this well again."

Our Lord responds to this skepticism by saying, "Go, call thy husband, and come hither" (v. 16). The woman answers, "I have no husband." Jesus commends her honesty and tells her, "You have had five husbands, and your present mate is not your husband" (vv. 17-18). The woman recognizes Jesus to be more than she had assumed; He was apparently a prophet. But she wanted to shift the discussion away from her marital and sexual history, and so she raises the key question between Jews and Samaritans: is it Mount Gerizim or is it Jerusalem that has the true temple? (vv. 19-20).

Jesus refuses to be drawn into such a discussion because He is the true and living Temple. Neither Jerusalem nor Samaria are the center. All the same, "salvation of the Jews," the promise of the great messianic redemption, comes from Judaea. The true worshipper will worship in the Spirit and in truth. God is not limited by space and time, because God is Spirit, and He can only be worshipped in Spirit and truth. He cannot be localized even in the greatest Temple, even in one built in terms of His word. In Himself, Jesus Christ is God incarnate, as the way, the truth, and the life (John 14:6); He is the revelation of the invisible God (vv. 21-24).

The woman recognizes that all this fits one person, the Messiah. She says, "When he is come, he will tell us all things" (v. 25). Our Lord says simply, "I that speak unto thee am he" (v. 26).

At this point the disciples returned, rather surprised that He was speaking to a woman. Rabbis usually felt that such teaching was below their station, but none commented on it (v. 27). The woman, however, went into the city to summon men to see Jesus. "He has," she said, "a knowledge beyond man's. Is this not Christ?" (vv. 28-30).

The disciples, having brought food, urged Jesus to eat. He, moved with the challenge of His ministry, spoke of the meat or food His calling provided His inner being (vv. 31-32). The uncomprehending disciples wondered who had fed Him, and He said, "My meat is to do the will of him that sent me, and to finish his work" (vv. 33-34). This finished work required the cross.

"It takes, in farming, four months for harvest time to come," Jesus said, "but, in the work of My calling, harvest time is here. The labors of men over the ages have prepared a harvest for you, My disciples, to reap" (vv. 35-38).

At this point, the woman returned with many Samaritan men who heard Him and believed as He spoke to them (vv. 39-42). This is the high point of this narrative. More than the Jews, and more than the disciples, these Samaritan men believed. The normal channels of Israel and the church are not necessarily God's channels. We cannot circumscribe God by our institutional boundaries, sacraments, or successions. What Israel could not do, the church also cannot do. God had to bypass Israel, and He, at times, bypasses the church when, in arrogance, the church sees itself as God's only means of expression.

The woman at the well was no remarkable person and was, in fact, of lowly status and probably in poor repute. She is, in fact, nameless to us. All the same, God in His grace, made her an important instrument of His Kingdom.

Chapter Nine
The Second Miracle: the Sign of Life
(John 4:43-54)

43. Now after two days he departed thence, and went into Galilee.
44. For Jesus himself testified, that a prophet hath no honour in his own country.
45. Then when he was come into Galilee, the Galilaeans received him, having seen all the things that he did at Jerusalem at the feast: for they also went unto the feast.
46. So Jesus came again into Cana of Galilee, where he made the water wine. And there was a certain nobleman, whose son was sick at Capernaum.
47. When he heard that Jesus was come out of Judaea into Galilee, he went unto him, and besought him that he would come down, and heal his son: for he was at the point of death.
48. Then said Jesus unto him, Except ye see signs and wonders, ye will not believe.
49. The nobleman saith unto him, Sir, come down ere my child die.
50. Jesus saith unto him, Go thy way; thy son liveth. And the man believed the word that Jesus had spoken unto him, and he went his way.
51. And as he was now going down, his servants met him, and told him, saying, Thy son liveth.
52. Then enquired he of them the hour when he began to amend. And they said unto him, Yesterday at the seventh hour the fever left him.
53. So the father knew that it was at the same hour, in the which Jesus said unto him, Thy son liveth: and himself believed, and his whole house.
54. This is again the second miracle that Jesus did, when he was come out of Judaea into Galilee. (John 4:43-54)

The response of the Samaritans was so good that our Lord spent two days in Sychar before going to Cana in Galilee. The response He received in Galilee was a good one, and yet He declares that "a prophet hath no honour in his own country" (v. 44). In Matthew 13:57, Mark 6:4, and Luke 4:24, we see the same comment again made. His reception on this occasion in Galilee was a good one. Why then the remark? The woman at the well and the men of Sychar had received Him *at His word* as the Messiah. The peoples of Galilee were more ready for the miracles than for Him. This was the difference. In v. 48, when the nobleman shows faith without a miracle as yet performed, Jesus turned to the Galileans to ask, "Will none of you believe without seeing signs and portents?" The contrast is between the royal officer, a foreigner, and the Galileans. This story and our Lord's question points at us. Our faith is lacking where action counts. Our Lord's miracles were many, but they did not in and of themselves result in faith in Him as the Messiah and Redeemer. John selects certain miracles as signs of more than themselves, as indications of the nature of our redemption. This is certainly true in this case.

Philip Schaff summed up the meaning of this miracle in these words: "Christ's word is as good as Christ's presence."[1]

The text in v. 46 speaks of "a certain nobleman," or, "a royal official," a *basilikos*, which can mean either someone of royal blood or a servant to such a person, one with status. The man asks that Jesus go to Capernaum to heal his son, who was at the point of death. Jesus answers, "Except ye see signs and wonders, ye will not believe" (v. 48). This was addressed to the other people present as much as to the nobleman, if not more so. It was the people who, while impressed by His miracles at Jerusalem (v. 46), were not ready to see Him in His office of Redeemer-Messiah. The "nobleman" pleaded (v. 49), and Jesus answered, "Go thy way: thy son liveth" (v. 50). The *basilikos* returned, to be met the next day by his servants, who reported his son's miraculous recovery. This recovery had taken place when Jesus had said, "Thy son liveth." The *basilikos* and his whole household believed in Jesus (vv. 51-53).

Then, in v. 54, we are told that this is our Lord's second miracle after departing from Judaea into Galilee (v. 54). This *can* mean that He did work another miracle after leaving Judaea, or, that after leaving Judaea, He performed a second miracle which could be called *a sign*, a revelatory act. The latter is the more likely meaning.

Moreover, the place is again Cana of Galilee, where the miraculous conversion of water into wine had occurred (John 2:1-11). In that first sign, our Lord turned one ordinary, natural thing, water, into another equally natural fact, wine. His presence glorifies the natural. His power raises the natural to a new level. The miracle points to the glorification of this world in His new creation, and of our lives by His regenerating and transforming power. He is the life-giver and the renewer of all things.

In the first miracle of Cana of Galilee, water is turned into wine, but a greater miracle occurs in the second Cana miracle: near death is turned into life. The word "signs" in v. 48 is the same Greek word translated in John 2:11 as "miracles."

In 1 Kings 17:23, Elijah resurrects the widow's dead son and returns him to his mother, saying, "See, thy son liveth." Here, our Lord echoes Elijah, saying, "Thy son liveth" (v. 51). The men of his day rejected Elijah, hunted him, and jeered him. In our Lord's day, He, having healed many, and raised them from the dead, was crucified. Men hate life because they hate God. Paul tells us, "the carnal mind is enmity against God: for it is not subject to the law of God, *neither indeed can it be*" (Rom. 8:7; James 4:4). The law is the redeemed man's way of life, and therefore those who hate God hate His

[1]. John Peter Lange, *John* (Grand Rapids, MI: reprint, n.d), 176.

law, and the people of His law. Because of this hatred of God, the *miracles* of our Lord commended him to many, but He Himself was despised and rejected of man.

The two miracles of Cana thus point to the fullness of life in Christ. They tell us that we are surrounded by an ocean of death, but also an ocean of life, and Christ is our only way, truth, and life (John 14:6).

The Samaritans recognized Christ as "the Savior of the world" (v. 42). We are now told that this nobleman and his whole house believed in Jesus as the Christ (v. 53). We are again confronted with the fact set forth in John 1:11: "He came unto his own, and his own received him not." Too often the church sees itself as the center and the miracle and thereby forgets Christ and His power. The living God can never be domesticated into an institution, and all attempts to do so are finally fatal to the would-be domesticators.

In our Lord's day, there were two "domesticators" of absolute power, or of divine power. The Roman Empire saw itself as the epitome of power. The Senate could make and unmake gods. Roman power covered the Mediterranean world, half of Europe, most of North Africa, and much of the near East. "Eternal Rome" was an apt term whereby Rome depicted itself as the order of the ages, the new and true world order.

The religious and civil rulers of Judaea were no less assured that they represented the divine order, which was to a degree true, but they also saw themselves as the *controllers* of that divine order. The well-known habit of the Pharisees to define God's law in terms alien to it made clear their arrogance. Keeping the Sabbath holy is God's law; the numerous rules created to tell the people how far they could walk on the Sabbath, or whether or not they could eat an egg laid on the Sabbath or an egg over which the hen had labored on the Sabbath, only to produce it two days later: all such rules supplanted God's law with man's definitions. Men then kept man-made rules rather than God's law.

In the world of that era, there were no hereditary titles of nobility: a nobleman, a *basilikos*, was simply a man of power. A *basilikos* was, in his domain or sphere, the personification of power. But, faced with a dying son, this *basilikos* was impotent. Confronted with the issues of life and death, the power of Rome, King Herod, or the Pharisees and Sadducees, was helpless and impotent.

What this miracle, this *sign* and *wonder*, tells us is simply this: neither church nor state nor any human power can conquer the ultimate, basic, and essential problems of life and death. Only the triune God who made us is sufficient unto the task.

This second sign (v. 54) of Cana of Galilee tells us that church and state *cannot* settle the problems of our life and world. Only the triune God who made us can ever resolve those problems: *to renew life or to resurrect it is nothing to Him who makes it.* Our being born again is such a miracle, and it tells us that we *cannot* bring about a rebirth in any sphere of life and thought apart from the triune God. *All efforts to do so are sin.* The signs and wonders in the Gospel of John are a condemnation of all attempts to effect a reformation in this world apart from the regenerating power of God and the sanctifying power of His law.

Chapter Ten

The Third Miracle: The Sign of Grace
(John 5:1-16)

1. After this there was a feast of the Jews; and Jesus went up to Jerusalem.

2. Now there is at Jerusalem by the sheep market a pool, which is called in the Hebrew tongue Bethesda, having five porches.

3. In these lay a great multitude of impotent folk, of blind, halt, withered, waiting for the moving of the water.

4. For an angel went down at a certain season into the pool, and troubled the water: whosoever then first after the troubling of the water stepped in was made whole of whatsoever disease he had.

5. And a certain man was there, which had an infirmity thirty and eight years.

6. When Jesus saw him lie, and knew that he had been now a long time in that case, he saith unto him, Wilt thou be made whole?

7. The impotent man answered him, Sir, I have no man, when the water is troubled, to put me into the pool: but while I am coming, another steppeth down before me.

8. Jesus saith unto him, Rise, take up thy bed, and walk.

9. And immediately the man was made whole, and took up his bed, and walked: and on the same day was the sabbath.

10. The Jews therefore said unto him that was cured, It is the sabbath day: it is not lawful for thee to carry thy bed.

11. He answered them, He that made me whole, the same said unto me, Take up thy bed, and walk.

12. Then asked they him, What man is that which said unto thee, Take up thy bed, and walk?

13. And he that was healed wist not who it was: for Jesus had conveyed himself away, a multitude being in that place.

14. Afterward Jesus findeth him in the temple, and said unto him, Behold, thou art made whole: sin no more, lest a worse thing come unto thee.

15. The man departed, and told the Jews that it was Jesus, which had made him whole.

16. And therefore did the Jews persecute Jesus, and sought to slay him, because he had done these things on the sabbath day. (John 5:16)

This is an unusual episode because of the setting, the pool of Bethesda. There were a number of such pools in ancient Jerusalem; then as now, people went to such spas for their sometimes real benefits. This particular pool has been discovered and excavated; it is on the property of the White Fathers near St. Anne's Church. A large pool, it was between 165 to 220 feet wide by 315 feet long, with a central partition. There were colonnades on the four sides and at the partition.[1] We are told that an angel at times

---

[1.] Raymond E. Brown, *The Gospel According To John I-XII* (Garden City, NY: Doubleday, 1966), 207.

45

"troubled the water" and that the first one to step in was healed (v. 4). Modernist scholars agree that this statement was not a part of the original text; clearly, they do not want to believe in this. Of course, there is not much that they will accept as historical in this Gospel or in the others. Tertullian (c. A.D. 200) attests to this verse, as do others. William Hendriksen, in *The Gospel of John*, vol. I (1953), sees it as probably historical, while others, such as Leon Morris, see possibly natural factors as responsible for the troubling of the waters.

Very clearly, the temptation has been a real one to discard this angel. This is a very unusual kind of miracle, obviously, but should by no means be dropped on that account. It is a part of the received text, and it does have attestation. If we try to understand this miracle and sign, we will hopefully come to know the significance of every part of it.

This miracle can be dated. The feast was on a sabbath day, and in A.D. 29 the first day of Purim, as various scholars have pointed out, was March 19. The Book of Esther gives us the origin of Purim (Esther 9:17-18). It was a time of rejoicing over the victory over God's enemies, and gifts were given one to another *and to the poor* (Esther 9:19, 22). If the common conclusion of scholars that this "feast of the Jews" was Purim, then our Lord was giving a gift to a poor man — *healing*. Whether or not it was Purim, it was a gift, but Purim makes it especially appropriate.

Returning to the angel, his presence was unusual and has little in the way of parallels elsewhere in the Bible. Why would God send an angel to supply miracles to a soon to be doomed nation? Is there a parallel between the cripple and Judaea? Both are very close to the source of all healing, and both are also very far from it. The man was partially paralyzed or partially crippled. His infirmity was of thirty-eight years duration; it could have been a condition which began in his childhood, and he might now be no more than a man in his early forties. Jesus asked him, "Wilt thou be made whole?" (v. 6). J. Stephen Hart very ably summed up the exchange:

> Christ does not receive a direct answer. The man feels himself blamed, and makes a grumbling excuse for not even trying the effect of the water. He tried in the past often enough, but he never got through the crowd in time, and he lost hope and gave up the attempt. He has accepted the life of a professional beggar, which he finds sufficient to bring him a sustenance wage of good clothing and a lodging somewhere near, though he may do some chores to earn that. He comes to Bethesda now for the sake of social intercourse with people like himself. Christ sometimes asked for faith in His applicants; this time it is hope that is lacking. He is reconciled to idle poverty, though he will not acknowledge that he prefers it to work, for that might deprive him of the alms he expects to receive. The external malady is

but the sign of the spiritual one, and its unfortunate cause, though it should not have been an effective one.[2]

Hart is right. The answer to the question, "Wilt thou be made whole?," should have been a quick and spontaneous "yes." We do not know how long this cripple had been there at the pool; thirty-eight years was the length of his malady, not of his presence at Bethesda.

In v. 16, John tells us that this miracle was seen by the religious leaders as a total affront, and they decided then on Jesus' death. At the same time, it is for John the third sign.

The parallel between Israel, or Judaea, and this cripple is a very important one. Both were close to the source of healing, and neither truly wanted it. In Luke 16:31, our Lord says of the ungodly, "If they hear not Moses and the prophets, neither will they be persuaded, though one rose from the dead." They were not persuaded by an angel's miracles, nor Christ's, nor by His resurrection. Why should they believe when their faith was opposed to God in the name of God?

By healing this man, Jesus so angered the religious and civil leaders that they sought His death (v. 16). The greater the good, the greater the hatred on the part of the ungodly. They will only have God on their terms, meaning God as their slave or not at all.

But Jesus healed the man even though the man did not ask for healing. He told him, "Rise, take up thy bed, and walk" (v. 8). The cripple was at once stopped for working on the sabbath by carrying his bed or pallet. He was as yet ignorant of the identity of Jesus. Jesus, finding him, told the man, "Behold, thou art made whole: sin no more (or, stop your sinning) lest a worst thing come unto thee" (v. 14). We are not told the nature of his sinning, if it had a particular form. The cured cripple went at once to the leaders and identified Jesus as his healer (v. 15), which tells us how poor in character he was.

This healing was an act of grace. All Christ's miracles were, but this instance was particularly so because it was not even asked for. In Luke 17:11-19, we are told of ten lepers whom Christ healed and ordered to report to the priests in order to be certified as healed. Afterward, only one of the ten came back to Jesus to thank Him. Here, the angel in the pool's turbulence, and Christ at the pool's side, gave a special grace to Judaea, and it was rejected. Christ's life and work was a far greater miracle and a revelation of God than the single troubling of the waters, but the people in both cases rejected God the Healer, nor were they truly interested in healing.

---

[2] J. Stephen Hart, *A Companion to St. John's Gospel* (Carlton, Victoria, Australia: Melbourne University Press, 1952), 85.

Our Lord's miracle and sign meant simply this: be healed, or perish. Jerusalem, rejecting the healer, was given over to destruction. The sign to our world is the same: be healed by Christ, or perish.

In Isaiah 57:18-21, we read:

> 18. I have seen his ways, and will heal him: I will lead him also, and restore comforts unto him and to his mourners.
> 19. I create the fruit of the lips; Peace, peace to him that is far off, and to him that is near, saith the LORD; and I will heal him.
> 20. But the wicked are like the troubled sea, when it cannot rest, whose waters cast up mire and dirt.
> 21. There is no peace, saith my God, to the wicked.

The contrast between a do-nothing Sabbath and a Sabbath surrendered to God's healing and working is like the difference between night and day.

Ernst Haenchen said of this miracle that the religious leaders "are unmoved by the miracle, either in this point or in what follows. They are concerned only with the observance of the sabbath law."[3]

When Jesus healed the man sick with palsy, He said, "Son, be of good cheer; thy sins be forgiven thee" (Matt. 9:2), a statement repeated to other men whom He healed. Here, the remark differs: "Behold, thou art made whole: sin no more, lest a worst thing come unto thee" (John 5:14). This warning could have been made to all Israel, even as it is now applicable to the whole world. In Hart's words, our Lord's warning had reference to the crippled man's sin: "The sin is the helplessness, hopelessness, and lack of moral energy that we have noted in him."[4] This is our failing also, and one we commit all too often.

This miracle is a sign of God's sovereign grace. It can heal the undeserving, and it can heal those who have no interest in it. To depend on ourselves is to depend on nothing; our mainstay and only hope is God's sovereign grace to the undeserving. Where that grace is external only, there is no hope. Where is it given to the whole man, it means redemption. At every point, this episode reveals the supernatural. In v. 6, we see that our Lord knew the man and his history before he spoke to him. He also knows us, and the very hairs of our head are all numbered (Matt. 10:30), so that we are totally in His providential care and grace. This grace was extended to this cripple, and it revealed to Israel the sign of His covenantal mercy, if they would hear, but they would not.

[3.] Ernst Haenchen, *A Commentary on the Gospel of John, Chapters 1-6* (Philadelphia, PA: Fortress Press, 1984), 246.
[4.] Hart, *op.cit.*, 86.

Chapter Eleven

Christt the Center
(John 5:17-47)

17. But Jesus answered them, My Father worketh hitherto, and I work.
18. Therefore the Jews sought the more to kill him, because he not only had broken the sabbath, but said also that God was his Father, making himself equal with God.
19. Then answered Jesus and said unto them, Verily, verily, I say unto you, The Son can do nothing of himself, but what he seeth the Father do: for what things soever he doeth, these also doeth the Son likewise.
20. For the Father loveth the Son, and sheweth him all things that himself doeth: and he will shew him greater works than these, that ye may marvel.
21. For as the Father raiseth up the dead, and quickeneth them; even so the Son quickeneth whom he will.
22. For the Father judgeth no man, but hath committed all judgment unto the Son:
23. That all men should honour the Son, even as they honour the Father. He that honoureth not the Son honoureth not the Father which hath sent him.
24. Verily, verily, I say unto you, He that heareth my word, and believeth on him that sent me, hath everlasting life, and shall not come into condemnation; but is passed from death unto life.
25. Verily, verily, I say unto you, The hour is coming, and now is, when the dead shall hear the voice of the Son of God: and they that hear shall live.
26. For as the Father hath life in himself; so hath he given to the Son to have life in himself;
27. And hath given him authority to execute judgment also, because he is the Son of man.
28. Marvel not at this: for the hour is coming, in the which all that are in the graves shall hear his voice,
29. And shall come forth; they that have done good, unto the resurrection of life; and they that have done evil, unto the resurrection of damnation.
30. I can of mine own self do nothing: as I hear, I judge: and my judgment is just; because I seek not mine own will, but the will of the Father which hath sent me.
31. If I bear witness of myself, my witness is not true.
32. There is another that beareth witness of me; and I know that the witness which he witnesseth of me is true.
33. Ye sent unto John, and he bare witness unto the truth.
34. But I receive not testimony from man: but these things I say, that ye might be saved.
35. He was a burning and a shining light: and ye were willing for a season to rejoice in his light.

36. But I have greater witness than that of John: for the works which the Father hath given me to finish, the same works that I do, bear witness of me, that the Father hath sent me.
37. And the Father himself, which hath sent me, hath borne witness of me. Ye have neither heard his voice at any time, nor seen his shape.
38. And ye have not his word abiding in you: for whom he hath sent, him ye believe not.
39. Search the scriptures; for in them ye think ye have eternal life: and they are they which testify of me.
40. And ye will not come to me, that ye might have life.
41. I receive not honour from men.
42. But I know you, that ye have not the love of God in you.
43. I am come in my Father's name, and ye receive me not: if another shall come in his own name, him ye will receive.
44. How can ye believe, which receive honour one of another, and seek not the honour that cometh from God only?
45. Do not think that I will accuse you to the Father: there is one that accuseth you, even Moses, in whom ye trust.
46. For had ye believed Moses, ye would have believed me: for he wrote of me.
47. But if ye believe not his writings, how shall ye believe my words? (John 5:17-47)

We have in these verses a statement by Jesus of His nature and authority. This follows after two miracles or signs, 1) the healing of the son of the nobleman or *basilikos* (John 4:46-54) and 2) the healing of the crippled man at the pool of Bethesda. The words of our text are, clearly, a statement on the nature of the Son and His relationship to the Father, but they also throw light on the *basilikos* and the cripple.

First, in vv. 19-29, we are told of the nature, authority, and prerogatives of the Son. Where this episode took place, we do not know, but vv. 18-19 make it clear that these words were spoken to some of the religious leaders who sought to kill Him. In part, the issue is this: who is Lord over the Sabbath? This is a secondary question. More importantly, who defines life and mortality, God or man? Our Lord begins by insisting on the absolute priority of God the Father to the incarnate God the Son, who is both God and man (v. 19). All the same, while the Son is totally directed by the Father, this is because of an identity of purpose, and it is a witness to their oneness. Separate action is not possible because of their unity, which is grounded on moral necessity and oneness. In A. Plummer's words, "The Father's love for the Son compels Him to make known all His works to Him; the Son's relation to the Father compels Him to do what the Father does."[1] The Son's work on earth was determined beforehand in heaven (v. 20).

[1.] A. Plummer, *The Gospel According to St. John* (Cambridge, England: Cambridge University Press, 1880, 1906), 128.

The great work of the Father and the Son is resurrection (v. 21). The primary reference here is to the resurrection of the spiritually dead, but there is also physical resurrection obviously in mind. This is the great work undertaken by the Son at the Father's direction. The Father has given all judgment into the hands of the Son (v. 22), so that all men should honor the Son as they ostensibly do the Father. Since atonement is the work of the incarnate Son, it follows that judgment is also, because Christ's atonement is the supreme act of judgment on all sin. Hence, Christ is supremely the Judge at the Last Judgment (Matt. 25:31-46). The modern church has made the atonement an instrument of sentimentality, whereas the Bible presents it as the evidence of deadly sin and the radical nature of judgment.

It follows therefore that all men should honor the Son even as they honor the Father, and failure to honor the Son is failure to honor the Father (v. 23). The law and justice of God are basic to the cross and to judgment. It is a logical to conclude from this that to hear Jesus Christ is to hear God. To believe in Christ is to have everlasting life, beginning now, and to escape from condemnation; it is passing from death into life (v. 24). We are now *legally* the heirs of eternal life, and our growth is now in terms of it.

There will come an hour in the world's history when all the spiritually dead hear the Son of God, and the elect ones hear and live (v. 25). Like the Father, the Son imparts life to whom He will. Both are alike the fountain of life; both are one God, one nature (v. 26). The Son is made judge with authority, made judge over the living and the dead because He is truly man, the atoner for men; He is the victor over sin and death. He has thereby authority to be the Great Judge over all men (v. 27). In due time, even the dead shall hear his voice (v. 28), and they shall arise to a resurrection of life or a resurrection of judgement (v. 29).

Our Lord now turns, in this *second* section, to the charge (v. 18) that He made Himself equal with God (vv. 30-38). He cites the witness of John the Baptist (vv. 30-35), then the witness of His own works (vv. 36-39). He begins by declaring, "I can of mine own self do nothing;" in all things, He reflects the will and the judgment of the Father (v. 30). There is no independent claim on His part: He sets forth God's truth (v. 31). His is not a self-attestation because it is not Himself *per se* that He represents (v. 32). John the Baptist's witness was a clear one, but Jesus does not rest His case on a man (vv. 33-34). He does take the occasion to call attention to John as a "burning and shining light" whom they accepted only up to a point — and only because of his priestly lineage (v. 35).

But our Lord has a greater witness than John: the *works* he does with empowerment from God witness to Him (v. 36). Moreover, God the Father witnesses to Jesus Christ's office, calling, and nature, but this is a witness they will not hear (vv. 37-38). They have separated themselves from His word.

Jesus now cites the witness of the Old Testament (vv. 39-40). "Search the scriptures," and you will see that they testify of Me (v. 39). But willfully, "ye will not come, that ye might have life" (v. 40). They want eternal life from the written word, the Scriptures, while ignoring the implications of the word itself.

Now, in the *third* section, vv. 41-47, in the words of B.F. Westcott, "Christ, starting from the fact of a want of will to believe in His hearers, unfolds the cause (vv. 41-44) of their rejection of Himself."[2] Our Lord does not receive His honor from men (v. 41) as His enemies do, who do not love God (v. 42). Where such people honor one another, they do so because their standards are alien to God's (vv. 43-44). Moses is their accuser before God; they profess to follow Moses, but they disbelieve his word, and so too Christ's word (v. 45-47).

We can now see the relevance of this to the two previous signs, the healing of the *basilikos'* son and of the lame man at the Bethesda pool. The *basilikos* heard and believed. His election and calling manifested itself in hearing ears and trust in Christ's words. The lame man and the religious leaders witnessed a word of grace and saw it as lawlessness: they concluded that Jesus must die. The lame man did not ask for healing; he gave no thanks for healing, and most likely the healing was no blessing to him: he now had to work for a living.

I recall years ago a comment made of a man: if you want to make him your enemy, do something good for him. What this meant specifically in his case, I do not know, but the experience of returning evil for good is a common one. The peoples of Judaea, and the lame man, were the particular beneficiaries of great and marvelous mercies, and yet the leaders of the people crucified the Christ.

Let us assume for a moment that the lame man thanked our Lord and then went his way, unconcerned about Jesus except as a healer. He would then have accepted the grace and mercy of healing but not the Healer. His status would have been no better. But he did not even give thanks.

Our Lord in this healing called attention to Himself as God's grace and judgment walking on earth. To receive only the healing and not the Healer would have been no less offensive. The center cannot be what happens to us, however much we want something, but Christ Himself. Christ was rejected by the religious leaders because His mission was greater than their hopes and plans. They wanted a Messiah on their terms, not on God's. Instead of being what God requires of us, these and all such men want God

2. B.F. Westcott, *The Gospel According to St. John* (Grand Rapids, MI: Eerdmans, 1881, 1954), 91.

to be what they require of Him. I vividly recall a dying woman in a hospital bed who insisted, after hearing me read a text, "I cannot believe in such a God," to which I answered, "But there is no other God."

The lame man was not happy to have God the Son reorder his life: he would have preferred to be left alone. This was to imagine a vain thing. No man can ever sidestep God.

The fact of sin involves all men, and sin requires atonement. Atonement means judgment. If Christ is not our vicarious substitute, then the judgment falls upon us. Hence the severity of the judgment on Jerusalem and Judaea in the war of A.D. 66-70. The fact that the lame man at Bethesda is nameless to us does not diminish the evil of his life, nor excuse him from judgment. Too many people like him today want God to leave them alone. This is to imagine a vain thing.

When the miracle occurred and, later, when the authorities questioned him, the lame man did not know who Jesus was. After Jesus identified Himself, it is almost a certainty that others told him that some believed Jesus to be the Great Prophet; others said He was the Messiah. The lame man resented having his life "messed up," and he wanted to be left alone.

Chapter Twelve

The Fourth Miracle: The Sign Against Magic
(John 6:1-15)

1. After these things Jesus went over the sea of Galilee, which is the sea of Tiberias.
2. And a great multitude followed him, because they saw his miracles which he did on them that were diseased.
3. And Jesus went up into a mountain, and there he sat with his disciples.
4. And the passover, a feast of the Jews, was nigh.
5. When Jesus then lifted up his eyes, and saw a great company come unto him, he saith unto Philip, Whence shall we buy bread, that these may eat?
6. And this he said to prove him: for he himself knew what he would do.
7. Philip answered him, Two hundred pennyworth of bread is not sufficient for them, that every one of them may take a little.
8. One of his disciples, Andrew, Simon Peter's brother, saith unto him,
9. There is a lad here, which hath five barley loaves, and two small fishes: but what are they among so many?
10. And Jesus said, Make the men sit down. Now there was much grass in the place. So the men sat down, in number about five thousand.
11. And Jesus took the loaves; and when he had given thanks, he distributed to the disciples, and the disciples to them that were set down; and likewise of the fishes as much as they would.
12. When they were filled, he said unto his disciples, Gather up the fragments that remain, that nothing be lost.
13. Therefore they gathered them together, and filled twelve baskets with the fragments of the five barley loaves, which remained over and above unto them that had eaten.
14. Then those men, when they had seen the miracle that Jesus did, said, This is of a truth that prophet that should come into the world.
15. When Jesus therefore perceived that they would come and take him by force, to make him a king, he departed again into a mountain himself alone. (John 6:1-15)

This miracle, the first feeding of a multitude, has an Old Testament precedent. In 2 Kings 4:42-44, we have Elisha using twenty loaves of barley bread and some grain to feed one hundred men. We are told, "they did eat, and left thereof." This miracle was a forerunner of the fall of Samaria and Israel, even as Christ's two miraculous feedings preceded the judgment on Judaea.

The setting was the seashore of Galilee, also known by the Roman name, the Sea of Tiberius. The names of seas, mountains, countries, and cities have often been changed throughout history to satisfy the whims of their conquerors, but God and His law never change. The judgment for sin is death, and the alternative to life is also death.

The disciples had sailed across Galilee, known also as Gennesareth and Gennesar. According to Josephus, the lake was sixteen by four and a half miles in size, but it is now twelve and a half by seven miles. It was then a prolific source of fish.

Jesus and the disciples took a boat to find refuge from the crowds by sailing to a remote coast of the sea, but a great crowd followed them, apparently by land, eager to receive miraculous healing in some cases and, in others, to witness it.

W. Robert Cook, in commenting on the signs cited by John, lists them as follows:

> 1. Jesus is self-revealed as the master of quality when He turns water into wine (John 2:1-11);
> 2. He is the master of space when He heals the son of the *basilikos* (John 4:46-54);
> 3. He is the master of time when He instantaneously cures the cripple at the pool (John 5:1-18);
> 4. He is the master of quantity when He provided the miraculous feeding of 5,000 with so little;
> 5. He is the master over natural law when He walks on water (John 6:16-21);
> 6. He is "the master of misfortune" when He heals the man born blind (John 9:1-41);
> 7. He is the master over death in resurrecting Lazarus (John 11:1-47).[1]

This is all very true, but there is much more to this particular sign.

Our Lord performs a great miracle. Matthew 14:21 tells us that the *men* numbered 5,000, "beside women and children." The actual count could have been up to twice 5,000 or more. The only available food was one boy's lunch, five barley "loaves" and two small fish. Out of this, our Lord fed all, and twelve baskets were left over. The baskets, no doubt, came from their ship.

From this miracle, the crowd came to a conclusion. This man is the great Prophet foretold in Deuteronomy 18:15. They therefore sought to take Christ by force and compel Him to be king (vv. 14-15). Since Jesus was born a king, as some believed, He was already the King. Isaiah 9:6 heralded his kingship and deity. Why then did the multitude, seeing His divine powers, not fall down before Him to worship and obey Him? Why did they seek to force kingship on Him?

To understand this, we must understand the difference between true religion and magic. In our time, as often before, the vast difference is obscured or denied. *The Westminster Shorter Catechism* begins by defining

---

[1.] W. Robert Cook, *The Theology of John* (Chicago, IL: Moody Press, 1979), 55f.

true religion: "Man's chief end is to glorify God and to enjoy Him forever." Man must conform Himself to the will and the word of God. He is not in charge: God is. It is God's will that must be done, not man's. The prayer of Jesus Christ as the Lamb of God and the innocent sin-bearer was, in Gethsemane, "Thy will be done" (Matt. 26:42). The prayer taught to us by our Lord declares, "Thy Kingdom come. Thy will be done in earth, as it is in heaven (Matt. 6:10).

The difference is a very great one: it is man's will versus God's will. Our Lord here witnesses to His kingship, its power and its meaning. The multitude wanted *specific* miracles: our Lord offered instead a miraculous life in Him. The attitude of the crowd, on seeing the miraculous feeding, was that this was a power *we* can use for Israel; therefore, let *us* make Him King. But Scripture declares the Messiah to be God's ordained King. According to Isaiah 9:6,

> For unto us a child is born, unto us a son is given: and the government shall be upon his shoulder: and his name shall be called Wonderful, Counselor, The Mighty God, The Everlasting Father, The Prince of Peace.

Men want a God they can control, and the goal of magic is man's freedom from God and "nature" and man's total control over all things. Modern science is essentially related to magic in its goals.

In theology, magic declares that man *elects* God to be God, and Christ to be King; both are placed under man's control and choice, and man's will is made into the constitution of God's government.

Thus, there is a radical conflict between doctrines which declare the sovereignty of God and those affirming the sovereignty of man. Both may affirm Jesus Christ, but for one He is the Lord and Savior and the absolute predestinator over all things, and for the other man chooses God. Our Lord, in John 15:16, declares,

> Ye have not chosen me, but I have chosen you, and ordained you, that he should go and bring forth fruit, and that your fruit should remain: that whatsoever he shall ask of the Father in my name, he may give it you.

Sovereignty resides with God in both choosing us and in giving to us.

This is clearly a sign against magic. Man since the Fall dreams of magic, to be his own god and law-maker, and the modern state works towards this, striving for total planning and control. It uses politics and the results of science to gain total power and to substitute man's decree of predestination for God's.

This is the dream of humanism, both in the church and in politics. In direct opposition to this age-old desire and hope, Jesus makes clear in this sign against magic that man cannot use God: he must rather be willingly and joyfully used by God.

Chapter Thirteen
The Fifth Miracle: The Sign of Transcendence
(John 6:16-21)

16. And when even was now come, his disciples went down unto the sea,
17. And entered into a ship, and went over the sea toward Capernaum. And it was now dark, and Jesus was not come to them.
18. And the sea arose by reason of a great wind that blew.
19. So when they had rowed about five and twenty or thirty furlongs, they see Jesus walking on the sea, and drawing nigh unto the ship: and they were afraid.
20. But he saith unto them, It is I; be not afraid.
21. Then they willingly received him into the ship: and immediately the ship was at the land whither they went. (John 6:16-21)

This is a miracle also recorded in Matthew 14:23-33 and Mark 6:47-52. In Matthew, we are told of Peter's request that he be made to walk on the water, of the fearfulness that endangered his life, and of our Lord's rescue of Peter. The attention in John's account focuses on our Lord's total power over all natural forces.

After the miraculous feeding, Jesus "went up into the mountain apart to pray," according to Matthew 14:23. At the same time, we are told in Matthew 14:22 that He "constrained" the disciples to enter the boat and sail to the other side. Since the crowd would have expected Jesus to go with the disciples, it was easier for our Lord to slip away from the people.

When the disciples were about half way across the sea, they saw Jesus coming to them and were afraid, assuming it was an apparition, "and they cried out for fear" (Matt. 14:26). The sea was subject to sudden storms and could be dangerous. They may have feared that the ostensible apparition was a sign of their near death.

The disciples were attempting to reach Bethsaida, according to Mark 6:45. John tells us they were going "toward Capernaum" (John 6:17), which was close to Bethsaida.

The multitude had wanted to make Jesus their king, but He escaped from them. His calling was neither to be a bread-king nor a miracle-king. In all that He did, He called attention to His redemptive work, not to the bread which passes away. Men can only know Christ on His terms, not on theirs. As Calvin commented, "And what avails the pretense of zeal, when by our disorderly worship we offer a greater insult to God then if a person were expressly and deliberately to make an attack on his glory?" Calvin stated also, "obedience is the foundation of true worship..." We must therefore abide by His word, "for as soon as we turn aside in the smallest degree, the truth is poisoned by our leaven, so that it is no longer like itself."[1]

William Hendriksen called attention to the fact that this miracle is "really four miracles in one." *First*, Jesus walks on the waters of the sea. *Second*, Matthew tells us that He caused Peter to walk on the sea also. *Third*, He causes the storm to cease when He enters the boat (Matt. 14:32; Mark 6:51f). *Fourth*, when He enters the boat, from a spot in the middle of the sea, they are suddenly on the shore.[2] Clearly, Jesus transcended all human limitations and powers, and yet the multitude and the disciples wanted Him to meet man's expectations, in this case, Judaean man. The people saw Jesus in terms of the miracles of the loaves and fishes, not in terms of who and what He was and had, in one way or another, declared Himself to be.

We know that even after the resurrection, and at the time of the ascension, the disciples themselves had Judaic expectations and hoped that Jesus would restore the kingdom to Israel (Acts 1:6). Our Lord told them that the coming of the Holy Spirit would give them a *world* perspective (Acts 1:7-8). G. Campbell Morgan was right in analyzing the disciples' failure:

> Now mark this carefully. None saw the sign (the miracle at sea) but His own disciples. It was a sign for them only. Why? I can only answer suggestively. It seems to me that when He sent them in that boat across the sea, He knew the keenness of their disappointment, and their perplexity, that He would not be made King. Perhaps they wondered and questioned as to whether after all, He had Kingly power and authority. So He gave them a demonstration of His present Kingship, and that in the realm of Nature. It was as though He had said, "I have refused to be crowned King upon the basis of bread, but make no mistake, I am King in every realm; King in the realm of Nature, contrary winds cannot hinder Me; the tossing sea cannot overwhelm Me. I am King.[3]

This sign, like the miraculous feeding, strikes at man's expectation that God meet man's requirements and hopes. The source of all determination is God, not man. The believer cannot play the unbeliever's game. Fallen man wants to be his own god and lawgiver. Redeemed man, because he now believes, cannot require God to meet his terms. Our faith cannot command God. The meaning of man's salvation is that now God's will, not ours, be done. Both signs require of us a God-centered life. We cannot expect God to please us: we must please Him. God is not man's happy servant, ready to jump at man's whims as soon as man has supposedly said "yes" to Jesus.

[1] John Calvin, *Commentary on the Gospel According to St. John*, vol. I (Grand Rapids, MI: Eerdmans, 1949 reprint), 233-234.
[2] William Hendriksen, *The Gospel of John*, vol. I (Grand Rapids, MI: Baker Book House, 1953), 227.
[3] G. Campbell Morgan, *The Gospel According to John* (New York, NY: Fleming H. Revell. n.d.), 102f.

Such views place churchmen in the same place as the scribes and Pharisees of old.

Raymond E. Brown was correct in saying that the multitude wanted a political Messiah, and this Jesus refused to be. He was far more than the terms "the Prophet" and "king" could imply, in that He interprets Himself, a sign that what He is can be fully expressed only by the divine name "I am."[4]

The hope of the people is in their nation, or self-realization, and it is, in their eyes, God's duty to bless their hopes. Far too many people reverse the *Westminster Shorter Catechism*'s opening statement, asserting that "The chief end of God should be to glorify man and to enjoy him forever." All this and more is expected for a simple, costless "yes" to Jesus. Perhaps one should not say *costless*. A woman of wealth and beauty was, some years ago, very angry with me for my theology and my post-millennial beliefs. How could God expect her to go through the tribulation when she had given up her two great loves, smoking and dancing, for His sake? When I reminded her that I was an Armenian, and my people had undergone great tribulation, and asked her why she should be spared, she dismissed my statement as irrelevant! This sums up the issue very clearly. The goal of humanism in the church, as in Israel of old, is to make our group the center, whereas Christ is alone the center.

Our Lord's miracle here is the sign of *transcendence*. We cannot limit God in terms of our vision and our hopes. He is the Lord, not man. Isaiah tells us of the arrogance of all attempts to control God, and in summary he states:

> 13. Who hath directed the Spirit of the Lord, or being his counselor hath taught him?
> 14. With whom took he counsel, and who instructed him, and taught him in the path of judgment, and taught him knowledge, and showed to him the way of understanding?
> 15. Behold, the nations are as a drop of a bucket, and are counted as the small dust of the balance: behold, he taketh up the isles as a very little thing.
> 16. And Lebanon is not sufficient to burn, nor the beasts thereof sufficient for a burnt offering.
> 17. All nations before him are as nothing; and they are counted to him less than nothing, and vanity. (Isaiah 40:13-17)

The arrogance of man in assuming his own supremacy over God is an amazing fact. In this miracle, the sign of transcendence, Jesus compels us to see that our lives must be God-centered, not fixed upon ourselves.

[4.] Raymond E. Brown, *The Gospel According to John* (i-xii), vol. I (Garden City, NY: Doubleday, 1966), 225.

Chapter Fourteen
To Believe on Him
(John 6:22-40)

22. The day following, when the people which stood on the other side of the sea saw that there was none other boat there, save that one whereinto his disciples were entered, and that Jesus went not with his disciples into the boat, but that his disciples were gone away alone;

23. (Howbeit there came other boats from Tiberias nigh unto the place where they did eat bread, after that the Lord had given thanks:)

24. When the people therefore saw that Jesus was not there, neither his disciples, they also took shipping, and came to Capernaum, seeking for Jesus.

25. And when they had found him on the other side of the sea, they said unto him, Rabbi, when camest thou hither?

26. Jesus answered them and said, Verily, verily, I say unto you, Ye seek me, not because ye saw the miracles, but because ye did eat of the loaves, and were filled.

27. Labour not for the meat which perisheth, but for that meat which endureth unto everlasting life, which the Son of man shall give unto you: for him hath God the Father sealed.

28. Then said they unto him, What shall we do, that we might work the works of God?

29. Jesus answered and said unto them, This is the work of God, that ye believe on him whom he hath sent.

30. They said therefore unto him, What sign shewest thou then, that we may see, and believe thee? what dost thou work?

31. Our fathers did eat manna in the desert; as it is written, He gave them bread from heaven to eat.

32. Then Jesus said unto them, Verily, verily, I say unto you, Moses gave you not that bread from heaven; but my Father giveth you the true bread from heaven.

33. For the bread of God is he which cometh down from heaven, and giveth life unto the world.

34. Then said they unto him, Lord, evermore give us this bread.

35. And Jesus said unto them, I am the bread of life: he that cometh to me shall never hunger; and he that believeth on me shall never thirst.

36. But I said unto you, That ye also have seen me, and believe not.

37. All that the Father giveth me shall come to me; and him that cometh to me I will in no wise cast out.

38. For I came down from heaven, not to do mine own will, but the will of him that sent me.

39. And this is the Father's will which hath sent me, that of all which he hath given me I should lose nothing, but should raise it up again at the last day.

40. And this is the will of him that sent me, that every one which seeth the Son, and believeth on him, may have everlasting life: and I will raise him up at the last day. (John 6:22-40)

There had been but one boat at the site of the first miraculous feeding, the disciples' vessel. The crowd had seen the disciples set out across the sea without Jesus. During the night, the storm arose, and the ships at sea put in to Tiberius for safety. The next morning, they used these ships to gain passage to the disciples' destination. On arriving, they found Jesus there also, so their immediate questioning of Him was, How did you get here? (vv. 22-25).

Our Lord does not answer this question. Curiosity governed it, and our Lord, like His written word, says nothing merely to satisfy man's curiosity. It is the characteristic of pretended revelations that they speak to curiosity and to trifles. In fact, our Lord tells them that they seek Him, not even for the sake of His miracles, but because His miraculous feeding provided food. Their concern is not with the power of God manifested in the miracle, but with the product, food (v. 26).

Our Lord summons them to seek not the physical food, but the spiritual manna or nourishment. He, as the Son of Man, can give them food for eternal life. He is the One whom the Father has sealed, whose life and work God has authenticated (v. 27).

The people then ask, how can we work the works of God (v. 28)? Their approach was humanistic. They assumed that all depended on their doing, rather than on what God does. Our Lord's answer is that what God requires of them is to believe on Him whom God had sent (v. 29).

At this point, the people again insisted on the priority of man: "What then doest thou for a sign, that we may see, and believe thee? What workest thou? Our fathers ate manna in the wilderness, as it is written, He gave them bread out of heaven to eat" (v. 30-31). The miraculous feeding was not enough for them. Their forefathers had eaten manna in the wilderness for forty years. What comparable miracle did Jesus have to offer? *The people insisted on their sovereign power to chose.* What did Jesus have to offer beyond this miraculous feeding? Could He provide free food for a generation?

Our Lord answers, the manna came not from Moses, but from God; it came from heaven, not from man (vv. 32-33). The true bread of life, come down from heaven, is He who gives life to the world (vv. 32-33). The true bread of life is a person, not food. There is a myth created by scholars that asserts that in John's Gospel our Lord reveals His Messiahship, while concealing it in Matthew, Mark, and Luke. However, the revelation of His Messiahship is everywhere clear, but it is always rejected. It led to His crucifixion, and to the charge nailed to the cross.

The response of the people was, "Lord, evermore give us this bread" (v. 34). This statement was a plea for manna, not for Jesus Christ. They insisted on the validity of their needs and wants against God's demands.

Jesus then plainly states the fact: "I am the bread of life: he that cometh to me shall never hunger; and he that believeth on me shall never thirst" (v. 35). This was not what they wanted to hear. They wanted *their* kingdom to be established, and they insisted on the priority of *their* needs and demands.

Therefore, our Lord said, You have seen me and have not believed on me (v. 36). Westcott said of v. 29, "Faith is the life of works; works are the necessity of faith."[1] Their lack of faith was a rejection of faith. Again, citing Westcott, "He himself was the sign which the Jews could not read. No other more convincing sign could be given."[2] More accurately, theirs was a *false* faith: they believed in the priority of themselves, of Israel and its earthly hope, and the Messiah had to meet their hope or be rejected. Men routinely expect God to say *Amen* to them and their wishes, and this is surely very commonplace in the churches. The crowd saw Jesus and His works, and they still rejected Him, nor would they ever accept Him except on their terms.

Their rejection did not alter God's eternal decree and plan: "All that the Father giveth me shall come unto me; and him that cometh to me I will in no wise cast out. For I am come from heaven, not to do mine own will, but the will of him that sent me. And this is the will of him that sent me, that of all which he has given me I should lose nothing, but should raise it up at the last day" (vv. 37-39). This is very plainly a statement about predestination. It is strange that those who emphasize the "spiritual" and "free will" aspects of the faith can so brazenly use John's Gospel which so strongly affirms predestination. Our Lord never stresses how *we* feel in reaction to Him, but what God has decreed through His word and Son concerning us and our salvation. The key fact is not what works *we* have done, not what *we* feel, but what He has done. To put our hope in our reaction can become demonic because it is distrust in what God has done.

Our Lord then declares what God's will is, "that every one which seeth the Son, and believeth on him, may have everlasting life: and I will raise him up at the last day" (v. 40). This is an often repeated promise. It tells us that the matter is a simple one.

When I was young, an outstanding pastor condemned all who strove to turn people over to perpetual spiritual turmoil and seeking, when we are simply to believe in the Lord Jesus Christ and be saved, saved to serve. He cited a phrase, not original with him, about the dangers of some spiritual quests, calling it a "perpetual St. Vitus' dance in no man's land." Ephesians 2:14 tells us that Christ is our peace. Those who tells us that we need a "second blessing" to have peace are proclaiming another "gospel," and it is

---

[1] B.F. Westcott, *The Gospel According to John* (Grand Rapids, MI: Eerdmans, 1881, 1954), 101.
[2] *ibid.*, 102.

not of Christ. Our Lord is very clear: to believe on Him, which means to *trust and obey*, is to do the work of God (v. 29). We must not complicate what our Lord has made so clear.

Chapter Fifteen

The Bread of Life: Christ's Humanity
(*John 6:41-58*)

41. The Jews then murmured at him, because he said, I am the bread which came down from heaven.
42. And they said, Is not this Jesus, the son of Joseph, whose father and mother we know? how is it then that he saith, I came down from heaven?
43. Jesus therefore answered and said unto them, Murmur not among yourselves.
44. No man can come to me, except the Father which hath sent me draw him: and I will raise him up at the last day.
45. It is written in the prophets, And they shall be all taught of God. Every man therefore that hath heard, and hath learned of the Father, cometh unto me.
46. Not that any man hath seen the Father, save he which is of God, he hath seen the Father.
47. Verily, verily, I say unto you, He that believeth on me hath everlasting life.
48. I am that bread of life.
49. Your fathers did eat manna in the wilderness, and are dead.
50. This is the bread which cometh down from heaven, that a man may eat thereof, and not die.
51. I am the living bread which came down from heaven: if any man eat of this bread, he shall live for ever: and the bread that I will give is my flesh, which I will give for the life of the world.
52. The Jews therefore strove among themselves, saying, How can this man give us his flesh to eat?
53. Then Jesus said unto them, Verily, verily, I say unto you, Except ye eat the flesh of the Son of man, and drink his blood, ye have no life in you.
54. Whoso eateth my flesh, and drinketh my blood, hath eternal life; and I will raise him up at the last day.
55. For my flesh is meat indeed, and my blood is drink indeed.
56. He that eateth my flesh, and drinketh my blood, dwelleth in me, and I in him.
57. As the living Father hath sent me, and I live by the Father: so he that eateth me, even he shall live by me.
58. This is that bread which came down from heaven: not as your fathers did eat manna, and are dead: he that eateth of this bread shall live for ever. (John 6:41-58)

The people who had been miraculously fed tried to seize Jesus to compel Him to be their King. Their desire was to elect God to be God, and to use Him. They wanted to say, We have chosen you, thus you bear fruit for us. Against this, Jesus now offers Himself as the bread of life. In His perfect humanity, in His body and blood, which point clearly to His atoning death and its commemoration in the sacrament of communion, there is life. He is the last Adam (1 Cor. 15:45-50), the head of the new humanity; we are not divinized in Christ, but we are humanized, made to know ourselves as God's covenant creatures. Calvin commented (on John 6:56):

> This is another confirmation; for while he alone has life in himself, he shows how we may enjoy it, that is, by *eating his flesh*; as if he had affirmed that there is no other way in which he can become ours, than by our faith being directed to his flesh. For no one will ever come to Christ as God, who despises him as man; and, therefore, if you wish to have any interest in Christ, you must take care, above all things, that you do not disdain his flesh.[1]

The goal of fallen man is self-deification, or *theosis*, to be as God (Gen. 3:5), whereas the goal of redeemed man is to be God's covenant man. Christ's perfect humanity is our standard, not His deity. We cannot have Christ as our God if we will not have Him as our true man, as our federal head. In the first Adam, we are born into sin and death; in the last Adam, we are born into justice or righteousness and life.

Our Lord's statement, I am the bread which came down from heaven, was resented by the people. They observed contemptuously that they knew His father, Joseph, and His mother, Mary, so how could He claim to have come down from heaven? (vv. 41-42). His *flesh* refers to Christ's perfect humanity; we cannot become deified, but we can in Christ be restored into a true humanity and the dominion mandate to serve God.

Our Lord was fully aware of their resentment against Him. He tells them that only God's chosen ones will come to Him, and He will not only govern them here and now, but will also raise them up at the last day. In saying of Jesus, we know His parentage (v. 42), the people were saying, How can He claim to be God? His response is that God's chosen ones not only come to Him, but are also taught of God; their coming to Jesus Christ is not of their volition but of God's determination. No man has seen God the Father except the incarnate Son (v. 46). We can all hear God through and in His word, but only the incarnate Son can see God. Our Lord in this statement implies that all the appearances of God in the Old Testament were the actual presence of God the Son.

In v. 47, we are told that here and now the believer has everlasting life. It is an emphatic statement that eternal life is a very present fact for the believer because Jesus is the bread of life (v. 48). The multitude, when miraculously fed, thought at once of manna in the wilderness. Our Lord reminds them that all who ate the manna still died in due time, and they were an unregenerate generation. Those, however, who are the redeemed of God and members of the new humanity in Christ have eternal life (vv. 48-49). Obviously, our Lord has in mind here the Last Supper and

---

[1] John Calvin, *Commentary on the Gospel According to John*, vol. I (Grand Rapids, MI: Eerdmans, 1949), 268.

communion, but only because the Last Supper and communion refer totally to Him as the last Adam and the head of the new humanity. Communion does not make us members or participants of the Godhead, but rather members of the new human race in Christ our covenant Head. In the first Adam, we are born to sin and death; in the last Adam, we are born to justice and life. We are told, in Revelation 21:4, "And God shall wipe away all tears from their eyes; and there shall be no more death, neither sorrow, nor crying; neither shall there be any more pain: for the former things are passed away." Justice triumphs, and history's vast evils will be recompensed in full (Rev. 18-19).

Jesus is the true bread of life, come down from heaven. His *flesh*, His true humanity, is our bread of life; this He gives for the life of the world. We are in Him no longer the sinful and death-bound sons of fallen Adam, but the just and life-bound people of the last Adam (vv. 50-51). The bread He gives us is His flesh, His glorious humanity, so that we are remade into people of righteousness and eternal life.

Our Lord's statements were taken literally. How can this man give us His flesh, nature, or humanity to eat? (v. 52). Our Lord's response is to challenge their deliberate literalness. You have no life, unless you partake of My humanity. Apart from Me, you are people of death (v. 53). Only those who eat My flesh and drink My blood, i.e., become members of My new human race, have eternal life and the promise of the resurrection (v. 54). Only My new humanity is life-giving: My flesh, My humanity, and My blood, My atonement, alone give eternal life (vv. 55-56). I am, says our Lord, the true manna, the bread of life come down from heaven. There is neither life nor future for those who will not live by Him (v. 57), but there is eternal life for those who are members of the last Adam (v. 58). This is what Paul means when he says, "we are members of his body, of his flesh, and of his bones" (Eph. 5:30).

The people wanted a savior who provided them with manna, with cradle to grave security. They wanted constant care and feeding, and they echoed the temptation of Satan to our Lord in the wilderness, "If thou be a Son of God, command that these stones be made into bread" (Matt. 4:3). This temptation is still present in those resolutions to political problems that define salvation in purely economic terms. Rome's answer was bread and circuses. The people wanted God to end history, not to conquer in it through them. Christ, however, will only end history when our conquest in His name is completed (1 Cor. 15:24-27).

We cannot have Christ as our God if we will not have the last Adam as our man, our federal head. We must recognize that in the first Adam we are born into sin and death; we want to be our own gods, to decide right and wrong on our own, and to command God and creation to serve us.

To feed on Christ is to know Him as the true man and our only hope for life. We become members of Him and serve His purpose, to bring every area of life and thought into captivity to Him.

Instead of demanding a god who serves us manna, a constant feeding and the Satanic temptation, we must serve God. Instead of requiring that God and Christ bow down and serve us, we must bow down and serve the triune God according to His word and by His Spirit.

The multitude was ready to accept and use Jesus when they saw the reality of His deity in the miraculous feeding, but they rejected Him when He declared that their necessary relationship was to His humanity instead. He offered incorporation into His humanity, but into His deity, never.

Men want an end to history, but Christ as the last Adam shall and must reign, until He has put all His enemies under His feet through His new human race, the redeemed of God (1 Cor. 15:25). Man's hopes of shortcuts are really abandonments of Jesus Christ.

Chapter Sixteen

The New Human Race
(John 6:59-71)

59. These things said he in the synagogue, as he taught in Capernaum.
60. Many therefore of his disciples, when they had heard this, said, This is an hard saying; who can hear it?
61. When Jesus knew in himself that his disciples murmured at it, he said unto them, Doth this offend you?
62. What and if ye shall see the Son of man ascend up where he was before?
63. It is the spirit that quickeneth; the flesh profiteth nothing: the words that I speak unto you, they are spirit, and they are life.
64. But there are some of you that believe not. For Jesus knew from the beginning who they were that believed not, and who should betray him.
65. And he said, Therefore said I unto you, that no man can come unto me, except it were given unto him of my Father.
66. From that time many of his disciples went back, and walked no more with him.
67. Then said Jesus unto the twelve, Will ye also go away?
68. Then Simon Peter answered him, Lord, to whom shall we go? thou hast the words of eternal life.
69. And we believe and are sure that thou art that Christ, the Son of the living God.
70. Jesus answered them, Have not I chosen you twelve, and one of you is a devil?
71. He spake of Judas Iscariot the son of Simon: for he it was that should betray him, being one of the twelve. (John 6:59-71)

Man wants to take credit for what God does. Dr. K. Schilder, in his book on heaven, pointed out that "No man cometh unto the Father except he be *drawn*," can be translated as *dragged* (John 6:44).[1] But we want credit for what happens, as so we insist in seeing ourselves as somehow determinative. No man comes to God of his own nature. God drags man to Him by His sovereign grace and mercy. We should rejoice in what He has done and to accept His further dragging of us in terms of His purpose. If we are hosts to a visitor, we can limit him to certain areas of the house, but God is the owner and the creator: He is not our guest; we are His.

The setting of our text is the Capernaum synagogue (v. 59). The conversations of vv. 26-71 begin at the seashore and continue in the synagogue. We have in John's Gospel the key points of the discussion.

Our Lord's stress on God's determination of all things offended not only the multitude, but also many of the disciples, and they left Him (vv. 60-61, 66). The idea of prior determination by God is offensive to man in his fallen

---

[1]. K. Schilder, *Heaven — What is It?* (Grand Rapids, MI: Eerdmans, 1950), 47.

estate. Because the redeemed are by no means fully sanctified, they too rebel against God's sovereignty. The disciples themselves said, "This is a hard message. Who can listen to it?" Like the multitude, they found it repulsive. In Matthew 16:15-23, we see that the disciples found it repellant to hear about the cross, or atonement. Here it is God's predestination that offends them. Both doctrines are totally alien to humanism, and their meaning distasteful to men (v. 60). Our Lord's response, "Doth this offend you?" (v. 61), is, as Hendriksen pointed out, literally, "Does this ensnare?," does this cause you to fall into a trap?[2] Most commentators limit the offense to the idea of eating the flesh and drinking the blood of Jesus Christ, but this is to limit its application. What our Lord tells us is that God's sovereignty over us is total: our coming to Him, our growth in Him by our participation in His new humanity, and our deadness apart from Him, are all offensive to man, who wants some credit for his life. The totality of grace in our approach to and life in Christ is too radical a doctrine for most men.

Our Lord then pushes the offense further in v. 62: How will you react to My ascension? A man-centered view of Jesus Christ would absorb His mission radically or even totally into history. The multitude, with its hope of making Jesus a human king, was not interested in transcendence, nor are men today. Escape may have its appeal, but it too is man-centered. Views of the "rapture" concentrate on man and what happens to him. The ascension points beyond a historical or man-centered focus.

Then our Lord declares that it is the Holy Spirit Who at the beginning created all things with the Father and the Son (Gen. 1:1ff), Who alone gives life. Man's created human nature is neither self-regenerating nor creative. Next our Lord makes a very remarkable statement: "the words that I speak unto you, they are Spirit, and they are life" (v. 63). The Holy Spirit is a Person in the Godhead. He it is Who gives us the written word, together with the Father and the Son. He is also present to us in the very words of Scripture, so that the Spirit and the word cannot be separated. As Calvin noted, our Lord not only connects *life* with *the Spirit*, but He also equates His spoken word with the word and the Spirit.[3]

Our Lord knew the unbelievers among His disciples, and He knew who would betray Him (v. 64). At this point, many of the disciples left Him (v. 66). He did not spare them, and He called attention to the presence of one still present, then unnamed, who would betray Him (vv. 70-71).

[2.] William Hendriksen, *The Gospel of John*, vol. I (Grand Rapids, MI: Baker Book House, 1953), 246.

[3.] John Calvin, *Commentaries on the Gospel According to John*, vol. I (Grand Rapids, MI: Eerdmans, 1949 reprint), 274.

There was, however, a telling confession of faith from Simon Peter, who, however ignorantly and weakly, still had a regenerate faith. His confession admits that he fails to understand much, but he also sees no choice:

> 68. Lord, to whom shall we go? Thou hast the words of eternal life.
> 69. And we believe and are sure that thou art that Christ, the Son of the living God. (John 6:68-69)

This is an acknowledgment by Peter that, however faulty and wrong in their thinking they may be, he and the others know that Jesus speaks the words of eternal life because He is the Messiah, the Son of the living God. Peter was bewildered and ignorant about much, but he was still a believer. Peter was emphatic: "we believe," are *sure*, or *know* that you are the Christ.

An important question is this: did the departing people and disciples misunderstand Jesus? Hugh J. Schonfield held that the listeners regarded Jesus' comments as akin to espousing cannibalism, i.e., masticating his flesh, and so on. That they chose to place a false interpretation on the words of our Lord can be assumed. But we must also recognize that if a *literal* meaning was understood, the matter would be one for ridicule, not dissent. There is no question that our Lord's words were upsetting. The covenant people were to avoid the taste of the blood of animals (Gen. 9:4; Lev. 17:10-16), and our Lord here states plainly that His flesh, His humanity, His blood, and His atoning death are the foundations of our covenant with God. The Book of Hebrews is implicit in what is said here. These were not welcome words. They clearly set forth the end of the old sacrificial system and the Temple. They witnessed to a new passover and a new covenant people.

The renewed covenant in Christ requires of the covenant people that they see Him as the bread of life, as the Passover sustenance come to earth. They must enter into this renewed covenant by means of the blood of atonement, His blood, and by partaking of, or becoming members of, His humanity, the new human race founded by Jesus Christ. They knew what they were rejecting.

Chapter Seventeen

The Great Warfare
(John 7:1-9)

1. After these things Jesus walked in Galilee: for he would not walk in Jewry, because the Jews sought to kill him.
2. Now the Jews' feast of tabernacles was at hand.
3. His brethren therefore said unto him, Depart hence, and go into Judaea, that thy disciples also may see the works that thou doest.
4. For there is no man that doeth any thing in secret, and he himself seeketh to be known openly. If thou do these things, shew thyself to the world.
5. For neither did his brethren believe in him.
6. Then Jesus said unto them, My time is not yet come: but your time is alway ready.
7. The world cannot hate you; but me it hateth, because I testify of it, that the works thereof are evil.
8. Go ye up unto this feast: I go not up yet unto this feast; for my time is not yet full come.
9. When he had said these words unto them, he abode still in Galilee. (John 7:1-9)

The incarnation was certainly not problem-free. One of its penalties was that our Lord was born into a family in which not all were at this time redeemed persons. At this time, we are told in v. 5, His brothers did not believe in Him. We do not know what their father, Joseph, may have told them while still alive, nor what Mary may have said. In any case, they were apparently resentful of the attention Jesus had brought to the family.

At the same time, Jesus was staying away from Judaea because He had more to do before the time for His atoning death arrived. As a result, He stayed in his home country, Galilee, comprised of the former territories of the northern Kingdom of Israel, with Samaria as its capital.

The Feast of Tabernacles fell on Tisri 15 - 22, sometime in our September - October, so that it was six months later than the events of John 6. This feast lasted a week, but an eighth day was often added in emulation of Leviticus 23:36.

The Feast of Tabernacles followed the yearly day of atonement. It is called also the feast of booths (*succoth*) and the feast of ingathering. The booths were slight structures of branches to give shade. The booths were a reminder of their wilderness life during the exodus. Sacrifices were prescribed for the festival. Certain psalms were sung, and the festival was limited to the covenant people.

Our Lord's brothers were right in holding that this feast was an appropriate occasion for Him to reveal Himself as whatever He said He was, but they apparently knew also that the leaders of the people wanted Jesus dead.

The brothers of our Lord refused to believe in man's depravity. In vv. 3-4 they urge Jesus to go and reveal Himself openly. They were evidentialists: provide the great crowds in Jerusalem for the festival with enough evidence, and they will surely believe. We have today many groups within the church who believe that the nation will be captured for Christ if only we make use of the right arguments and technologies: they refuse to acknowledge that men hate the truth and want no part of it. This false view of man marks much of modern evangelicalism. They can "vindicate" themselves by pointing to their own numerical gains, but they cannot claim legitimate Kingdom advances.

The brothers of our Lord tried to command Him: "Depart hence" (v. 3), or, leave here and go, is blunt; He is also told, "be known openly," or be open and honest about Yourself and Your claims. If you are the Messiah, and if You have miraculous powers, why hide Yourself? For them, the matter was a simple one. As evidentialists, they believed that the authorities in Jerusalem would give a fair and impartial hearing to Jesus. He could present them with proofs that would demand a favorable answer. Like all evidentialists, these men did not know the reality of the Fall and of sin.

Our Lord did not tell them that He would not go. He simply said, "I go not up *yet* unto the feast; for my time is not yet fully come" (v. 8). He had more to do, not least of which was the training of the twelve disciples. "Your time is always ready" (v. 6) because your appearance at the feast requires no great price for you. The disciples were aware of Jesus' miraculous powers, but they were still ready to instruct Him as though He were lacking in common sense. They told Him to go and to work miracles, as though this summed up His life's work. Because His brethren were friends of the world, they could not see that Jesus would pay a price for an open appearance. They wanted Him to make a public display of His power.

This is why our Lord says, "The world cannot hate you" (v. 7). You are a part of it, and My failure to be a part of it is not due simply to poor public relations, but also to a radical difference of a moral and religious nature.

The world hates Me, because I call attention to its evil nature and works, He tells them (v. 7). The fundamental difference among men is moral and religious, and it is precisely this difference that mankind wants ignored. They resent anyone or anything which calls attention to the moral question. A saying of the era of the 1960's on moral revolution holds, "Whether I'm right, or whether I'm wrong, I've got to be me." Our Lord could therefore say to His brothers, "your time is always ready" (v. 6).

In vv. 6 and 8, when our Lord says that His *time* is not yet come, the word used for *time* is not *hora*, meaning God's destined hour, but is rather *kairos*, which means the opportune moment.[1]

As Barclay observed of this episode, "It is impossible to force Jesus' hand." To date, Jesus had performed only one miracle in Jerusalem, the curing of the man at the pool at Bethesda (John 5:1ff.).[2] The brothers held that Jerusalem was the proper place for miracles, since bigger crowds of spectators and more important people were likely to be present. Provide them with the evidence, and they will believe!

In v. 1, John uses twice a word, *periepatei*, first, then *peripatein*, translated *first*, as *walked*, then as *walk*. As John Marsh pointed out, this was a word which was "the regular description for a peripatetic Rabbi, and the tense he uses indicates, in the Greek, that this peripatetic activity of Jesus went on for a considerable time."[3]

On v. 7, Marsh commented,

> 'The world cannot hate you, but it hates me because I testify of it that its works are evil': This is more than to acknowledge that Jesus is a moral critic of the world; it is a claim (like that made in 3:18 etc.) that by his actual presence the world is being judged, judged by its reaction to him.

The hatred for Christ was intense and total because He was in His person an indictment of this fallen world. It should not therefore surprise us that some of this hatred is manifested against all who try to be faithful to Him. The war of the ages is this fallen world against Christ and His new human race.

[1.] William Barclay, *The Gospel of John*, vol. I (Philadelphia, PA: Westminster Press, 1955, 1956), 231.

[2.] *ibid.*, 232.

[3.] John Marsh, *Saint John* (Harmondworth, Middlesex, England: Penguin Books, 1968, 1977), 319.

Chapter Eighteen

Righteous Judgment
(John 7:10-24)

10. But when his brethren were gone up, then went he also up unto the feast, not openly, but as it were in secret.
11. Then the Jews sought him at the feast, and said, Where is he?
12. And there was much murmuring among the people concerning him: for some said, He is a good man: others said, Nay; but he deceiveth the people.
13. Howbeit no man spake openly of him for fear of the Jews.
14. Now about the midst of the feast Jesus went up into the temple, and taught.
15. And the Jews marvelled, saying, How knoweth this man letters, having never learned?
16. Jesus answered them, and said, My doctrine is not mine, but his that sent me.
17. If any man will do his will, he shall know of the doctrine, whether it be of God, or whether I speak of myself.
18. He that speaketh of himself seeketh his own glory: but he that seeketh his glory that sent him, the same is true, and no unrighteousness is in him.
19. Did not Moses give you the law, and yet none of you keepeth the law? Why go ye about to kill me?
20. The people answered and said, Thou hast a devil: who goeth about to kill thee?
21. Jesus answered and said unto them, I have done one work, and ye all marvel.
22. Moses therefore gave unto you circumcision; (not because it is of Moses, but of the fathers;) and ye on the sabbath day circumcise a man.
23. If a man on the sabbath day receive circumcision, that the law of Moses should not be broken; are ye angry at me, because I have made a man every whit whole on the sabbath day?
24. Judge not according to the appearance, but judge righteous judgment. (John 7:10-24)

After His brothers went to the Feast of Tabernacles, our Lord Himself went to the feast, not openly but secretly (v. 10). The leaders in Jerusalem, expecting Jesus to be there, tried to locate Him (v. 11). Added to that was the public expectation. Jesus had aroused nation-wide interest, and the curious pilgrims looked for Him, some saying, "He is a good man," while others labelled Him a deceiver (v. 12). At the same time that this widespread interest and murmured talk went on, all kept quiet for fear of the leaders (v. 13). These leaders are described by John as "the Jews." The reason for this curious designation by John, a Jew and one related to prominent leaders, was a religious one. Our Lord's followers were Jewish also, but John sees the term *Jew* as a religious description, even as *Christian* came to be a like term. By following Jesus, they were no longer Jews.

In the middle of the eight day festival, Jesus went to the Temple and began to teach openly (v. 14). By making His appearance so public, He forestalled a secret arrest. The people marvelled at His teaching, asking, How did this man gain so much learning since He lacks formal schooling or teaching? (v. 15).

Our Lord's answer is of central importance to John's Gospel: "My doctrine is not mine, but his that sent me." Moreover, to know God's doctrine, we must do God's will. Then we will know whether Christ speaks from God or from ordinary human sources (vv. 16-17). This knowledge has a *moral and religious foundation*. If any man *wills* to do God's will, if he seeks actively and earnestly to obey God's law, he will know God's requirements. Such knowledge is not simply an intellectual exercise. It requires a harmony of man's will and life to the law of God (v. 18).

Moreover, if any man seeks his own glory rather than the glory of God, he is outside of God and there is no truth in him. Those who seek God's glory are *true*, and there is no injustice or unrighteousness in them (v. 18).

What our Lord says goes against everything in the philosophical and intellectual tradition from Plato to the present. That heritage insists on the ability of man's reason, whether pure or practical, to come to a knowledge of truth irrespective of the moral character of the thinker. This means that, on every kind of issue, the reasoning of a murderer, a homosexual, or a habitual liar or criminal, is as good as the reasoning of a moral man. The premise of such thinking is that moral character has no effect on thinking. Such thinking denies the fact of the Fall. Evidentialists within the church believe that the ungodly can be converted by rational proofs, which means they discount the Fall and human depravity and insist on a neutral rationality common to all men. It is this that our Lord rejects totally. Man is not objective Reason: he is a fallen created being who is at war with his Maker. There is not a neutral bone in his body, and his every atom is a part of his revolt against God. Reason is a tool whereby fallen man denies his fallen being to assert an independence which he claims in order to separate himself from God.

As Ronald A. Ward wrote,

> The law, especially in its commandments, expresses the will of God (cf. Matt. 22:36). They do not obey it any more than they believe in Him; then how can they recognize the origin of His teaching? How

can they "see" the Word? They are seeking His death (cf. 5:18; 8:59; 10:31), though they deny it (7:19-20).[1]

Our Lord's words are an indictment of all philosophies that begin with man and his judgments, experiences, and reasoning.

Then in v. 19 our Lord makes a statement that exposes their faulty and vicious thinking: "Did not Moses give you the law, and yet none of you keepeth the law? Why go ye about to kill me?" They profess to be followers of Moses, but the law given by Moses condemns them. Our Lord tells them, in A. Plummer's paraphrase, "Ye are all breakers of the law, and yet would put Me to death as a breaker of it."[2] Our Lord here, *first* of all, makes public the plan to kill Him, and He thereby confounds their plans. So public a statement made it difficult to do anything against Jesus without confirming His charges. *Second*, the people against Him denied that they sought Jesus' death. His statement had left them in an indefensible position. *Third*, they countered also with accusations of demon possession, a ridiculous charge against a miracle worker who had done good. The miraculous feeding and other miracles had to be common knowledge.

Then our Lord turns to the miracle of healing at the Bethesda pool (v. 21). A man could be circumcised on the Sabbath, according to the religious leaders, without breaking God's law given by Moses. Why then is a miracle of healing on the Sabbath morally wrong? (v. 23). The law required circumcision on the eighth day, according to the common interpretation. We know now that only then does the newborn boy's blood coagulate to prevent bleeding to death. The law thus required *waiting* seven days, but, as it was then interpreted, it supposedly *required* circumcision on the eighth day. If this eighth day fell on the Sabbath, the circumcision was still required and was not regarded as Sabbath-breaking.

This legal nicety is illustrative of Phariseeism. The emphasis was shifted from circumcision into the covenant to a strict requirement that it be done on the eighth day.

Then (v. 24) our Lord says, "Judge not according to the appearance, but judge righteous judgment." In terms of the Pharisaic rules, the healing at Bethesda was a violation of the Sabbath, but circumcision on the Sabbath was not. In such a perspective, legalism has replaced morality. The details of the law replace the spirit of the law. When Paul tells us, "the letter killeth, but the spirit giveth life" (2 Cor. 3:6), refers to this kind of Pharisaic practice.

---

1. Ronald A. Ward, *The Gospel of John* (Grand Rapids, MI: Baker Book House, 1961), 50.
2. A. Plummer, *The Gospel According to St. John* (Cambridge, England: Cambridge University Press, 1880, 1906), 166.

This point is a very important one because too many churchmen are guilty of the same Phariseeism. To illustrate, Matthew 7:1-2 is commonly used with Pharisaic intent by many:

> Judge not, that ye be not judged. For with what judgment ye judge, ye shall be judged, and with what measure ye mete, it shall be measured to you again.

It is a common interpretation on the part of idiots within and without the church that this text forbids all judgment, whereas, in fact, it tells us that if we judge with false, non-Biblical measures or standards, we shall be similarly judged. What is required of us, as our text tells us, is to "judge righteous judgment," with God's law as our measure of justice. Earlier, in v. 16ff., our Lord had made clear that His message and work were from God. The rabbinic method of teaching was to cite authorities for all statements, and our Lord cited His: His came from the Almighty One, God. Jesus then used the example of circumcision on the Sabbath to vindicate healing on the Sabbath. The Jews to whom He spoke could not answer Him from the Bible; He had clearly confounded them by His use of the Bible, so they accused Him of being demonic. He therefore summons them to stop their evil judgements and to "judge righteous judgment." This meant a moral judgment instead of one based on legal technicalities.

Today our legal system is Phariseeism. It relies on technicalities, not on the meaning and spirit of the law. It is therefore evil and anti-Christian.

Chapter Nineteen

Living Water
(John 7:25-44)

25. Then said some of them of Jerusalem, Is not this he, whom they seek to kill?

26. But, lo, he speaketh boldly, and they say nothing unto him. Do the rulers know indeed that this is the very Christ?

27. Howbeit we know this man whence he is: but when Christ cometh, no man knoweth whence he is.

28. Then cried Jesus in the temple as he taught, saying, Ye both know me, and ye know whence I am: and I am not come of myself, but he that sent me is true, whom ye know not.

29. But I know him: for I am from him, and he hath sent me.

30. Then they sought to take him: but no man laid hands on him, because his hour was not yet come.

31. And many of the people believed on him, and said, When Christ cometh, will he do more miracles than these which this man hath done?

32. The Pharisees heard that the people murmured such things concerning him; and the Pharisees and the chief priests sent officers to take him.

33. Then said Jesus unto them, Yet a little while am I with you, and then I go unto him that sent me.

34. Ye shall seek me, and shall not find me: and where I am, thither ye cannot come.

35. Then said the Jews among themselves, Whither will he go, that we shall not find him? will he go unto the dispersed among the Gentiles, and teach the Gentiles?

36. What manner of saying is this that he said, Ye shall seek me, and shall not find me: and where I am, thither ye cannot come?

37. In the last day, that great day of the feast, Jesus stood and cried, saying, If any man thirst, let him come unto me, and drink.

38. He that believeth on me, as the scripture hath said, out of his belly shall flow rivers of living water.

39. (But this spake he of the Spirit, which they that believe on him should receive: for the Holy Ghost was not yet given; because that Jesus was not yet glorified.)

40. Many of the people therefore, when they heard this saying, said, Of a truth this is the Prophet.

41. Others said, This is the Christ. But some said, Shall Christ come out of Galilee?

42. Hath not the scripture said, That Christ cometh of the seed of David, and out of the town of Bethlehem, where David was?

43. So there was a division among the people because of him.

44. And some of them would have taken him; but no man laid hands on him. (John 7:25-44)

The city of Jerusalem was full of pilgrims at the time of this festival, some from Galilee and Judaea, and others from the territories of the Dispersion or Diaspora. Those of Jerusalem were not as familiar with Jesus as were other Judaeans and Galileans, and so they wondered at the boldness of His speech. Why were the rulers silent? Did they recognize this Jesus as the Messiah (v. 25f.)? However, the people felt that Jesus could not be the Messiah because His origin was known, whereas, they held that when the Christ comes, no man will know from whence He came (v. 27).

Jesus, teaching in the Temple, told the people, You know Me and My origin. I am not here on My own authority but God's. You do not know God, nor do you recognize His truth, "But I know him: for I am from him, and he hath sent me" (v. 28f.). Earlier, the people had called Jesus demonic. This was a way of evading a decision or considering what He said. By discrediting the messenger, they discredited and evaded the message. Our Lord's words, however, push them towards a decision they do not want to make: are His word and works true? Our Lord tells them He is from God and knows God (v. 29). As a result, some of the people sought to kill Him (v. 30). They were unwilling to hear anything that would compel them to take Jesus' message seriously.

However, there were many who believed Jesus. Their argument was a simple one: "When Christ cometh, will he do more miracles than these which this man hath done?" (v. 31). This was an unanswerable argument. On hearing this, the Pharisees sent officers to arrest Jesus. The situation was close to getting out of hand (v. 32).

Then, in vv. 33-34, our Lord tells the people that His stay with them will not be too long. Later, when they need Him, they will not find Him. The time of opportunity will have passed. In not too many years, the Jewish-Roman War of A. D. 66-70 would mean the end of the Temple, of Judaea, and its local peoples.

But the people refused to understand Him. Was Jesus planning to go out of the country to teach the Dispersion? Did He plan to teach the Gentiles? They regarded His language as outrageous (vv. 35-36).

Men will not hear what they religiously and morally reject. Their thinking is governed by their presuppositions, and if God is not their starting point, they have no place for Him in their lives and thought.

We have next a reference to the last day of the feast, the eighth day (Lev. 23:39; Num. 29:35; Nehemiah 8:18). Jesus makes a statement, which apparently had reference to a custom which had developed in connection with the Feast of Tabernacle and was observed in the seven days thereof. In Plummer's words,

> The conjectural reference to the custom of pouring water at the Feast of Tabernacles is probably correct. On all seven days water was brought from the pool of Siloam and poured into a silver basin on the western side of the altar of burnt offering, a ceremony not mentioned

in O. T. Apparently this was *not* done on the *eighth* day. Accordingly Christ comes forward and fills the gap, directing them to a better water than that of Siloam.[1]

Many say it was a golden pitcher. Our Lord's actions and words are important in more ways than one. Too many zealots over the centuries have had a misplaced zeal. Had they been present, they would have condemned the practice of pouring water into a silver basin on the west side of the altar. They would have damned the practice as unbiblical, which it was. Majoring in minors, they would have stressed the practice as unlawful, and so on. On the other hand, our Lord, when He condemned anything, did it with a total relevance. The Pharisees then and now are *unduly* concerned with relatively minor details.

Instead, our Lord speaks of the water of life. "If any man thirst, let him come unto me and drink" (v. 37). Moreover, "He that believeth on me, as the scripture hath said, out of his belly shall flow rivers of living water" (v. 38). The reference is to several verses: Isaiah 44:3; 58:11; Zechariah 13:1; 14:8; etc. We must have water to live, and so we take it in daily. But our Lord says that those who believe in Him will instead give out the water of life like a living fountain or spring.

Our Lord here spoke of the Holy Spirit, Who was not yet a normative part of the life of the believer (v. 39). After Christ's glorification, the Holy Spirit became the Christian's indwelling power, and the purpose of this was and is that Christ's work be carried on.

The response of many people to this statement was to recognize that Jesus spoke from God, either as the great Prophet or as the Christ (v. 40). There was an intense dispute over the messiahship. It was assumed that Jesus was a Galilean, because Nazareth was the family home, whereas the prophecy of Micah 5:2 hailed Bethlehem as the place from whence the Messiah would come (vv. 41-42).

This dispute was a passionate one, and some men, on their own, were ready to seize Jesus and take Him to the Sanhedrin to settle the matter, but no man was ready to take the initiative (vv. 43-44).

Basic to this text is the statement of our Lord that all who believe on Him will become springs of the water of life. Our Lord makes us, as our new Adam, members of His new human race. According to Ezekiel 47:1-12, in the new temple of the messianic era, a river will issue forth out of the threshold of the temple eastward. It will enliven and heal all that it touches (Ezek. 47:9; Zech. 14:8). This stream of the water of life will grow larger and wider, and it will create a new world.

[1.] A. Plummer, *The Gospel According to St. John* (Cambridge, England: Cambridge University Press, 1880, 1906), 271.

Believers are new and living temples of Christ and His Spirit (Gal. 4:6; Rom. 8:9; 1 Cor. 3:16). The new creation began with our Lord's resurrection, and it continues with our regeneration. As the life of the faithful continues, and as the people of the new creation increase and succeed in their service, so too the waters of the river of life nourish all the world.

This is a depiction of the world triumph of Christ's Kingdom. We are repeatedly told of that victory in the Scriptures. John 7:38 and Ezekiel 47:1-12 tell us that we, as living temples of Christ, are God's means whereby the world is made new. The importance of the believer and his calling are thus affirmed. The triumph of the faith rests upon the people of faith. Before that victory is possible, the believer must see that he is not the *end* of God's purpose, but a means whereby God's Kingdom is realized on earth.

Chapter Twenty
Evil
(John 7:45-53)

45. Then came the officers to the chief priests and Pharisees; and they said unto them, Why have ye not brought him?
46. The officers answered, Never man spake like this man.
47. Then answered them the Pharisees, Are ye also deceived?
48. Have any of the rulers or of the Pharisees believed on him?
49. But this people who knoweth not the law are cursed.
50. Nicodemus saith unto them, (he that came to Jesus by night, being one of them,)
51. Doth our law judge any man, before it hear him, and know what he doeth?
52. They answered and said unto him, Art thou also of Galilee? Search, and look: for out of Galilee ariseth no prophet.
53. And every man went unto his own house. (John 7:45-53)

In this text, we come face to face with the fact of evil, and its enormity. Mankind is in the main unwilling to acknowledge the true nature of evil. In the twentieth century, a higher percentage of mankind has been killed by war, mass murder, torture, slave labor camps, famine, religious persecution, and so on and on, than ever before, and yet we boast of our high civilization and our enlightenment. Not only that, but, during the long butchery and horror of the Soviet Union, politicians, intellectuals, the media, many of the clergy, educators, and more, insisted that the Soviet Union was a great and noble experiment, the greatest of its kind in history. To be critical of the Soviet Union was to be obviously morally derelict and evil.

Far worse than this, within the so-called "free West," abortion, homosexuality, and euthanasia have been legalized. The Soviet Union, like other revolutionary regimes, claimed it was killing its enemies. How are unborn babies enemies? *Evil now wears a smiling face and is pharisaical to the core.*

We should not be surprised that the religious leaders of Judaea saw Jesus Christ as their enemy. These men were the ostensible champions of God's law, which they had reinterpreted, and of the Temple, which they had defiled. Our Lord repeatedly spoke bluntly of their hypocrisy, as witness these words from Mark 12:38-40:

38. ...Beware of the scribes, which love to go in long clothing and love salutations in the market places,
39. And the chief seats in the synagogues, and the uppermost rooms at the feasts:
40. Which devour widows' houses, and for a pretense make long prayers: these shall receive greater damnation.

88   *The Gospel of John*

This is one of the briefer condemnations by our Lord. It clearly cites the pretensions of the religious leaders and their immorality. To rob widows of their homes by fraud is especially evil in the sight of God. The defenseless must be protected, not exploited.

The essence of evil is that it claims to be the true good, and it calls the good, evil. The whole moral order is reversed. The hatred of God, morality, and the people of God marks the evil ones. The Soviet Union proclaimed itself as the true order; the ungodly within the churches insist on their superiority to Christ's flock, whom they despise and denigrate.

In our text, we see this passionate and religious, if ungodly, contempt. *First*, the officers who were to arrest Jesus returned to the chief priests and Pharisees to report that this man was no transgressor: "Never man spake like this man" (v. 46). For this they garnered contempt. Notice the unity here between the chief priests, Sadducees, and the Pharisees. These usual enemies were united in their hatred for Jesus.

Second, their standard is radically humanistic: "Have any of the rulers or of the Pharisees believed on him?" (v. 48). The elite of the nation are against Jesus; how dare the officers have another opinion? Today men would say, Neither the U. S. Supreme Court nor Congress recognize the "claims" of Jesus or the Bible. It is the superstitious people who do.

Third, the leaders recognized that the people largely believed in Jesus, so "this people who knoweth not the law are cursed" (v. 49). The people, whose leaders they ostensibly were, received only contempt. Today, those who proclaim democracy most are least ready to respect the people. They use and abuse them.

Fourth, Nicodemus spoke up to question the sense of their condemnation before any formal hearing. As rulers and judges over the people, how could they condemn any man without a hearing? Biblical law does not even allow passing sentence on a confession without corroboration. How then could they speak as they did?

Fifth, the people are called "cursed" (v. 49). In effect, these leaders were excommunicating the whole nation without going through the open procedure of doing so. Unless the people obeyed them, the people were nothing; if they followed them, the people were still stupid fools in their eyes.

Sixth, the people are described as ignorant of the law (v. 49). In reality, the people were very well educated in the law. It was the Pharisaic additions to it, and the Sadducean beliefs regarding it, that the people did not know. An American may know the U. S. Constitution very well, and yet be remarkably ignorant of the U. S. Supreme Court's reinterpretations of it, but this does not make him ignorant of the fundamental law of the land.

Seventh, the rulers had challenged the officers, saying, "Have any of the rulers or of the Pharisees believed on him?" (v. 48). Almost at once Nicodemus challenges their attempts against Jesus as lawless, undermining their statement that Jesus had no worthy supporters. As a result, they were contemptuous of Nicodemus. They said in effect that anyone who disagreed with them could have no standing. This is still a common tactic. Nicodemus had not spoken in favor of Jesus, only in favor of *lawful* proceedings. He insisted on justice, not lynch law. They refused to acknowledge that Nicodemus was right. They chose instead to interpret his remarks as a defense of Jesus, a defense because Nicodemus insisted on justice!

We are again face to face with evil and its intense self-righteousness. Our inability to confront evil often begins with ourselves. One man, a monster of egocentricity and contempt for all others, including family and kin, held that, as "a good man," he was ready to take his chances with heaven. He could not understand how God could reject him, given his track record! If we fail to appreciate our own sinful dispositions, we will hardly be able to recognize the dimensions of sin in the world around us. Too many people, faced with evil, collapse because such knowledge is too much for them.

The vision of evil is a terrifying one because it makes too clear the enormity of what is against us. Evil can only be counteracted by the vision of God in Christ. Evil cannot accomplish more than God permits.

Our Lord's Prayer includes this petition: "Lead us not into temptation, but deliver us from evil" (Matt. 6:13). Some have translated this latter clause as, "Deliver us (or, save us) from the Evil One," while others question this possible reading. What is clear is that, while we are *not* to concentrate on evil, we are to pray for deliverance from it. We are not to be victims of it, but rather conquerors over it.

Chapter Twenty-One

The Woman Taken In Adultery
(John 8:1-11)

1. Jesus went unto the mount of Olives.
2. And early in the morning he came again into the temple, and all the people came unto him; and he sat down, and taught them.
3. And the scribes and Pharisees brought unto him a woman taken in adultery; and when they had set her in the midst,
4. They say unto him, Master, this woman was taken in adultery, in the very act.
5. Now Moses in the law commanded us, that such should be stoned: but what sayest thou?
6. This they said, tempting him, that they might have to accuse him. But Jesus stooped down, and with his finger wrote on the ground, as though he heard them not.
7. So when they continued asking him, he lifted up himself, and said unto them, He that is without sin among you, let him first cast a stone at her.
8. And again he stooped down, and wrote on the ground.
9. And they which heard it, being convicted by their own conscience, went out one by one, beginning at the eldest, even unto the last: and Jesus was left alone, and the woman standing in the midst.
10. When Jesus had lifted up himself, and saw none but the woman, he said unto her, Woman, where are those thine accusers? hath no man condemned thee?
11. She said, No man, Lord. And Jesus said unto her, Neither do I condemn thee: go, and sin no more. (John 8:1-11)

This famous episode was not popular with many in the early church. St. Augustine tells us that many men cut these verses out of their copies of the Gospel to prevent their wives from thinking adultery could be condoned.[1] The death penalty for adultery in Biblical law could not be exercised under Rome. As a result, substitute penalties were legislated. The Council of Ancyra required seven years penance; St. Basil's Canons, fifteen years penance. The Council of Eliberis in Spain required a five year penance for a single act, and ten years if repeated. As against all this, our Lord, who upheld the law, still said, "The publicans and the harlots go into the Kingdom of God before you" (Matt. 21:31f.). This He said to the religious leaders of the nation.

Our Lord was teaching in the Temple when the scribes and the Pharisees triumphantly brought before Him for judgment a "woman taken in adultery, in the very act" (v. 4). They demand a decision from Him as to her judgment, and their purpose was to destroy Him. If Jesus forgave the

---

[1.] Cited from Augustine's *De Conjug. Adult.* by J. C. Ryle, *Expository Thoughts on the Gospels, St. John*, vol. II (London, England: William Hunt, 1869), 76.

woman, He was then setting aside God's law, and He could be condemned as faithless to it. If he demanded judgment in terms of it, then Jesus would run afoul of Roman law and popular opinion, which favored laxity. This was a staged episode in order to destroy His credibility. Either answer meant trouble.

The woman had in fact been taken in adultery. That was true enough, but adultery is not a solitary act! Where was the man? The Pharisees and the scribes showed their own false standard clearly. They were condoning in the man what they would not excuse in the woman. The man had been allowed to go his way, but the woman was taken to the Temple ostensibly to be publicly shamed, as Jesus would also be in whatever answer He gave. "What sayest thou?" (v. 5), they demanded. But Jesus acted as though He had not heard them; He stooped down and wrote on the ground. They continued their demands for an answer, certain they had Jesus in a thorough bind, and, finally, "He lifted up himself, and said unto them, He that is without sin among you, let him first cast a stone at her" (v. 7). Judges, witnesses, and executioners had to have clean hands in dealing with an offender and an offense, in this case adultery. All of them were guilty men, adulterers, and their consciences convicted them (v. 9). As a result, all left quietly, "beginning with the eldest, even unto the last." Correct form required that men wait for the eldest to leave first, and, even in their sin, they maintained proper form, like good churchmen. Finally, "Jesus was left alone, and the woman standing in the midst" (v. 9). The Pharisees and scribes were all gone; only His disciples, and the people who had been there to hear His teaching, remained.

"When Jesus had lifted up himself, and saw none but the woman, he said unto her, Woman, where are those thine accusers? hath no man condemned thee?" (v. 10). Her answer was, "No man, Lord."

The men who had brought her to Jesus had called Him "Master" (v. 4). The word "Master" is in the Greek *diduskale*, teacher. The woman taken in adultery could not have been ignorant of Jesus' existence. Seeing Him here in action, her spontaneous reaction is to call Him *Lord*. By the grace of God, she had now come to know who He was, and her response reflected it.

Our Lord's response was direct, simple, and final: "Neither do I condemn thee: go, and sin no more" (v. 11).

He had not set aside the law, the religious leaders had; the law cannot be used to commit sin, and the purpose of the scribes and Pharisees was thoroughly evil. *First*, whereas the purpose of God's law here is to make the family, the basic institution in society, secure against treason to it, the accusers were all guilty men, adulterers, and *their use of the law was evil and obscene*. Moreover, they limited its application to the woman and allowed the man to go his way. Because a man has more authority in God's law, he also has greater responsibility and culpability. Our Lord Himself declares, "For unto whomsoever much is given, of him shall be much required: and to whom men have committed much, of him they will ask the more" (Luke 12:48). Men are always held more accountable by God because headship has been given to them. Their sins are thus more culpable in the sight of God. The Pharisees and scribes had a double standard that gave men permission for sexual sins, while severely denying them to women. This double standard is offensive to God, and it does incur God's judgment.

Second, this double standard was revealed in their arrest of the woman and not the man, so that they thereby incurred for themselves a greater offense: they had used God's law to confirm their sinful order. It is a serious enough offense to break God's law, but even worse to use His law to further a sinful situation. There is a long history of the evil use by men of laws against adultery. The abuses have been done in the name of protecting the family, but, since husbands are the head of their families, their sins are far more serious in God's sight.

Third, God makes very clear that, when men will not obey Him, He will not punish the sins of their wives and daughters, so that their families become free to sin as a judgment on their own apostasy and sin. We are told in Hosea 4:12-14,

> 12. My people ask counsel at their stocks, and their staff declareth unto them: for the spirit of whoredoms hath caused them to err, and they have gone a whoring from under their God.
> 13. They sacrifice upon the tops of the mountains, and burn incense upon the hills, under oaks and poplars and elms, because the shadow thereof is good: therefore your daughters shall commit whoredom, and your spouses shall commit adultery.
> 14. I will not punish your daughters when they commit whoredom, nor your spouses when they commit adultery: for themselves are separated with whores, and they sacrifice with harlots: therefore the people that doth not understand shall fall.

Those who have authority must exemplify obedience to the law of God from their heart and in all their being, or else God's judgment will in time turn against them, rather than those under their authority. During most of history, men with power and authority have seen themselves as above the law, whereas God requires them, most of all, to obey it, "for unto whomsoever much is given, of him shall be much required" (Luke 12:48).

God's judgment in history shatters the centers of authority, because they are the derelict ones of whom much is required. They have betrayed their trust, and therefore God condemns them. Well before the fall of Jerusalem and Judea, it was recognized that commonplace disobedience to the law had led God to abandon *personal* judgment. In A. D. 66-70, national judgment followed. We live now in an age asking for judgment by its sins.

Chapter Twenty-Two

The Question of Authority
(John 8:12-20)

12. Then spake Jesus again unto them, saying, I am the light of the world: he that followeth me shall not walk in darkness, but shall have the light of life.
13. The Pharisees therefore said unto him, Thou bearest record of thyself; thy record is not true.
14. Jesus answered and said unto them, Though I bear record of myself, yet my record is true: for I know whence I came, and whither I go; but ye cannot tell whence I come, and whither I go.
15. Ye judge after the flesh; I judge no man.
16. And yet if I judge, my judgment is true: for I am not alone, but I and the Father that sent me.
17. It is also written in your law, that the testimony of two men is true.
18. I am one that bear witness of myself, and the Father that sent me beareth witness of me.
19. Then said they unto him, Where is thy Father? Jesus answered, Ye neither know me, nor my Father: if ye had known me, ye should have known my Father also.
20. These words spake Jesus in the treasury, as he taught in the temple: and no man laid hands on him; for his hour was not yet come. (John 8:12-20)

These words are part of a confrontation between Jesus and the Pharisees. At issue is authority. In Matthew 21:23, we are told that, in the Temple, the chief priests and the elders of the people came to Jesus, "*as he was teaching*," to demand, "By what authority doest thou these things? and who gave thee this authority?" Neither our Lord's miracles nor His teachings were specified, because they wanted no examination of Christ's record, but simply to challenge His right to do or say anything.

In the incident in Matthew, our Lord put these leaders on the spot by asking, "The baptism of John, whence was it? from heaven, or of men?" (Matt. 21:25). The religious leaders were unwilling to answer Him, and so He would not answer them. In this episode, He uses the opportunity to indict them and to set forth His own person.

He begins by declaring, "I am the light of the world: he that followeth me shall not walk in darkness, but shall have the light of life" (v. 12). The occasion, the Feast of Tabernacles, was a reminder of the wilderness journey, during which the pillar of fire lighted the way of the wandering Israelites and protected them from harm (Ex. 13:21). By declaring Himself to be "the light of the world," the light of all who follow Him, and their light of life, Jesus declared Himself to be one with God the Father. In effect, He invited the Pharisees to challenge openly His self-identification. This they did not dare to do. The miraculous feeding clearly invited comparison to the wilderness manna, and this question they had no desire to raise. Jesus' statement was in effect *a summons to follow Him out of the new Egypt, Judaea*, into the wilderness and freedom. *Now Egypt is Jerusalem*, and Revelation 11:8 speaks of the "great city, which spiritually is called Sodom and Egypt, where also our Lord was crucified." Nothing could be plainer: not only is Jerusalem compared to Egypt, but also to the depraved Sodom. Christ says, I am the pillar of fire which alone can lead you out of the present day Egypt and Sodom.

The Pharisees did not pursue this point. The people might not fully agree with Christ's declaration of Himself, but too many had a low regard for the religious leadership of their day. The rise of Christianity and the Jewish-Roman War of A. D. 66-70 left a partially leaderless people, and the Pharisees came to the fore, but we cannot read their success backwards in time.

Instead of answering, the Pharisees said, "Then bearest record of thyself; thy record is not true" (v. 13). The law requires corroboration of any testimony before it can be accepted (Deut. 17:6; 19:15). The Pharisees insisted on discounting anything Jesus said as lacking corroboration.

Jesus answers by saying, I do bear record of Myself, and My record or witness is true; its truth is self-evident, and so it needs no corroboration. At what point will you challenge Me? The miracles are real and evident. I know My origin and My destination. You are so blinded that you cannot say whence I came from or where I shall go (v. 14).

You condemn "after the flesh," as fallen men, but I judge no man. My mission now is simply to save and to heal those who will be so blessed (v. 15).

However, if I judge, My judgment is always true, because My judgment is never alone, for God judges with Me (v. 16). My judgment, in other words, has behind it the judgment of God the Father. Can you question what I have said and done without questioning the Father? You require, quite properly, because God's law requires it, two witnesses (v. 17). I bear witness, and the Father confirms My witness (v. 18).

This was a direct challenge to the Pharisees to *examine* His works and words instead of *challenging* His authority. His works and words had an inherent testimony and authority. The challenge to Him was comparable to university professors telling Thomas Alva Edison that they could not accept as valid his harnessing of electricity to give light until he presented appropriate university credentials. With such tests, nothing becomes acceptable.

The response was again evasive. Instead of looking to the Scriptures for validation or non-validation, the Pharisees asked, "Where is thy Father?" (v. 19). Our Lord simply dismissed them. "Ye neither know me, nor my

Father." They had not asked, "Who is thy Father?," but "Where is He?" Were they implying Christ came from hell? Their malevolence was clearly great.

We again see *the enormity of evil*. The modern faith is in *facts*. As a result, where men's *faith* militates against the facts, the facts are declared null and void. The clear-cut evidence of our Lord's life and works is denied by those who refuse to admit His truth, power, and person. Modernism and unbelief are exercises in a false faith, not an honest consideration of the truth.

Men hate the truth and love a lie unless they are truly made new in Christ. *How we know* has its foundation in *what we are*. True knowledge has moral foundations, and the modern illusion that facts are determinative is a dangerous one. Courts of law become courts of injustice if God's Son and God's law do not govern them. Our courts today grow more and more evil; at times the innocent victims and the police seem more on trial than the accused.

In v. 20, we are told that our Lord had been teaching in or at the treasury, the place where thirteen bronze chests were placed for the people to drop their offerings. These were at the Court of Women, near to the place where the Sanhedrin met. It was close to the seat of religious authority, yet "no man laid hands on him; for his hour was not yet come" (v. 20). The confrontation was of God's ordination, and the confrontation had become an evasion. No honest consideration was given to our Lord's words and works. Instead, hatred governed the challenge of the religious leaders.

The Pharisees had in effect denied the Father as well as the Son, in favor of themselves, a choice still common in the church.

Chapter Twenty-Three

"Who Art Thou?"
(*John 8:21-29*)

21. Then said Jesus again unto them, I go my way, and ye shall seek me, and shall die in your sins: whither I go, ye cannot come.
22. Then said the Jews, Will he kill himself? because he saith, Whither I go, ye cannot come.
23. And he said unto them, Ye are from beneath; I am from above: ye are of this world; I am not of this world.
24. I said therefore unto you, that ye shall die in your sins: for if ye believe not that I am he, ye shall die in your sins.
25. Then said they unto him, Who art thou? And Jesus saith unto them, Even the same that I said unto you from the beginning.
26. I have many things to say and to judge of you: but he that sent me is true; and I speak to the world those things which I have heard of him.
27. They understood not that he spake to them of the Father.
28. Then said Jesus unto them, When ye have lifted up the Son of man, then shall ye know that I am he, and that I do nothing of myself; but as my Father hath taught me, I speak these things.
29. And he that sent me is with me: the Father hath not left me alone; for I do always those things that please him. (John 8:21-29)

The question (in v. 25), "Who art thou?," is an evasion. Very often, people ask questions, not to learn or to gain answers, but to postpone and obscure the obvious facts that confront them. One thing was clear about Jesus: His *powers* so obviously came from God that it was clear *He* either came from God or was God incarnate.

In vv. 21-24, our Lord tells the religious leaders, ostensibly the very pillars of orthodoxy and conservatism, that they shall die in their sin. The expression, to die in one's sin, is an Old Testament one (Ezek. 3:18 f., 18:18). It means dying under God's curse. With death, a great, impassable gulf will separate Him from them, because there is already a gulf between them. This is a guilt that words cannot bridge, because words can only reveal the moral gap: they cannot cross it. Too many people have an unwarranted faith in words; a little more talking or nagging is held to be the means of changing others, whereas essential change is a religious, not a verbal, matter. Because of the moral gulf between them, where Jesus goes, the religious leaders cannot follow.

These leaders chose to misunderstand Jesus: "Will he kill himself?" Suicide is a sin, so, by raising this question, they were stressing their perspective as the true one: This man is a sinner because He is not on our side. We cannot follow Him because this would lead us to Hell.

Our Lord (v. 23-24) tells them that the division between Himself and them is moral and religious. They are of this world, of the race of the fallen

99

Adam, and they therefore hate God and His moral order. However much they claimed to be the true religious leaders, they were still of the false religion and the fallen humanity. Their focus was humanistic; God's purpose, as they saw it, was to ratify their faith and to support them. There are two worlds and two moral orders; the one is God-centered, the other is man-centered. These two worlds do not merge one into the other, although men seek to blur the division. They are moral contraries.

Their refusal to believe that Jesus is God, the "I am," means that they shall die in their sin (v. 24). Jesus makes very clear that He is God incarnate without actually stating it in so many words.

Verse 24 in the Greek has no "he" after "I am." God's self-identification as the "I am" is most clear in Exodus 3:14, where, when Moses asks God to define Himself, Who is He?, God simply answers, "I AM THAT I AM," I am the eternal One, the Creator; I can be defined by nothing, because all things else are My creation. I am therefore beyond definition. *I cannot be defined, but I can be known in my self-revelation*: I am the God of Abraham, Isaac, and Jacob (Ex. 3:15). Exodus 3:14-15 is basic to the doctrine of God, and therefore basic to the doctrine of Christ. Jesus cannot be understood naturalistically, nor can He and His teachings be reduced to an aspect of the first century's configuration of events. He is in history but His origin is in eternity. He is not of this world (v. 23). By rejecting Him the Jews would die in their sins; by refusing to know Him as God incarnate, they would know eternal death instead.

When these Jews asked, "Who art thou?" (v. 25), our Lord does not answer them directly. They had rejected His every self-identification, and they deserved nothing more. He is the same as He was in the beginning. Their question, "Who art thou?," is contemptuous; He has just told them, and they rejected it with disdain. His answer is that He has hidden nothing from the beginning. He has been open and plain-spoken. He has much to speak about to them, but His coming is becoming one of judgment. God, who sent Him, is true, and what He teaches comes from God (v. 25).

Because what He has to say comes from God the Father, it is true. Moreover, as Judge over all creation, He is mindful of the conduct of these religious leaders. For the present, He speaks as the Father would have Him speak (v. 26).

At this point, we are told, "They understood not that he spake to them of the Father" (v. 26). But, earlier, (v. 18ff.), He had clearly told them of God the Father, and of Himself as the "I AM." Why now did they fail to understand? Up until now, they had shown a perverse refusal to take Him seriously. Now they *cannot* understand. He had just spoken to them about having many things to say and "to judge of you," and they failed to grasp His meaning. If God is at best simply a great *Idea*, then judgment becomes an absurd concept, and men then administer the Idea: it cannot judge in any active sense. For Jesus to speak of Himself as potentially their Judge was impossible for them to grasp. In our time also, many can believe in an after-life, in the advisability of having a moral code and to instruct the people in it, but they cannot see God as an acting Person. He is simply the great Idea. For Jesus to speak of being their Judge was to baffle them, because the term to them implied a *human* office, not God.

Our Lord's response was that, when they lifted Him up, meaning on the cross, then they would know who He was. This would not change them, but it would instead deepen their guilt. Our Lord says further that they would know that the Father taught Him, and that He does nothing of Himself. The cross will be a revelation, whether openly acknowledged as such or not. It will bring them knowledge even as it hardens their hearts (v. 28).

In v. 29, our Lord says that He is never alone, and that He does only those things that please the Father. He can therefore speak as He does because He and the Father are one (John 10:30).

Our Lord clearly answered their question, "Who art thou?," but it only led to ignorance on the part of the Jews because God was never the *living* God for them. For too many then and now, God is the greatest Idea of history, but the action belongs to men. John's prologue (1:1-18) tells us that God is He who works in history. He is the transcendent God who created all things, but He does not hesitate to incarnate Himself, to walk the dirt roads of Palestine, to mingle with the crowds, and to heal and teach them. The question, "Who art thou?," is thus always pertinent. The great modernist illusion has been "the search for the historical Jesus," that is, the premise that Jesus was entirely a product of history because no active and personal God exists, only an Idea, or, at best, a vague Spirit. An Idea can do nothing outside of men, and so it is held, "God has no hands but mine to use," a blasphemous and pharisaic concept. On the other hand, others see only the activity of the Spirit, a charismatic act which affects persons, not history *per se*.

The living God made all things, governs all things, decrees all things, and judges all things. He is *the Lord*.

But men seek to reduce God to an Idea they can obliterate, or one they can reshape. Philosophical Idealism and Hegelianism have sought to do this. The Unitarian, Octavius Brooks Frothingham (1822-1895), defined God thus:

> The interior spirit of any age is the spirit of God; and no faith can be living that has that spirit against it; no Church can be strong except in

that alliance. The life of the time appoints the creed of the time and modifies the establishment of the time.[1]

Such thinking has shaped the twentieth century. It is basic to the concept of "political correctness." *First,* it means that God, i.e., the interior spirit of an age, is inspired and infallible as expressed through the "philosopher-kings" of an era. *Second,* this truth and this god are evolving, and "The life of the times appoints the creed of the times." This is relativism glorified into a religion.

Those who hold to such thinking regard the historic Calvinists as hopelessly backward and out of touch with truth. They themselves are truth incarnate because they represent the spirit of the age.

But God, the Lord, the King, remaineth.

---

[1]. O. B. Frothingham, *The Religion of Humanity* (New York, NY: G. P. Putnam's Sons, 1875, third edition), 7f.

Chapter Twenty-Four

Truth and Freedom
(John 8:30-49)

30. As he spake these words, many believed on him.
31. Then said Jesus to those Jews which believed on him, If ye continue in my word, then are ye my disciples indeed;
32. And ye shall know the truth, and the truth shall make you free.
33. They answered him, We be Abraham's seed, and were never in bondage to any man: how sayest thou, Ye shall be made free?
34. Jesus answered them, Verily, verily, I say unto you, Whosoever committeth sin is the servant of sin.
35. And the servant abideth not in the house for ever: but the Son abideth ever.
36. If the Son therefore shall make you free, ye shall be free indeed.
37. I know that ye are Abraham's seed; but ye seek to kill me, because my word hath no place in you.
38. I speak that which I have seen with my Father: and ye do that which ye have seen with your father.
39. They answered and said unto him, Abraham is our father. Jesus saith unto them, If ye were Abraham's children, ye would do the works of Abraham.
40. But now ye seek to kill me, a man that hath told you the truth, which I have heard of God: this did not Abraham.
41. Ye do the deeds of your father. Then said they to him, We be not born of fornication; we have one Father, even God.
42. Jesus said unto them, If God were your Father, ye would love me: for I proceeded forth and came from God; neither came I of myself, but he sent me.
43. Why do ye not understand my speech? even because ye cannot hear my word.
44. Ye are of your father the devil, and the lusts of your father ye will do. He was a murderer from the beginning, and abode not in the truth, because there is no truth in him. When he speaketh a lie, he speaketh of his own: for he is a liar, and the father of it.
45. And because I tell you the truth, ye believe me not.
46. Which of you convinceth me of sin? And if I say the truth, why do ye not believe me?
47. He that is of God heareth God's words: ye therefore hear them not, because ye are not of God.
48. Then answered the Jews, and said unto him, Say we not well that thou art a Samaritan, and hast a devil?
49. Jesus answered, I have not a devil; but I honour my Father, and ye do dishonour me. (John 8:30-49)

Verse 30 is often included as a part of vv. 12-29, and this is entirely possible, but its inclusion with vv. 31-47 has importance also. The intense confrontation of vv. 31-47 has as its reason the fact stated in v. 30, that "many believed on him" because of His declaration in vv. 12-29. The hatred and confrontation increased as a result.

Now, to those who believed Him, Jesus said, "If ye abide in my word, then are ye truly my disciples; and ye shall know the truth and the truth shall make you free." Plummer's paraphrase reads, "If ye abide in My word, so that it becomes the permanent condition of your life, then are ye My disciples in truth, and not merely in appearance after being carried away for the moment." The words *ye* and *Me* are the focal points. To *abide* means to obey His word and more: it becomes the condition and nature of our lives. Then we are in the Truth, Jesus Christ, who makes us free (vv. 31-32).

In v. 33 "They answered him." The question has been raised, who are they? Does it refer to those who believed, or to His enemies? The cynicism of the question indicates non-believers. As Abraham's seed, they held that they had never been in bondage to any. This was an absurd statement, because Israel and Judaea had a long history of bondage and were currently in bondage to Rome. They were perhaps referring to personal enslavement.

Our Lord's answer is to define slavery as a religious fact: "Whosoever committeth sin is the servant (or, slave) of sin" (v. 34). The reference to committing sin means to continue in sin; where sin becomes second nature to us, we are in slavery to it. Our freedom then is gone, and an outside power is needed to restore it.

In terms of Biblical law, slavery was bond-service. A distinction is here drawn between freedom and bondage. The bond-servant is not fully a member of the family; he can be sent away when his tenure is ended, whereas a son remains as a member of the family (vv. 35-36).

In v. 37, Jesus openly calls attention to the plan by the religious leaders to kill Him. They call themselves "Abraham's seed," and they are physically Abraham's descendants. But they are not spiritually Abraham's family because they seek Jesus' death. Because they are religiously alien to Abraham, our Lord's words have no place in the their lives. Their hostility is to Christ's word, and they are not of Abraham's covenant, or they would hear His word.

In v. 38, our Lord calls attention to their diverse parentage. Jesus is the Son of God and also Abraham's true son. The leaders' religious parentage is an alien one. Religiously and covenantally, they were far from Abraham, and their words and works manifest their foreign nature.

Their indignant response was, "Abraham is our father" (v. 39). But, Jesus answers, "If ye were Abraham's children, ye would do the works of Abraham." There is a unity between faith and action. To profess to be of the true covenant while denying it in practice is a contradiction. In modern terms, they were antinomians. They professed the covenant in name only, not in faith and works.

Because of this, the Jews seek to kill Him who told them the truth of God: "this did not Abraham" (v. 40).

But in this they are consistent, for Abraham is not their true father. They answered to maintain that they were not born in fornication, implying that Jesus was a bastard and not they. They boast of their physical descent and do not deal with the covenantal issue. Moreover, they added, "we have one Father, even God" (v. 41).

But our Lord now tells them that the issue is a moral and covenantal one: if they were God's children, they would love His Son (v. 42). Because they did not, they became liable in time for all the sins from Adam to the present. This is very clearly stated by our Lord in Luke 11:47-51:

> 47. Woe unto you! for ye build the sepulchres of the prophets, and your fathers killed them.
> 48. Truly ye bear witness that ye allow the deeds of your fathers: for they indeed killed them, and ye build their sepulchres.
> 49. Therefore also said the wisdom of God, I will send them prophets and apostles, and some of them they shall slay and persecute.
> 50. That the blood of all the prophets, which was shed from the foundation of the world, may be required of this generation:
> 51. From the blood of Abel unto the blood of Zacharias, which perished between the altar and the temple: verily I say unto you, It shall be required of this generation.

Very clearly, we are all heirs, not only genetically and in terms of properties, but also morally. We are either covenantal heirs or judgment heirs. Our Lord therefore requires that we know the truth and be faithful to it.

Morally, the religious leaders were blind and deaf. They could not hear His speech, the outward expression, nor His word, His meaning (v. 43).

The reason for this is plainly stated in v. 44: their parentage is alien; their father is the devil, tempter of Eden. There is a personal devil, a power for evil, and you, his religious heirs, are manifesting his nature. As his children, you will express his nature, and you will do his will. He was a murderer from the beginning, and he hated and denied the truth "because there is no truth in him." When he lies, he speaks out of his own nature.

The inability of the religious leaders to believe Jesus when He speaks the truth (v. 45) rests in the fact that they belong to the world of the lie. The fundamental lie is that every man is his own god and lawmaker, his own determiner of good and evil (Gen. 3:5). Note the recurring pattern: people sell themselves to the devil in some form or another, prosper for a time, and are then betrayed. No one who sees himself as god will do other than betray rival claimants to godhood.

None can convict Jesus of ever sinning. It therefore follows that, as the sinless One, He speaks the truth. Because He says truth, and His being expresses truth, they do not believe Him (v. 46). The implicit fact is that they disbelieve Him because they love and revel in the lie.

"He that is of God heareth God's words; ye therefore hear them not, because ye are not of God" (v. 47). Their moral nature determines what they will hear.

The religious leaders' absurd answer to this was to accuse Him of being a Samaritan. Had He not spent a few days in Samaria? On top of that, He is the one Who is devil-possessed! (v. 48).

Our Lord's answer is brief: "I have not a devil;" rather, "I honor my Father, and you dishonor Me and therefore my Father" (v. 49).

Clearly, He binds the doctrine of truth to His person. In John 14:6, He says, "I am the way, the truth, and the life: no man cometh unto the Father, but by me." Truth is at least a moral fact, but supremely it is Jesus Christ. In the modern world, truth has been separated from *morality* and limited to *factuality*. Thus, 2 + 2 = 4 is truth, while to say that homosexuality is evil is held to be an opinion because Biblical morality cannot, by definition, also be true.

Our Lord not only grounds truth on morality but on His Person as God incarnate, as *the truth* of all creation, of all being. There can be no freedom in God's creation except on God's terms, so that every effort to find freedom and truth apart from the triune God is a step towards death. The truth alone can make us free and alive, because Christ, the Truth, is Life.

All this is stated by John in his prologue. The Word, who is God, made the world and has now come into the world to redeem His fallen handiwork. "Grace and truth came by Jesus Christ" (John 1:17), in His Person; the world could not comprehend, understand, or encompass that truth (John 1:5), but it shall be judged by Him.

Chapter Twenty-Five

War Against God
(John 8:50-59)

50. And I seek not mine own glory: there is one that seeketh and judgeth.
51. Verily, verily, I say unto you, If a man keep my saying, he shall never see death.
52. Then said the Jews unto him, Now we know that thou hast a devil. Abraham is dead, and the prophets; and thou sayest, If a man keep my saying, he shall never taste of death.
53. Art thou greater than our father Abraham, which is dead? and the prophets are dead: whom makest thou thyself?
54. Jesus answered, If I honour myself, my honour is nothing: it is my Father that honoureth me; of whom ye say, that he is your God:
55. Yet ye have not known him; but I know him: and if I should say, I know him not, I shall be a liar like unto you: but I know him, and keep his saying.
56. Your father Abraham rejoiced to see my day: and he saw it, and was glad.
57. Then said the Jews unto him, Thou art not yet fifty years old, and hast thou seen Abraham?
58. Jesus said unto them, Verily, verily, I say unto you, Before Abraham was, I am.
59. Then took they up stones to cast at him: but Jesus hid himself, and went out of the temple, going through the midst of them, and so passed by. (John 8:50-59)

The confrontation between Jesus and the religious leaders now reaches its climax. As is often the case, then as now, religious leaders often believe that they have a monopoly on religion, and that God has no other voice but their own.

Jesus had previously called attention to their wilful misunderstanding of Him, and their efforts to defame and dishonor Him. So be it. If, in the face of this animosity, a man honor Jesus and His word, even as others seek His dishonor, then he shall never see death: because he already possesses eternal life (vv. 50-51). He is already a member of God's Kingdom.

Because Jesus disagreed with the religious leaders, they accused Him of being devil-possessed. They had suspected it previously, but, they say, "Now we know!" Because they reject Him, they reject His words and deeds. The miracles are discounted, and His words are rejected. In their own eyes, they are good and are the guardians of true religion; Jesus must then be devil-possessed. After all, is He not attacking them? Abraham is dead: he died long ago. The Pharisees were now speaking as Sadducees. They professed to believe in life after death, but Abraham was not a living person to them.

107

The Pharisees also distort his comment that those who "keep" His saying, who ground their lives on Him, "shall never see death." In their version, Jesus said, "he shall never taste of death." A common image in antiquity was the *bitterness* of death. Even those who believed in life after death saw it as a shadow life, and the dead as "shades" or pallid ghosts; such was the Greek view expressed by Homer. The echo of this pagan view of death as bitter indicates the extent to which Greco-Roman culture had influenced them (v. 52).

Then they accuse Jesus of making Himself greater than Abraham and the prophets. But they already know He is greater. Abraham and the prophets, with rare exceptions (e.g., Elijah and Elisha), worked no miracles. Our Lord's life and works were without equal. The purpose of their judgment was ridicule, not truth.

But Jesus answers, despite your persistent attempts to dishonor Me, God the Father honors Me. You call God your Father, but you pay no attention to His obvious confirmation of My person and work. I do not need to honor Myself; self-honor is nothing (v. 54).

Jesus has again opened the door to them for an acknowledgment of His person, His word, and His works. They have called Him demonic, but they have rejected the evidence to the contrary. They reject all evidence that does not conform to their evil presuppositions. The Father has glorified Jesus in all His works, but they reject Jesus because they reject God the Father. Having falsely glorified themselves, using God's name, they now reject the Father by rejecting Jesus.

You have not known the Father, whom I know, Jesus tells them. I would be a liar like you if I said otherwise. You cannot recognize the hand and presence of God. I keep the Father's saying, i.e., I live in obedience to Him. If I deny who and what I am, I will be a liar like you (v. 55).

Earlier, in v. 44, Jesus had declared the father of these religious leaders to be the devil, a liar and a murderer from the beginning. Now He demonstrates to them that "relationship" is proved by action."[1]

This is a fact the world chooses to ignore. Morality is revelational of our character. Empty professions of faith are all too common. Our premise must be, "by their fruits shall ye know them" (Matt. 7:20). Pietism has replaced the priority of faith revealed through works with empty words. Pious words are no evidence of faith in too many cases. These religious leaders saw themselves as pillars of faith.

In v. 56, our Lord boldly says, "Your father Abraham rejoiced to see my day: and he saw it, and was glad." He rejoiced, meaning he was over-joyed and exulted. Since this statement is in the past tense, it could mean that

---

[1] G. Campbell Morgan, *The Gospel According to John* (New York, NY: Fleming H. Revell, n.d.), 158.

Abraham, while on earth, had a vision of Christ's coming (Gen. 12:3). Perhaps, as Morris posits, he all his life exulted over the future coming of the Messiah.[2] According to Plummer, "The Old Testament saints in Paradise were allowed to know that the Messiah had come. *How* this was revealed to them, we are not told; but here is a plain statement of fact."[3] Whether Morris or Plummer is right, it is hard to say, but we do know that Abraham rejoiced to see Christ's day, however he saw it.

The religious leaders were quick to answer, again taking Christ's words in as wrong a sense as possible. "Thou are not yet fifty years old, and hast thou seen Abraham?" (v. 57). Fifty meant maturity to them, and Jesus was in His early thirties. How could He speak so familiarly of a man dead perhaps two thousand years?

Jesus said, "Verily, verily, I say unto you, Before Abraham was, I am" (v. 58). Before Abraham ever existed, I was the eternally self-existent One. Jesus once again identifies Himself as God Incarnate. In his prologue, John speaks of Jesus the Christ as the eternally preexistent and self-existent God the Son, the *Logos*. God's supreme self-identification to Moses was exactly this: *I Am* (Ex. 3:14-15). There was no mistaking what He said, and the religious leaders knew it. Their response was to pick up stones to kill Him. The Temple was under expansion, and building stones were apparently lying nearby. Our Lord simply hid Himself in the crowd and left (v. 59).

Jesus made clear, *first*, that He knew Abraham, their father, in a way that they did not. *Second*, He is God incarnate, the eternal *Logos*. *Third*, this means that He is the Messiah of prophecy. All that they professed to believe in, *He was and is*, and yet they refused to know Him.

The implications are clear: the religious leaders were indeed evil. They professed to believe in God and in His Messiah, but, face to face with Him, their response was attempted murder.

This raises the greater question: can men murder God? This has been and is the goal of much of man's activity, in both the church and the world, to eliminate God somehow. It is an idiotic goal. Man thinks that by blinding himself to God, and by killing God's people here on earth, he will eliminate God! Man is at war against God, and it is a war he must lose.

[2.] Leon Morris: *The Gospel According to John* (Grand Rapids, MI: Eerdmans, 1971), 470-472.
[3.] A. Plummer, *The Gospel According to John* (Cambridge, England: Cambridge University Press, 1880, 1906), 195.

Chapter Twenty-Six

The Sixth Miracle: The Challenge
(John 9:1-7)

1. And as Jesus passed by, he saw a man which was blind from his birth.
2. And his disciples asked him, saying, Master, who did sin, this man, or his parents, that he was born blind?
3. Jesus answered, Neither hath this man sinned, nor his parents: but that the works of God should be made manifest in him.
4. I must work the works of him that sent me, while it is day: the night cometh, when no man can work.
5. As long as I am in the world, I am the light of the world.
6. When he had thus spoken, he spat on the ground, and made clay of the spittle, and he anointed the eyes of the blind man with the clay,
7. And said unto him, Go, wash in the pool of Siloam, which is by interpretation, Sent. He went his way therefore, and washed, and came seeing. (John 9:1-7)

We have here a key miracle, in that, as v. 14 later tells us, it was performed on the Sabbath. It was a deliberate challenge to the religious leaders and their unbiblical sabbatarianism. Jesus, as He passed by, stopped before a man who was blind from birth.

Healing the blind is a very important kind of miracle. Blindness due to a variety of causes was once a common affliction. Even in my lifetime, blindness was a devastatingly prevalent fact world-wide: many were blind from birth, and many became blind by their forties. In this area, many Christian and non-Christian missions have been most noteworthy in reducing this ancient curse. Much good will for the United States has been gained by such medical work over the years. An older generation saw Americans as the people who restored sight.

When the disciples saw the blind man, they raised a theological question. They assumed that sin was the cause of blindness, so their question was, whose sin? Did this man sin while in his mother's womb? It was then held falsely, in reference to Genesis 25:22 and Psalm 51:5 and like verses, that the unborn baby, as already a person, could sin.[1] Perhaps, the disciples suggested, his parents sinned, and they were punished by a blind child (v. 2).

Their thinking was man-centered. They wanted an explanation that would place causality in man, whereas God is the supreme cause in all history and nature. Our Lord's answer was blunt. Neither the child nor the parents sinned. God ordained this so that His works should be revealed in this man (v. 3). J. H. Bernard observed, in his comments on this verse:

[1.] A. Plummer, *The Gospel According to St. John* (Cambridge, England: Cambridge University Press, 1880,1906), 198.

The doctrine of predestination is apparent at every point in the Fourth Gospel, every incident being viewed *sub specie aeternitatis*, as predetermined in the mind of God.[2]

As Luthi pointed out, we are all here so that God's works can be made manifest in us. "There is no life under the sun that is without meaning or reason."[3] It is our duty to recognize that God created us for His purposes, not for our own purposes.

Then our Lord says, "I must work the works of him that sent me while it is day; the night cometh when no man can work" (v. 4). This He said for the disciples and for us. While we are alive, we must serve our God, not ourselves; death comes soon, and the time for our work here is then ended.

At issue are questions of *focus* and *causality*. The question of the disciples, Whose sin caused this blindness?, was man-centered. Because they were man-centered in their view of causality, they were man-centered in their focus. For them, there had to be an answer to such questions in terms of *this* life, the here and now, whereas our Lord tells them their focus must be eternity. Why do some people experience so much pain, grief, and trouble? If we seek a man-centered answer in terms of this world and this time-frame, we will be ignorant and miserable. If we seek the answer in God, we know that our focus will have eternity in mind. Our common failure is to limit our reaction to what we can see, and this warps our focus.

Our Lord then declares, "As long as I am in the world, I am the light of the world" (v. 5). Ernst Haenchen commented that, while for us He is indeed the light of the world, He here tells the disciples why He "performs the miracle now to be narrated: the miracle will make it obvious that he is the light of the world."[4] Jesus, the Light of the world, gives light to a man blind from birth. If we follow the Light, we will ourselves give light by doing His works in all spheres of life and thought. In Alford's words,

> As before the raising of Lazarus (ch. xi. 25), He states that He is *the Resurrection and the Life*; so now, He sets forth Himself as the source of the archetypical spiritual light, of which the natural, now about to be conferred, is only a derivation and symbol.[5]

Westcott noted, "Christ is 'light to the world' as well as 'the one light of the world.'"[6] The implications of this text are far-reaching. Calvin, in his commentary, observed:

[2] J. H. Bernard, A. H. McNeile, *A Critical and Exegetical Commentary on the Gospel According to St. John*, vol. II (Edinburgh, Scotland: T. & T. Clark, 1928, 1972), 325.
[3] Walter Luthi, *St. John's Gospel, An Exposition* (Edinburgh, Scotland: Oliver and Boyd, 1960), 117.
[4] Ernst Haenchen, *John, 2* (Philadelphia, Pennsylvania: Fortress Press, 1984), 38.
[5] Henry Alford, *The New Testament for English Readers* (Chicago, IL: Moody Press, n.d.), 548.
[6] B. F. Westcott, *The Gospel According to St. John* (Grand Rapids, MI: Eerdmans, (1884) 1954), p. 145.

For he compares himself to the sun which, though it illuminates the whole earth by its brightness, yet, when it sets, takes away the day along with it. In this manner he states that his death will resemble the setting of the sun; not that his death extinguishes or obscures his light, but that it withdraws the view of it from the world. At the same time, he shows that, when he was manifested in flesh, that was truly the time of the day-light of the world.[7]

The apostolic writings give us that sense of having beheld His glory, of having been history's most privileged people; 1 John 1:1 makes this emphatically clear.

Our Lord then mixed some of His spit with the clay on the ground to anoint the blind man's eyes (v. 6). He ordered the blind man to go to the pool of Siloam, called Sent because the waters came gushing out, and there to wash his eyes. With his eyes covered with clay, it was necessary for the blind man, whether he wanted to or not, to go to this nearby pool. He had no choice but to do so. Nothing was promised him: he was simply ordered to go and wash up. This is clear from v. 15, when the man answers the question of the Pharisees. He had been told nothing other than to wash the clay off his eyes.

This was an unasked for miracle. It was performed on the Sabbath. It was a direct challenge against false religion. The Pharisees were the epitome of zealous and self-righteous piety. They saw themselves as the guardians of the faith. Our Lord confronts them with a miracle that challenges their Sabbatarian rules. It was a confrontational act because it required them to choose between their self-styled holiness and a miracle from God. They too had to face the question of *causality*: who was responsible for this miracle? Was a miracle of healing more important than their man-made rules? Also, there was the matter of focus: the Pharisees saw their rules about the Sabbath as more binding than the obvious work of God. They judged Jesus, but God judged them.

---

7. John Calvin, *Commentary on the Gospel According to John*, vol. I (Grand Rapids, MI: Eerdmans, 1940 reprint), 368.

Chapter Twenty-Seven

The Sign of Truth
(*John 9:8-16*)

8. The neighbours therefore, and they which before had seen him that he was blind, said, Is not this he that sat and begged?
9. Some said, This is he: others said, He is like him: but he said, I am he.
10. Therefore said they unto him, How were thine eyes opened?
11. He answered and said, A man that is called Jesus made clay, and anointed mine eyes, and said unto me, Go to the pool of Siloam, and wash: and I went and washed, and I received sight.
12. Then said they unto him, Where is he? He said, I know not.
13. They brought to the Pharisees him that aforetime was blind.
14. And it was the sabbath day when Jesus made the clay, and opened his eyes.
15. Then again the Pharisees also asked him how he had received his sight. He said unto them, He put clay upon mine eyes, and I washed, and do see.
16. Therefore said some of the Pharisees, This man is not of God, because he keepeth not the sabbath day. Others said, How can a man that is a sinner do such miracles? And there was a division among them. (John 9:8-16)

Like all the miracles reported by John, this is, *first*, a *sign*. Of that, more, later. *Second*, this was a miracle which occurred on the Sabbath. The gospels tell us of *seven miracles of mercy wrought on the Sabbath*.

1. the withered hand (Matt. 12:10-13);
2. the demoniac at Capernaum (Mark 1:21-26);
3. Simon's mother-in-law (Mark 1:29-31)
4. the crippled woman (Luke 13:14)
5. the man with dropsy (Luke 14:2-4)
6. the paralytic at Bethesda (John 5:1-9)
7. the man born blind (John 9:1-7).[1]

Each of these miracles violated the Sabbath rules of the Pharisees, and each was a challenge to false religion. This healing of the man born blind, coming as it did when the Pharisees planned His death, was especially an affront to the Pharisees because it was a very deliberate condemnation of their stand. Is true religion made up of a handful of pious man-made rules, or is it obedient faithfulness to God? We cannot relegate the application of this stand to the religious leaders of Jerusalem. It applies equally to the churchmen of our time. The Pharisees then, and too often churchmen now, demanded *conformity* rather than *faith*. But conformity is commonly to men and to institutions, whereas our faith and primary obedience must be to the triune God.

---

[1]. A. Plummer, *The Gospel According to St. John* (Cambridge, England: Cambridge University Press, 1880,1906), 201.

Among other things, this miracle is a sign of what counts with God. Our self-created piety is of no value. His truth alone matters, and His truth must command us. The whole of our being must be under His command. We can try to govern ourselves by our own will, or we can be governed by God, His word, and His Spirit. This miracle is a sign of *truth*: are we ruled by our will, or by the truth of God? The religious leaders had made their decision; the man born blind now had to decide whom to follow.

After the miracle, the formerly blind man was the subject of comment: was this the former blind beggar? Some said, "This is he," others, "he resembles the blind beggar, but he can see." The man said, "I am he" (vv. 8-9). His neighbors asked, How is it that you now can see? (v. 10). For a blind man, blind from birth, to gain his sight was a startling thing. The man recounted what had happened to him. He also identified his healer, "A man that is called Jesus" (v. 11).

The next question was, "Where is he?" (v. 12). This is important: they did not ask, Who is he? Everyone knew. Jesus was a mighty healer, perhaps the Messiah. It was unnecessary to ask more. The answer was, "I know not." A man born blind receives vision in a strange world; everything is unfamiliar and unaccountable. Suddenly this man found that he was expected to know much more than he could know.

Word of the miracle spread, and the once blind beggar found himself taken to the Pharisees, perhaps by officers, perhaps by "concerned" persons (v. 13).

In v. 14 we are told the critical fact, that the miracle was performed on the Sabbath day. The Sabbath has always been God's ordained day. The Temple, the synagogue, and too often the church have made it *their* day. But our Lord had earlier told certain Pharisees, "the Son of man is Lord also of the Sabbath" (Luke 6:5). The full context is given in Mark 2:23-28. This important statement precedes Jesus' declaration that He is Lord of the Sabbath: "The sabbath was made for man, and not man for the sabbath" (Mark 2:27). The Sabbath is intended as a blessing for man, not as a burden, as a freedom, not as a bondage. The stand of the seventeenth century Puritans of England against Sabbath labor won the working peoples to their side. Their condition in so-called Merry England had been one of enslavement while the wealthy made merry. Sabbath rules meant liberation for them.

The Pharisees wanted to preserve their Sabbath rules and regulations. The liberation of a man born blind meant nothing to them. In Matthew 12:9-14, we see the issue joined:

9. And when he was departed thence, he went into their synagogue:

10. And, behold, there was a man which had his hand withered. And they asked him, saying, Is it lawful to heal on the sabbath days? that they might accuse him.

11. And he said unto them, What man shalt here be among you, that shall have one sheep, and if it fall into a pit on the sabbath day, will he not lay hold on it, and lift it out?

12. How much then is a man better than a sheep? Wherefore it is lawful to do well on the sabbath days.

13. Then saith he to the man, Stretch forth thine hand. And he stretched it forth: and it was restored whole, like as the other.

14. Then the Pharisees went out, and held a council against him, how they might destroy him.

The argument of Pharisees against this position would have as its premise, *first*, no work of any kind on the Sabbath. *Second*, this man's condition is not new: the healing can therefore wait until another day. *Third*, it is therefore lawless to heal on the Sabbath when the healing can wait until the morrow. A sheep in a pit is an *emergency*. A man with a withered hand, and also a man born blind, are not emergencies. This is a *logical* argument, but an immoral one.

The Sabbath is the *Lord's* day. To do good on the Lord's day is not a sin. It is always lawful to do good, to serve God, on the Sabbath, and healing is an act of restoration.

The Pharisees persisted in questioning the healed beggar, who was now capable of work and a life of freedom and usefulness. How did he gain sight? Again they were told of Jesus' healing power (v. 15).

Some of the Pharisees refused to associate the miracle with Jesus and His mission. "This man is not of God, because he keepeth not the sabbath day." Of course, our Lord observed the Sabbath as God's law requires, not as the rules of the Pharisees stipulated.

Some, apparently a minority, asked, "How can a man that is a sinner do such miracles?" The result was a division in the meeting (v. 16). It is important to remember that the early church, apparently for a few generations, was predominately Jewish. In fact, well into the "Middle Ages," many churchmen and some popes were Jewish. In Acts 6:7 we are told that "a great company of the priests were obedient to the faith."

At this point, the minority insisted that the starting point of the discussion should be the miracle Jesus performed, whereas most began with the priority of their man-made rules. The starting point, or presupposition, determined the conclusion in either case. If our presupposition is not the triune God and His enscriptured word, we will presuppose that our own will, rules, or conclusions are the truth. A variety of humanistic premises is routinely established as the ground for truth. But a Christian must maintain that the truth is not in us; we are not the source of truth because God alone is. Hence, if we want to know the truth, we must begin with the

God of Scripture and His infallible word. False premises lead to false conclusions, and man is a false premise in and of himself. His essential presupposition is set forth in Genesis 3:5, man as his own god, knowing or determining for himself what constitutes good and evil, right and wrong, and law and morality. The Pharisees were earnest and moral men as compared with other men of their time, but their false premise led them to reinterpret and, in effect, alter God's law to make themselves the law-givers. This practice is still with us.

Chapter Twenty-Eight
False Priorities
(John 9:17-34)

17. They say unto the blind man again, What sayest thou of him, that he hath opened thine eyes? He said, He is a prophet.
18. But the Jews did not believe concerning him, that he had been blind, and received his sight, until they called the parents of him that had received his sight.
19. And they asked them, saying, Is this your son, who ye say was born blind? how then doth he now see?
20. His parents answered them and said, We know that this is our son, and that he was born blind:
21. But by what means he now seeth, we know not; or who hath opened his eyes, we know not: he is of age; ask him: he shall speak for himself.
22. These words spake his parents, because they feared the Jews: for the Jews had agreed already, that if any man did confess that he was Christ, he should be put out of the synagogue.
23. Therefore said his parents, He is of age; ask him.
24. Then again called they the man that was blind, and said unto him, Give God the praise: we know that this man is a sinner.
25. He answered and said, Whether he be a sinner or no, I know not: one thing I know, that, whereas I was blind, now I see.
26. Then said they to him again, What did he to thee? how opened he thine eyes?
27. He answered them, I have told you already, and ye did not hear: wherefore would ye hear it again? will ye also be his disciples?
28. Then they reviled him, and said, Thou art his disciple; but we are Moses' disciples.
29. We know that God spake unto Moses: as for this fellow, we know not from whence he is.
30. The man answered and said unto them, Why herein is a marvellous thing, that ye know not from whence he is, and yet he hath opened mine eyes.
31. Now we know that God heareth not sinners: but if any man be a worshipper of God, and doeth his will, him he heareth.
32. Since the world began was it not heard that any man opened the eyes of one that was born blind.
33. If this man were not of God, he could do nothing.
34. They answered and said unto him, Thou wast altogether born in sins, and dost thou teach us? And they cast him out. (John 9:17-34)

A stubborn fact faced the religious leaders: for a man born blind to gain sight as a mature man was an unheard of miracle, and the miracle-worker was Jesus. Their strategy was, *first*, to question the miracle. Was he really born blind, or was this a pretension? *Second*, if indeed the man was born blind, their goal was to separate the miracle from Jesus.

They questioned again the man who had been born blind. What was his opinion of the man who healed him? The answer was clear-cut: "He is a prophet" (v. 17). Whatever more he may have believed, this answer was enough to anger them. They refused to believe anything he said until they called his parents. The parents, for fear of excommunication from the synagogue, confirmed his blindness from birth, but, as to his healing, they said, "he is of age, ask him" (v. 18-23). The fact of his blindness from birth was thus confirmed. This meant that a miracle had taken place.

The approach of the religious leaders was now to separate the miracle from Jesus: "Give God the praise: we know that this man is a sinner" (v. 24). They were denying *causality*. Somehow, Jesus had nothing to do with the miracle because He was for them *a sinner* by definition.

This rejection of causality should not surprise us, because it is very much with us today. The homosexuals are insistent that AIDS was caused by Christians, not by their own sins. More than a few boast of their infection as a battle wound incurred in the battle against Christianity. Their insistent denial of causality is commonplace in their thinking. Again and again in history, men and nations have forsaken rationality, denied causality, and insisted that reality be redefined to suit them. This is a mark of original sin, the will to be god and to know or establish truth, law, and morality in terms of one's own will.

We also see that the religious leaders are again called "the Jews" by John. Perhaps the key reason for this was the religious leaders' identification of themselves as *the people*. They regarded the Galileans, who were not concerned about the ways and goals of either Pharisees or Sadducees, as not really believers or true Israelites. The Jews who did not follow them were also seen as not "the people." John, knowing them well, calls attention to this self-identification. In our time, we see similar stands: both the right and the left in the United States tend to see themselves alone "true Americans."

The healed man said, "Whether he be a sinner or no, I know not: one thing I know, that, whereas I was blind, now I see" (v. 25). He insisted on keeping the miracle in the forefront. Trying to break down his witness, the Pharisees asked him to recount what had happened (v. 36). The healed man answered, "I have told you already, and ye did not hear." Why are you asking again and again? Do you want to be His disciples? (v. 27). This statement brought out their malice. They reviled him and said, "Thou art his disciple; but we are Moses' disciples" (v. 28). Jesus had again and again called attention to their betrayal of Moses and the law, but they were determined to pit Moses, safely dead, against Jesus, dangerously alive. They continued, "We know that God spake unto Moses: as for this fellow, we know not from whence he is" (v. 29). Both in vv. 24 and 29, the religious leaders are determined to deny any causal relationship between Jesus and the miracle.

William Hendriksen called attention to the syllogisms employed by the religious leaders. Syllogisms are methods of deductive reasoning. They consist of a major premise, a minor premise, and a conclusion. A dictionary example is, Every virtue is praiseworthy; kindness is a virtue; therefore, kindness is praiseworthy. This syllogism can also be called a false syllogism, however, because kindness to murderers and rapists is *not* a virtue in many cases. An obviously false syllogism is, All men are mortal; my dog is mortal; therefore, my dog is a man.

The religious leaders had two faulty syllogisms in mind, Hendriksen pointed out:

1. Major premise: People who are from God keep the Sabbath.
2. Minor premise: This Jesus does not keep the Sabbath.
3. Conclusion: Jesus is not from God.

The other syllogism is:

1. Major premise: The ungodly alone suffer great afflictions.
2. Minor premise: This man was born blind and grew to maturity blind.
3. Conclusion: This man is wicked and ungodly.[1]

Basic to the thinking of these religious leaders was a presupposition which excluded Jesus Christ. Our thinking is always presuppositional: we begin with a pre-theoretical, pre-reflective belief which governs our faith and thinking. Only as men's presuppositions are changed can their thinking be changed, and this conversion from the premise of fallen man to that of redeemed man is an act of God.

The healed man answered with a wisdom beyond himself: "Why herein is a marvellous thing, that ye know not from whence he is, and yet he hath opened mine eyes" (v. 30). He went on to say that this was a new event in history, for a man blind from birth to have his sight restored (v. 32). You are right, he said, that God does not hear sinners (v. 31). "If this man were not of God, he could do nothing" (v. 33).

The response was a furious one. You were totally born in sin. Do you think that you are fit to teach us? (v. 34). The Pharisees therefore excommunicated the healed man.

The conflict was a religious one. It could not be solved by rational discourse. The religious leaders began with radically different premises, and the discussion simply hardened them in their resolution. The miracle had not made Jesus more obviously a prophet or the Messiah, as far as they were concerned, but rather a threat to religion, a stumblingblock for naive people.

---

[1] William Hendriksen, *New Testament Commentary. Exposition of the Gospel According to John*, vol. II (Grand Rapids, MI: Baker Book House, 1954), 88-92.

The healed man was in their eyes a *nobody*, a person of no account. But they saw the nation as made up of too many such nobodies, all potentially dangerous if Jesus made them His followers. As a result, the conclusion was soon stated openly by Caiaphas: "Ye know nothing at all, nor consider it expedient for us, that one man should die for the people, and that the whole nation perish not" (John 11:49f). The preservation of the political entity was of primary importance to them. It would be wrong to say that such a goal was not important; the world is full of important things, but they all pale before the mandate, "Seek ye first the kingdom of God and his righteousness; and all these things shall be added unto you" (Matt. 6:33). The Pharisees saw themselves as good men, the best men, but their priorities were false.

Chapter Twenty-Nine

Blindness and Knowledge
(*John 9:35-41*)

35. Jesus heard that they had cast him out; and when he had found him, he said unto him, Dost thou believe on the Son of God?
36. He answered and said, Who is he, Lord, that I might believe on him?
37. And Jesus said unto him, Thou hast both seen him, and it is he that talketh with thee.
38. And he said, Lord, I believe. And he worshipped him.
39. And Jesus said, For judgment I am come into this world, that they which see not might see; and that they which see might be made blind.
40. And some of the Pharisees which were with him heard these words, and said unto him, Are we blind also?
41. Jesus said unto them, If ye were blind, ye should have no sin: but now ye say, We see; therefore your sin remaineth. (John 9:35-41)

The man born blind was excommunicated. That term has lost much of its meaning in our time, except in a few religious communities, but it once meant total separation from one's family and community. In its Hebrew and Jewish forms, *herun* was once a living death because all ties were severed, as is still the case with some churches. The healed man was thus sentenced to something none of the disciples experienced, because the miracle of his healing testified so powerfully concerning Jesus.

Jesus sought the man out, even as others were avoiding him, to ask him, "Dost thou believe on the Son of God?" (v. 35). The man's answer was simply this: "Who is he, Lord, that I might believe on him?" (v. 36). His question indicates an eagerness to know and believe on the Son of God. He asks the question of Jesus because he obviously believes that Jesus *can* give him the answer. Jesus then identified Himself as the Son of God (v. 37).

The man answered, "'Lord, I believe.' And he worshipped him" (v. 38). He saw Jesus as God incarnate, and so he worshipped Him, which was at the time an act of prostration.

David well described the character of God in Psalm 27:10, "When my father and my mother forsake me, then the Lord will take me up." It is quite likely that the healed man's parents, already fearful, may have observed the excommunication and severed their son from his home. Our Lord's approach to him was to give him a new family. Although we hear no more of him, this does not mean he went uncared for or neglected.

Then Jesus made a devastating statement: "For judgment I am come into this world." According to Plummer, the word translated as *judgment* "signifies not the *act* of judging (v. 22, 24, 27, 30) but its *result*, a 'sentence' or 'decision' (Matt. vii.2, Mark xii.40, Rom. ii.2,3, etc.)." He had come to save men, but judgment resulted for those who rejected Him. They "passed sentence on themselves."[1] To tell the truth is to expose a lie. Christ's presence was a judgment on all His enemies. For this reason, Jesus Christ is still hated because, in all His word and works, He is a continuing judgment on the ungodly. By His coming, "they which see not might see." Religious leaders believed then and now that wisdom and vision belonged to them, and they despise the simple believers of whom our Lord said,

> I thank thee, O Father, Lord of heaven and earth, because thou hast hid these things from the wise and prudent, and hast revealed them unto babes. (Matt. 11:25)

Wisdom and vision do not belong to high office, nor do they mark the high and the mighty of the world. The men in charge of guiding others are often blinded by their unbelief.

God's goal is "that they which see might be made blind" (v. 39). St. Paul states this same fact in 1 Corinthians 1:18-31: God will "destroy the wisdom of the wise, and will bring to nothing the understanding of the prudent" (v. 19). The religious leaders believed that their program of excommunication and persecution would destroy Jesus. Instead, they destroyed themselves and the entire nation.

Verse 40 is interesting, because it confirms what is repeatedly seen in the Gospels: many Pharisees followed Jesus, out of interest, sometimes out of dawning belief, and at other times as spies. We know from Acts 6:7 that many priests became Christians.

Some of these Pharisees, critical ones, took exception to His words, saying, "Are we blind also?" (v. 40). One of the distressing aspects of the Gospels is that we see so many peoples, disciples and enemies alike, questioning and challenging our Lord's words. We do the same by our disobedience. Sometimes the comments were intended as corrections, as though this miracle-worker would go astray without their guidance. We have an example of this in Matthew 16:21-28, where Peter seeks to correct Jesus when He speaks to the disciples about His coming death.

Our Lord's answer to these Pharisees was blunt: "If ye were blind, ye should have no sin: but now ye say, We see; therefore your sin remaineth" (v. 41). If you had any awareness of your spiritual blindness, of your sin, you would be on the road to salvation, to freedom from sin. Very much to the contrary, you feel confident that your vision is sound, that religiously you are the wise ones, and therefore your sin remains basic to your being.

The fact stated by our Lord is one which is still basic to theology and philosophy. Men try to make *knowing* an intellectual and rational matter, whereas it involves man in all his being and is founded on his religious and

---

[1]. A. Plummer, *The Gospel According to St. John* (Cambridge, England: Cambridge University Press, 1880, 1906), 208.

moral nature. Original sin is man's will to be his own God and lawmaker. Sin governs man's being totally, and it orders what he knows and why he knows it. The subject of how we know is called epistemology in philosophy, and the perspective is, apart from the school of Calvin and Van Til, man-centered. Too many churchmen are man-centered in their epistemology.

Such epistemologies begin with man's reason, man's experience, or some aspect of man's capabilities. As against this, our Lord here tells us that there can be no other foundation for knowledge other than Himself, that any other premise leads to compromise or falsification of knowledge.

Our Lord is emphatically clear that there can be no foundation other than Himself. He declares, "I am the way, the truth, and the life; no man cometh unto the Father, but by me" (John 14:6). We cannot come to the Father, nor to a knowledge of His creation, apart from Him. All non-Christian knowledge is borrowed knowledge. If creation is not the handiwork of God, then it is the product of chance, in which case knowledge is impossible. Everything is a surd. The ungodly gain limited knowledge by denying chance in practice while affirming it in theory.

Our Lord here contrasts the clear knowledge of an unlettered man born blind with the spiritual blindness of the highly literate men who rejected Him. He called the leaders blind men, and such blindness still governs too much of the world.

Chapter Thirty

Hearing His Voice
(John 10:1-6)

1. Verily, verily, I say unto you, He that entereth not by the door into the sheepfold, but climbeth up some other way, the same is a thief and a robber.
2. But he that entereth in by the door is the shepherd of the sheep.
3. To him the porter openeth; and the sheep hear his voice: and he calleth his own sheep by name, and leadeth them out.
4. And when he putteth forth his own sheep, he goeth before them, and the sheep follow him: for they know his voice.
5. And a stranger will they not follow, but will flee from him: for they know not the voice of strangers.
6. This parable spake Jesus unto them: but they understood not what things they were which he spake unto them. (John 10:1-6)

Much of the Bible is a closed book to us because we are unfamiliar, in many cases, with its use of rural images, especially sheep. Sheep are not highly regarded by cattlemen, and sheep do have their liabilities. *First,* sheep are dirty and often smelly. Their wool catches pebbles, twigs, and dirt and usually becomes quite filthy if they are pastured in the hills and mountains. Sheep cannot clean themselves. We are called sheep because, like them, we cannot clean ourselves of our sins and offenses. *Second,* sheep lack the intelligence to be free. If they see a trail, they will follow it, even if it leads them over a cliff. Sheep need a shepherd, someone to care for them and lead them, as do we. God, in calling us sheep, is not paying us a compliment. *Third,* sheep are defenseless. They need to be protected, or predatory animals will kill them at will. We need God's shepherding care to avoid destruction. *Fourth,* sheep are not only dirty, unintelligent, and defenseless, but they are also great complainers. Go by a few penned sheep who have been well fed, and they will bleat for more.

In vv. 1-5, we have a clear account of the life of shepherds and sheep. My father's experience as a boy echoes these verses. In the summer, or beginning in the spring as soon as grass was available but not too green, the sheep were parcelled out to young boys, a few to each boy. At night, the sheep were either taken to the nearest stone corral or to the home base. The stone corral was built high enough to keep out predatory animals. The entry way was only wide enough to allow the sheep to enter, and for the shepherd to unfold his bedroll there. "The porter" was the man in charge of the boy shepherds. David very early was such a shepherd. The boy shepherds called their little bands, six or more sheep, by names they gave them. The sheep quickly learned their shepherd's voice; they recognized their own name, and they responded when called. The boy shepherd

127

enjoyed calling his sheep by name, and the lambs were very playful companions.

The sheep thus followed their shepherd because they knew his voice; they would not respond to the voice of a stranger or a thief.

The Bible repeatedly speaks of God as our Shepherd, as witness Psalm 23. When Jesus declares Himself to be the Good Shepherd (John 10:11; cf. Matt. 18:12f.; Luke 15:3-7; Jer. 23:1-8; Ezek. 34), it also reveals that He is God incarnate. Pagan rulers often spoke of themselves a their people's shepherd, thereby asserting either their divinity or the deity inherent to their status. In G. Campbell Morgan's words:

> The shepherd always represented kingship, full and final authority. It was Homer who said, "All kings are shepherds of the people." That saying embodies the Eastern idea. The shepherd is the king, the king is the shepherd; and his authority is based upon his care for the sheep.[1]

In John 10:1-18, our Lord states clearly that He is the Good Shepherd and that His status is given Him by God, His Father. He is thus both King and God.

In our text there is a stress on the shepherd's voice and the thief's voice. According to Paul E. Kretzmann, actual tests have demonstrated that the sheep do not follow the shepherd's scent, nor his clothes, nor his dog — only his voice.[2] The implications are clear. The faithful sheep, the true members of Jesus Christ, follow the called under-shepherds of Christ, while those who are not of Christ will follow the hirelings. In our time, in countries like Australia and the United States, men have sheep by the hundreds and thousands, and they are thus not as familiar with the sheep as were the shepherds of the Near East, or of Scotland in much of history.

The parable tells us that, if men do not have Christ as their Shepherd, they will have thieves and murderers as their shepherd. We are also told that the false shepherds use devious means. We are not given any shades of gray between the Good Shepherd and the thieves. Men are either Christ's under-shepherds, or *pastors*, or they are the devil's. The word *pastor* means *shepherd* in Latin, and it comes from a verb meaning *to feed*. No man is a pastor under Christ who does not feed people from the Word of God.

A *fold* of sheep is a number of sheep under one shepherd; a *flock* is the totality of all the sheep under their great Shepherd. A church is thus a *fold*.

The bluntness of the Gospels is very much evident in John's Gospel. The Christian is plainly defined as one who hears Christ's voice. In vv. 2-5, we have the repeated statement that the true sheep hear His voice. This means that they do not quibble over God's Word: they accept it as is. They do not

---

[1.] G. Campbell Morgan, *The Gospel According to John* (New York, NY: Fleming H. Revell Company, n.d.), 173.

[2.] Paul E. Kretzmann, *Popular Commentary of the Bible, The New Testament*, vol. I, "The Gospels" (St. Louis, MO: Concordia, 1921), 466.

regard certain texts as not meaning what they say, nor do they bypass certain doctrines because they dislike them: His sheep hear His voice. Their authority is not their own verdict concerning God's Word, but God's Word as it is.

We are also told that the only true approach to the sheep is through the Shepherd, who is the Door (John 10:7).

This statement was certainly provocative, because, to the religious leaders, the only true Shepherd was God alone, not Jesus Christ. This statement therefore only strengthened their resolve to kill Him. To say that those who harkened to His voice were the only true sheep of God was a further affront, since the leaders rejected His voice. This denied to the religious leaders the status they claimed, namely, that they were the true and elite people of God. Our Lord makes clear that God's true people hear and recognize His voice in Him, Jesus. G. H. C. Macgregor commented:

> Sir G. A. Smith (*Historical Geography of Palestine*, p. 312) gives a good illustration: "Sometimes we enjoyed our noonday rest beside one of the Judaean wells, to which three or four shepherds come down with their flocks. The flocks mixed with each other, and we wondered how each shepherd would get his own again. But after the watering and the playing were over, the shepherds one by one went up different sides of the valley, and each called out his peculiar call, and the sheep of each drew out of the crowd to their own shepherd, and the flocks passed away as orderly as they came.
>
> "They will not follow a stranger, they will run from him, because they do not know the voice of strangers." Plummer tells the story of a Scottish traveller who changed clothes with a Jerusalem shepherd and tried to lead the sheep; but the sheep followed the shepherd's voice and not his clothes."[3]

Thus, the point is an emphatic one. All hearing is governed by a moral factor. We either hear His voice, or we are not His people, the sheep of His pasture. In this matter, ignorance is no excuse. If we examine our own past, we can recognize the times when, however respectful we were, we became aware that we were not hearing our Shepherd's voice.

Men want to reduce everything to an intellectual or an emotional base, to reasoning or to feeling. We are here told that Christ's sheep hear His voice, not that of a thief or a hireling. We cannot excuse people on the ground that they failed to grasp the intellectual content of a false gospel. The critical component in all decisions is the moral judgment. Our decisions reveal our character. In this parable, our Lord denies implicitly to all who follow false shepherds the validity of their excuses. The voice they harkened to was the voice of a false shepherd, a wolf. Their decision revealed what they were, wolves in sheep's clothing.

[3.] G. H. C. Macgregor, *The Gospel of John* (London, England: Hodder and Stoughton), 235f.

Chapter Thirty-One

Our Enemies, In and Out of the Church
(John 10:7-16)

7. Then said Jesus unto them again, Verily, verily, I say unto you, I am the door of the sheep.
8. All that ever came before me are thieves and robbers: but the sheep did not hear them.
9. I am the door: by me if any man enter in, he shall be saved, and shall go in and out, and find pasture.
10. The thief cometh not, but for to steal, and to kill, and to destroy: I am come that they might have life, and that they might have it more abundantly.
11. I am the good shepherd: the good shepherd giveth his life for the sheep.
12. But he that is an hireling, and not the shepherd, whose own the sheep are not, seeth the wolf coming, and leaveth the sheep, and fleeth: and the wolf catcheth them, and scattereth the sheep.
13. The hireling fleeth, because he is an hireling, and careth not for the sheep.
14. I am the good shepherd, and know my sheep, and am known of mine.
15. As the Father knoweth me, even so know I the Father: and I lay down my life for the sheep.
16. And other sheep I have, which are not of this fold: them also I must bring, and they shall hear my voice; and there shall be one fold, and one shepherd. (John 10:7-16)

In v. 7, our Lord says that He is "the door of the sheep." This is a reference baffling to people today, but it was once well understood. A shepherd out in the hills or mountains would, in some cultures, bed his sheep down at night in a stone corral. The stone walls were high enough to keep out local predators such as bears, coyotes, wolves, cougars, and lions. The entrance into this stone corral was a narrow one, just wide enough for the shepherd to spread out his bedroll. He literally was the door to the sheep. They could not enter except over his body. In our Calaveras and Tuolumne County areas, there are three such sheep corrals. Our Lord tells us that, as long as we stay in His corral, in His care, we are safe from the predators. We can go and come in the security of His care (v. 9).

Our Lord then describes in various terms some of the persons whose concern with the sheep, with Christ's people, may be good or bad.

These are the wolf, the thief or robber, and the hireling. *First,* the wolf's only purpose with respect to the faithful is to destroy them. They are his prey. Christ's flock is seen only in terms of exploitation, and the wolf's purpose is openly evil. Implicit in what our Lord here says is the warning not to trust ourselves to evil men, to human wolves. If our trust in Christ is at all abated, we will trust in men who are actual or potential wolves.

The world outside of Christ is not neutral. It has no good will towards Jesus Christ, nor towards us. It believes not in salvation, but in self-fulfillment at the expense of others.

Second, there are the thieves and robbers. These are many, and the appeal of the flock is the possibility of self-enrichment. By calling Himself the Good Shepherd, our Lord contrasts Himself to all careless ones, men whose care for the sheep is lacking. The animal-enemies of the sheep are predatory creatures, and neither the sheep nor the Good Shepherd are predatory. To become a Christian means, from one perspective, to be disarmed. The most common weaponry used against the Christian is slander, lies, misrepresentation, and deceit. Against these things, the Christian can only respond with honesty and truth, which are of little interest to the ungodly. We thus must face the fact that many people want to believe evil of us. The church has often had thieves and robbers within its leadership, and the price it pays for such infiltration is a grim one.

Third, there is the hireling, working essentially for the money, an under-shepherd who is in with the sheep without a sacrificial concern for them. The care he gives is careless, and, at the sight of danger, he flees, or he protects himself rather than the sheep. Because of his unwillingness to risk everything in the sheep's defense, the hireling becomes an implicit ally of the wolf or of the robber.

Fourth, by way of contrast, Jesus Christ, supremely the Good Shepherd, gives His life for the sheep (v. 11). "I am the good shepherd, and know my sheep, and am known of mine" (v. 14). "As the Father knoweth me, even so know I the Father: and I lay down my life for the sheep" (v. 15). Here our Lord tells us that He and the Father have a common nature. But, because Jesus Christ is the incarnate one, not only very God of very God, but very man of very man, He also knows us, not only as His sheep, but as fellow members of the new human race. His complete knowledge of us has its consummation in the completeness of His atoning sacrifice. We do not share in Christ's deity, but, by His perfect humanity, and by His atoning and regenerating work, He makes us His new creation. We are members of His humanity, and in Him we are linked eternally to the Father and to the new creation.

Lest His followers see the true sheep, or the true humanity, in purely Jewish terms, our Lord states emphatically that He has other sheep, "which are not of this fold." These He shall bring in, so that there will be one *flock*, and one shepherd, Himself (v. 16). The translation here should read one *flock*, not one *fold* or subordinate group. This clearly sets forth the premise that the church is much more than one racial or national group. The underlying principle of unity is not found in the common origin of the members, but in Jesus Christ. There is no evil in a church which is solely German, Italian, or Jewish in its membership. The evil begins when leaders and members confine the church to such a group. The membership of the church is not defined by the people, but by Jesus Christ. Very early, there were those who attempted to limit the church in terms of Judaic antecedents, and these groups perished. Since then, many similar nationalistic definitions have been current, and their failures are notable.

This tells us that the dangers to the church exceed the hirelings, false shepherds, wolves, thieves, and robbers. They include all Christians who want to place limitations on what is not theirs; they are Christ's property, not His overlords. Thus, the otherwise devout believer can become as dangerous as these alien threats if he tries to erect his prejudices into barriers not of Christ's making.

Our Lord does not compliment us by calling us sheep. Sheep are foolish and stupid animals, blind followers, and devoid of the ability to keep themselves clean. Our Lord's parable tells us what we are, and also the protection that is ours if we follow Him faithfully. Jesus Christ alone defines the church, not man, and all man-made definitions are an implicit warfare against Him.

Chapter Thirty-Two

The Credulity of the Ungodly
(John 10:17-21)

17. Therefore doth my Father love me, because I lay down my life,
that I might take it again.
18. No man taketh it from me, but I lay it down of myself. I have
power to lay it down, and I have power to take it again. This
commandment have I received of my Father.
19. There was a division therefore again among the Jews for these
sayings.
20. And many of them said, He hath a devil, and is mad; why hear ye
him?
21. Others said, These are not the words of him that hath a devil. Can
a devil open the eyes of the blind? (John 10:17-21)

Our Lord in these words speaks of His messianic calling. He is God
incarnate, the Good Shepherd. He has come to make atonement for sin. In
Acts 2:22-36, Peter speaks of Christ's voluntary acceptance of His role as
the atoning sacrifice, while at the same time declaring it to be "the
determinate counsel and foreknowledge of God." God's absolute
predestination and the willing response of Jesus are both stressed. This is
the plain emphasis of vv. 17-18. "Therefore doth the Father love me,
because I lay down my life, that I *might* take it again" (v. 17). To bring about
the restoration of man into God's grace, Kingdom, and purpose, God the
Son offers Himself as the atonement. Hence the Father's love of the Son.
Jesus Christ lays down His life that He may take it again.

In v. 18 we are told, "No man taketh it from me, but I lay it down of
myself." Verses 17-18 speak of the perfect coincidence of God's
predestination and Christ's course of action. There is no compulsion, only
perfect agreement. Jesus was judicially murdered, but this is not the point
made by the Gospels, which all stress His readiness to submit to an act that
had eternal implications. "I have power to lay it down, and I have power to
take it again" (v. 18). As Hendrikson noted, this is a unique power. "No one
has a *right* to lay down his life, but Jesus did have that right. He had the
right both to lay it down and to take it again."[1] The word translated as *right*
can also be rendered as *authority, freedom,* or *power.* It is a clear statement
of Christ's divine power and authority, His right and freedom. The word
is an apt one, because Jesus reveals His authority and His freedom.

He adds, "This commandment have I received of my Father" (v. 18).
Through His obedience He opens up eternal life for His people (John

---

[1] William Hendriksen, *The Gospel of John*, vol. II (Grand Rapids, MI: Baker Book
House, 1954), 115.

12:49-50; cf. 14:31). A new human race is created by His atoning sacrifice, and the world now has a new direction.

The result of His sayings was a division *again* among the peoples (v. 19). The opinion of some was that he was demon-possessed or mad (v. 20).

Others objected, saying, "These are not the words of him that hath a devil. Can a devil open the eyes of the blind?"

This argument about the nature of Jesus continues today, on different levels, it is true, but with one and the same purpose of denying the deity of Jesus Christ. According to G. H. C. Macgregor:

> Both Cross and Resurrection are part of the Father's commission to the Son. The Son's freedom consists in spontaneously obeying the Father's commandment, for (note how admirable is the connection resulting from the transposition of 29-30), "I and my Father are one" (cf. 17:21-22). The unity here claimed is ethical rather than metaphysical, a unity of will rather than of essence and personalities, a mystical unity implying two separate personalities as in 38 below and 1:1 — "the Logos was with God." Christ never claims even in this Gospel to be in essence with God (see note on 5:18). The unity with the Father which he does claim is a similar unity of will and purpose to that which he prays may exist between Christian and Christian (17:11). An indivisible unity of nature in Father and Son is not implied, as Jesus himself makes clear when in verse 36 he interprets his present claim as meaning not "I am God," but "I am God's Son." [2]

If Macgregor is right, and he is not, then there can be no atonement, because Jesus was, like us, totally human. He simply overlooks the conclusion of John 1:1, "the Word was God." There is for Macgregor no incarnation, simply a moral union between a man named Jesus and God. He holds that we are all capable of effecting such a union. All can also become God's sons, not by the adoption of grace through Christ, but by our own mystical unity with God. This is not Biblical religion, but ancient paganism masquerading as Christianity. The virgin birth is set aside, as is everything that makes clear the supernatural origin and power of Jesus Christ.

Macgregor's commentary was an important one, part of a series of studies in *The Moffatt New Testament Commentary*. So-called scholarship was used to battle historic Christianity, and orthodox Christology was undermined.

Any honest reading of the New Testament tells us that Jesus Christ is revealed to us as God incarnate, truly God and truly man. Scholars encourage us to discount the Biblical accounts on the grounds of the popular credulity of that era. This is an absurd approach, because people have been gullible in every age, including our own. Anyone glancing at the

[2.] G. H. C. Macgregor, *The Gospel of John* (London, England: Hodder and Stoughton, 1928, 1933), 241.

array of supermarket tabloids, which sell heavily, will soon realize that we have millions of credulous people around us. Similarly, there were skeptics then as now, so that unbelief is not a new problem. To discount the evidence of the New Testament on the grounds of first century credulity is an evasion of the facts, and it rests on the presupposition that facts are only facts if certain men so decree them to be.

The problem faced by Jews and Gentiles when confronted by the New Testament and its claims was one of accommodation. How could they fit New Testament history into their idea of history? Moreover, if Jesus Christ were what He and the New Testament set forth, then the whole of their worldview was radically wrong.

As a result, thinkers began to reshape Jesus into an acceptable form. He was not easily dismissed. However much shunned by intellectual leaders, Jesus Christ shattered all the worldviews of antiquity. He was both God and man in a unique incarnation. His atonement for sin was beyond the capacity of any other person to reproduce or to repeat.

Here was a force without equal, a threat then as now to the systems of the world. As a result, while many rejected Him, many sought also to fit Him into their fallen world systems. This effort is still with us, and Macgregor's pathetic "solution" is one of many. Modernism is a form of ancient paganism's effort to minimize Jesus Christ in order to revive the march of the human spirit towards self-divinization.

As v. 21 makes clear, there were those present when this episode occurred who realized that madness cannot be matched with miracles. The effort to make such a connection was illustrative of the idiocy of the ungodly. To deny God is to be a credulous fool. If a man refuses to place his faith in the triune God of Scripture, there will be no limit to the lies he will believe.

Chapter Thirty-Three
The Evidentialists
(John 10:22-30)

22. And it was at Jerusalem the feast of the dedication, and it was winter.
23. And Jesus walked in the temple in Solomon's porch.
24. Then came the Jews round about him, and said unto him, How long dost thou make us to doubt? If thou be the Christ, tell us plainly.
25. Jesus answered them, I told you, and ye believed not: the works that I do in my Father's name, they bear witness of me.
26. But ye believe not, because ye are not of my sheep, as I said unto you.
27. My sheep hear my voice, and I know them, and they follow me:
28. And I give unto them eternal life; and they shall never perish, neither shall any man pluck them out of my hand.
29. My Father, which gave them me, is greater than all; and no man is able to pluck them out of my Father's hand.
30. I and my Father are one. (John 10:22-30)

The occasion for this incident was the feast of dedication, also called the festival of lights. It commemorated the purification and rededication of the Temple in 165 B. C., after the defilement by Antiochus Epiphanes (1 Mac. 1:59; 4:52, 59; etc.) It was an eight-day festival celebrating deliverance from a powerful foreign tyrant. In 166 B. C., the Temple had been profaned by Antiochus Epiphanes, and the deliverance was celebrated annually in mid-December. While there was no cessation of work or business, it was a time of joy and of feasting. The elation of victory colored Judaean life for generations. It was winter, we are told, and Jesus was walking inside the Temple, in Solomon's porch or portice where there was protection from the rain. We are told in v. 24 that the Jews, meaning the religious leaders, surrounded Jesus to demand, "How long dost thou make us to doubt? If thou be the Christ, tell us plainly" (v. 24). Our Lord's language had been plain enough, but what was demanded was explicit language that would hold up in court. His condemnation was already more or less decided upon; what they wanted was language that could be used against Him.

Jesus answered, "I told you, and ye believed not" (v. 25). Already (vv. 1-18) our Lord had spoken of His sheep, and of hirelings, thieves, and robbers. Whether directly or indirectly, the religious leaders were well aware of this, and they knew that they were clearly seen as neither sheep nor shepherds, but as wolves, strangers to God's flock, and exploiters. They refuse to believe, and there is no integrity in them. Both His words and His works plainly revealed Him to be the Messiah, but, as our Lord says, probably in the present tense, "ye *believe* not." "The works that I do in my Father's name, they bear witness of me" (v. 25).

The religious leaders were evidentialists. They held that, if the evidence were provided them, *then* they would believe. E. J. Carnell, a consummate evidentialist said, "Bring on your revelations! Let them make peace with the law of contradiction and the facts of history, and they will deserve a rational man's assent."[1] Carnell made *rational* man, whether regenerate or unregenerate, judge over God and His Word. Since Carnell saw adherents of rationalistic apologetics like himself as the true judges, he implicitly denied truth to any revelation if unapproved by himself. Such apologists make themselves gods over God.

The religious leaders of our Lord's day were determined that they alone could assess Jesus' the credentials. They rejected *both* His words and His works, our Lord reminds them. But Jesus does not let the matter rest there. "But ye believe not, because ye are not of my sheep, as I said unto you" (v. 26). His sheep know their Shepherd's voice. Here was a plain statement of His nature and being. The religious leaders knew that God speaks of Himself as the Good Shepherd, as did Jesus. Could anything point more plainly to Jesus as the Messiah, as God's anointed One?

Two basic statements have been made. *First*, "I am the good shepherd" (v. 11), i.e., I am God, the one true Shepherd. *Second*, "ye are not my sheep" (v. 26). You are reprobate, and you are pretenders. A more blunt denunciation is hard to imagine. He is God, and you are not of God, but rather against Him.

"My sheep hear my voice, and I know them, and they follow me" (v. 27). They *hear*, and they *follow*. The religious leaders did neither. They collected evidence to condemn Him. Hendriksen called attention to the fact that in vv. 27-28 we are told of three things that Christ's sheep must do: *First*, they listen to Christ's voice; *second*, they follow Him; and, *third*, they shall never perish, because of His grace. Jesus also says of Himself, *first*, I know my sheep; *second*, I give them everlasting life; and, *third*, no power will ever take them out of His hand.[2]

Despite the quibblings of some, vv. 27-28 plainly tell us of our eternal security in Christ. Because our salvation depends, not on what we do, but on what He has done, no man, nor anything in heaven or on earth, can take away our salvation. This is even more plainly stated in v. 29: "My Father, which gave them me, is greater than all; and no man is able to pluck them out of my Father's hand." It is a remarkable fact of man's persistent egocentricity that so plainly stated a doctrine is rejected. On occasion, non-professionals, i.e., men who are not theologians or clergymen, have stated their objection honestly: they do not want either their salvation or their

[1] E. J. Carnell, *An Introduction to Christian Apologetics* (Grand Rapids, MI: Eerdmans), 178.
[2] William Hendriksen, *The Gospel of John*, vol. II (Grand Rapids, MI: Baker Book House, 1954), 122.

personal security or perseverance to slip out of their hands. They want God's help, but not His control and government. As a result, they prefer an uncertain salvation to eternal security.

There is a double security for us in this text. In v. 28, our Lord says, "neither shall any man pluck them out of my hand." In v. 29, we are told, "no man is able to pluck them out of my Father's hand." The essential and total power of God the Father and God the Son assures our eternal security. If it depended on us, our security could never be eternal: we might experience ten million years of salvation, and then lose it all due to our own imperfections.

Our Lord then tells them plainly, "I and my Father are one" (v. 30). By using the *plural*, "*are* one," our Lord distinguishes between the two Persons of the Trinity. They are *one* in essence but *two* Persons. Those who choose to deny the doctrine of the Trinity simply bypass texts like this which set forth the oneness of essence while maintaining a distinction of Persons.

The discussion began with the demand, "If thou be the Christ, then tell us plainly" (v. 24). When He told them, they picked up stones to kill Him (v. 31). Their evidentialism simply meant, supply us with the evidence to convict or to kill you: we will never believe you no matter how compelling the evidence may be.

Chapter Thirty-Four
The Shepherd-King
(*John 10:31-42*)

31. Then the Jews took up stones again to stone him.
32. Jesus answered them, Many good works have I shewed you from my Father; for which of those works do ye stone me?
33. The Jews answered him, saying, For a good work we stone thee not; but for blasphemy; and because that thou, being a man, makest thyself God.
34. Jesus answered them, Is it not written in your law, I said, Ye are gods?
35. If he called them gods, unto whom the word of God came, and the scripture cannot be broken;
36. Say ye of him, whom the Father hath sanctified, and sent into the world, Thou blasphemest; because I said, I am the Son of God?
37. If I do not the works of my Father, believe me not.
38. But if I do, though ye believe not me, believe the works: that ye may know, and believe, that the Father is in me, and I in him.
39. Therefore they sought again to take him: but he escaped out of their hand,
40. And went away again beyond Jordan into the place where John at first baptized; and there he abode.
41. And many resorted unto him, and said, John did no miracle: but all things that John spake of this man were true.
42. And many believed on him there. (John 10:31-42)

Our text begins grimly: "Then the Jews took up stones again to stone him" (v. 31). Jesus had answered them as they had requested: "If thou be the Christ, tell us plainly" (v. 24). They wanted Him dead, and this they now revealed. Today, religious leaders and scholars raise up stones of criticism against Him. They will accept Him only on their terms.

Jesus raised the question, I have shown you many good works which obviously come from my Father. For which of these do you stone Me? (v. 32). Again the religious leaders insisted on separating the man and His works. We are not stoning you for the miracles, but for blasphemy. You, a man, "makest thyself God" (v. 33). They conceded that the miracles were good, but they refused to connect them with His person and being. Their statement was a denial of causality; they had already called Him a devil and stated implicitly that God had worked the miracles through a devil. This was a strange position, because its obvious implication was that they, God's religious leaders, had been bypassed by God in favor of a devil! They were the priests who guarded the Holy of Holies, and yet Gold had somehow chosen to use one whom they called a devil! Theirs was the logic of insanity.

In vv. 34-35, our Lord refers to Psalm 82:6-7. The reference in that psalm, in vv. 1 and 6, to *gods* is to *judges*, who, because they administer God's law, are called *elohim*, authorities who are like gods. Because they are faithless to their calling and judge unjustly, because they fail to defend the poor and the fatherless, the afflicted and the needy, the religious leaders shall die like guilty men (vv. 2-5, 7). When judges neglect or are faithless to God's law, "all the foundations of the earth are moved" and shaken (v. 5).

So now the religious leaders of Judaea are false judges who have shaken and altered the foundation of society. You, as the religious leaders, are especially bound to judge all things in terms of God's law, "and the scripture cannot be broken" (v. 35). Instead of judging Me by God's law, you judge Me in your sin. To judge apart from God's law is to destroy all religious and civil order. Public trust is shattered, and society becomes a place of injustice. Jesus tells them that they have shattered the foundations of justice, as men have today.

Jesus makes clear that not only is He part of the eternal order, but He is also the One by whom the Father sanctified the foundation of that order. He *is* the Son of God, and, if saying so is blasphemy to them, then by implication they are in blasphemy (v. 36).

Again our Lord states the causal fact. Did He or did He not do His Father's works (v. 36)? If the works He did were godly miracles, as the leaders recognized, how could they deny Him His calling? "If I do not the works of my Father, believe me not" (v. 37). You who claim to be godly have admitted the validity of the miracles. Why not then admit Who I am? (v. 38). The Father is obviously, very obviously, with Me and present in Me (v. 38).

Again they tried to arrest Him, "but he escaped out of their hand" (v. 39). He left for the wilderness area beyond Jordan where John had earlier baptized. There He resided for a time (v. 40).

Many who had earlier followed John now followed Jesus into that area. They compared John and Jesus, both seen as men of God. But John the Baptist performed no miracles, while Jesus did. As a result, many of these believed on Jesus (vv. 41-42).

Two aspects of our text require special attention. *First*, Jesus repeatedly in this chapter speaks of Himself as the Good Shepherd, especially in v. 14. For us, this image is a purely pastoral one. In antiquity, it had a much broader significance, both political and religious. The Good Shepherd is the Divine King, the Shepherd-King. The image is one of the fulness of religious and political oversight and care. The Shepherd-King is the ideal king, one whose care and concern is without equal. This Jesus Christ declares concerning Himself: He is the pastor, protector, and lord. The image of the Shepherd-King was one even tyrants, such as Antiochus IV

Epiphanes, used as they tried to convince people of their benevolent purposes. For our Lord to use this image was a declaration of His deity as well as His royal status and power. He declared Himself the God King.

The use of Psalm 82 by our Lord reinforces His claim to deity and to the status of lawgiver. As the Shepherd-King, He tells the religious leaders or judges of Israel, the *elohim*, that they shall die like convicted men because they have despised both the Lawgiver and His law.

Second, John 1:17 tells us that "the law was given by Moses," but the law came from the triune God. It was and is the law of God the Son no less than the law of the Father and the Spirit. In Matthew 7:29, we are told of Jesus that "he taught them as one having authority, and not as the scribes." Exactly. Because He was expounding His own law, the expression of the nature of the Godhead, He spoke with authority and without hesitation. When asked about marriage in the resurrection, He answered with a full knowledge of life in that age (Matt. 22:23-33).

When faced by Jesus, the scribes and Pharisees, who saw themselves as the guardians of the law, found themselves face to face with the law incarnate. Jesus manifested the true law of God, not the pharisaic versions of it, in all His being. In the hands of the religious leaders, the law had become *a yoke of bondage* (Gal. 5:1), not *the perfect law of liberty* (James 1:25; 2:12). The law as a burden was not God's law, but rather the pharisaic reinterpretations thereof. In John 10:10, our Lord declares, "I am come that they might have life, and that they might have it more abundantly." As against the niggardly images of popular religions, our Lord speaks of the fulness of blessings, full measures heaped up and running over (Luke 6:38). Our Lord never minimized the hatred and evil of our enemies, nor the persecutions we must endure, but He always tells us of God's greatness and assured victory. The Shepherd-King is our Lord and Savior.

Chapter Thirty-Five
The Raising of Lazarus
(John 11:1-46)

1. Now a certain man was sick, named Lazarus, of Bethany, the town of Mary and her sister Martha.

2. (It was that Mary which anointed the Lord with ointment, and wiped his feet with her hair, whose brother Lazarus was sick.)

3. Therefore his sisters sent unto him, saying, Lord, behold, he whom thou lovest is sick.

4. When Jesus heard that, he said, This sickness is not unto death, but for the glory of God, that the Son of God might be glorified thereby.

5. Now Jesus loved Martha, and her sister, and Lazarus.

6. When he had heard therefore that he was sick, he abode two days still in the same place where he was.

7. Then after that saith he to his disciples, Let us go into Judaea again.

8. His disciples say unto him, Master, the Jews of late sought to stone thee; and goest thou thither again?

9. Jesus answered, Are there not twelve hours in the day? If any man walk in the day, he stumbleth not, because he seeth the light of this world.

10. But if a man walk in the night, he stumbleth, because there is no light in him.

11. These things said he: and after that he saith unto them, Our friend Lazarus sleepeth; but I go, that I may awake him out of sleep.

12. Then said his disciples, Lord, if he sleep, he shall do well.

13. Howbeit Jesus spake of his death: but they thought that he had spoken of taking of rest in sleep.

14. Then said Jesus unto them plainly, Lazarus is dead.

15. And I am glad for your sakes that I was not there, to the intent ye may believe; nevertheless let us go unto him.

16. Then said Thomas, which is called Didymus, unto his fellow disciples, Let us also go, that we may die with him.

17. Then when Jesus came, he found that he had lain in the grave four days already.

18. Now Bethany was nigh unto Jerusalem, about fifteen furlongs off:

19. And many of the Jews came to Martha and Mary, to comfort them concerning their brother.

20. Then Martha, as soon as she heard that Jesus was coming, went and met him: but Mary sat still in the house.

21. Then said Martha unto Jesus, Lord, if thou hadst been here, my brother had not died.

22. But I know, that even now, whatsoever thou wilt ask of God, God will give it thee.

23. Jesus saith unto her, Thy brother shall rise again.

24. Martha saith unto him, I know that he shall rise again in the resurrection at the last day.

25. Jesus said unto her, I am the resurrection, and the life: he that believeth in me, though he were dead, yet shall he live:

26. And whosoever liveth and believeth in me shall never die. Believest thou this?

27. She saith unto him, Yea, Lord: I believe that thou art the Christ, the Son of God, which should come into the world.

28. And when she had so said, she went her way, and called Mary her sister secretly, saying, The Master is come, and calleth for thee.

29. As soon as she heard that, she arose quickly, and came unto him.

30. Now Jesus was not yet come into the town, but was in that place where Martha met him.

31. The Jews then which were with her in the house, and comforted her, when they saw Mary, that she rose up hastily and went out, followed her, saying, She goeth unto the grave to weep there.

32. Then when Mary was come where Jesus was, and saw him, she fell down at his feet, saying unto him, Lord, if thou hadst been here, my brother had not died.

33. When Jesus therefore saw her weeping, and the Jews also weeping which came with her, he groaned in the spirit, and was troubled,

34. And said, Where have ye laid him? They said unto him, Lord, come and see.

35. Jesus wept.

36. Then said the Jews, Behold how he loved him!

37. And some of them said, Could not this man, which opened the eyes of the blind, have caused that even this man should not have died?

38. Jesus therefore again groaning in himself cometh to the grave. It was a cave, and a stone lay upon it.

39. Jesus said, Take ye away the stone. Martha, the sister of him that was dead, saith unto him, Lord, by this time he stinketh: for he hath been dead four days.

40. Jesus saith unto her, Said I not unto thee, that, if thou wouldest believe, thou shouldest see the glory of God?

41. Then they took away the stone from the place where the dead was laid. And Jesus lifted up his eyes, and said, Father, I thank thee that thou hast heard me.

42. And I knew that thou hearest me always: but because of the people which stand by I said it, that they may believe that thou hast sent me.

43. And when he thus had spoken, he cried with a loud voice, Lazarus, come forth.

44. And he that was dead came forth, bound hand and foot with graveclothes: and his face was bound about with a napkin. Jesus saith unto them, Loose him, and let him go.

45. Then many of the Jews which came to Mary, and had seen the things which Jesus did, believed on him.

46. But some of them went their ways to the Pharisees, and told them what things Jesus had done. (John 11:1-46)

We come now to the seventh miracle or sign, the raising of Lazarus from the dead. Lazarus lived in Bethany with his sisters Mary and Martha. John identifies Mary as the woman who anointed Jesus with a precious oil (Matt. 26:6-13; Luke 7:37-48; and John 12:3 cite incidents of anointing).

When Lazarus became very ill, his sisters sent word to Jesus to come (v. 3), but Jesus delayed going, remaining two days more where He was. When

Jesus returned to Bethany, Lazarus was already dead and buried four days. This means that when the messengers reached Jesus, Lazarus was already dead (vv. 17, 39). Jesus was somewhere in Galilee (v. 7). Because Lazarus was dead, there was no rush to return, so that Jesus finished whatever He had come into Galilee to do.

What He did say for the benefit of the disciples and the messenger or messengers was that the outcome of this sickness was not death, but for the glory of God, and "that the Son of God might be glorified thereby" (v. 4). We are told that Jesus loved Martha, Mary, and Lazarus (v. 5). The delay had as its purpose the glory of God.

In two previous miracles, our Lord had raised the dead, Jairus' daughter (Matt. 9:23-31; Mark 5:23-43; Luke 8:42-56) and the son of the widow of Nain (Luke 7:11-17). In these instances, no great time had elapsed after the deaths, nor had burial yet taken place.

When Jesus announced His plan to return to Judaea, the disciples objected because the threat to His life was a very serious one (vv. 7-8). Why would He return to an area where His murder was likely?

Our Lord's answer begins, "Are there not twelve hours in a day? If any man walk in the day, he stumbleth not, because he seeth the light of the world. But if a man walk in the night, he stumbleth, because there is no light in him" (vv. 9-10). This is proverbial and idiomatic language. There are twelve daylight hours daily when a man can work without fear of stumbling. I know what I am doing, and I am returning because it is still time for me to work. The disciples are wrong in assuming that His return to Bethany is a mistake. Our Lord uses the opportunity to perform a miracle of staggering dimensions. The raising of Lazarus from the dead reveals Jesus to be the Lord over life and death, equal to God in His power and authority; His eventual condemnation thus becomes all the more clearly *evil* in its nature.

In vv. 11-14, Jesus tells them Lazarus is dead, and He will awaken him out of his sleep. The disciples, not eager for a return, because their lives, too, may be at stake, initially choose to misunderstand Him. If he is asleep, he will recover, they say, and Jesus responds plainly, "Lazarus is dead." He adds that He is glad for their sake that Lazarus is dead, because they will now see the fulness of the messianic power of Jesus (v. 13). The attitude of the disciples is that a return is suicidal, but, says Thomas, "Let us go also, that we may die with him" (v. 16). Thomas is a Hebrew name; Didymus is its Greek counterpart, meaning *twin*.

When Jesus reached Bethany, Lazarus was four days in the grave (v. 17). Bethany was about two miles from Jerusalem (v. 18), so that Jesus was once again close to the religious leaders who plotted to kill Him. Many of the leading people in Jerusalem had come to Bethany to comfort Martha and

Mary (v. 19). Martha, on hearing that Jesus was near, went out to meet Him
(v. 20). She said to Jesus, "Lord, if thou hadst been here, my brother had
not died" (v. 21). Then she added, "But I know, that even now, whatsoever
thou wilt ask of God, God will give it thee" (v. 22). Jesus' response was,
"Thy brother shall rise again" (v. 23). Martha assumed that Jesus spoke of
the resurrection at the last day (v. 24), but Jesus said, "I am the resurrection
and the life: he that believeth in me, though he were dead, yet shall he live:
and whosoever liveth and believeth in me shall never die. Believest thou
this?" (v. 26). Martha had affirmed her faith in an *event*, the general
resurrection at the end of the world. Jesus now told her He, Himself, in His
Person, was the resurrection and the life, so that the event was the work of
His Person. Without His Person, there can be neither life nor resurrection.
Martha's reaction was to go to her sister Mary, telling her that the Master
had come and was asking for her. The word *secretly* in v. 28 modifies *saying*;
she so spoke so as not to be overheard by the enemies of Jesus. Mary at once
arose and went to the place where Martha had left Jesus, perhaps not too
far from the grave (v. 30). Everyone followed Mary as she left, assuming
that she was going to the grave (v. 30). Mary, weeping, fell at Jesus' feet and
said, "Lord, if thou hadst been here, my brother had not died" (v. 32). Jesus
asked to be led to the tomb, and He wept (vv. 33-35). The people from
Jerusalem commented on this, some observing that Jesus obviously had
loved Lazarus. Others asked why a man who could heal the blind did not
prevent the death of a friend (vv. 36-37). When Jesus came to the grave, He
ordered the stone to be removed. Martha said, "Lord, by this time he
stinketh: for he hath been dead four days" (v. 39). Jesus responded, "Said I
not unto thee, that, if thou wouldest believe, thou shouldest see the glory
of God?" (v. 40). The stone was removed from the mouth of the cave.

Jesus then prayed, a prayer of amazing audacity, in open defiance of the
religious leaders. He thanked God for having already heard His prayer and
for hearing Him always. I make this prayer, openly and publicly, so that
these, my enemies, may hear Me and also witness Your answer (vv. 41-42).
The reason? "That they may believe that thou hast sent me." Some will be
saved, but others will perish in their staggering unbelief.

Then, with a loud voice, He called, "Lazarus, come forth" (v. 43).
Lazarus, still more or less bound with the graveclothes, did just that. Jesus
ordered them, "Loose him, and let him go." (v. 44).

Many of the witnesses believed then and there (v. 45), but some reported
the miracle to the Pharisees (v. 46). The Pharisees were supposedly the
strictest believers, but they surpassed all others in wanting the death of
Jesus. The question, of course, is this: belief in what? In the name of God,
and nowadays in the name of Jesus Christ, men can and do erect many
idols, false gods that bear a close resemblance to themselves; in so doing,
they reveal the depths of their hatred for the true and living God.

There is an important aspect to this miracle or sign, to which B. F. Westcott has somewhere called attention: both the first miraculous sign, the turning of water into wine at Cana in Galilee (John 2:1-11), and this, the seventh, the raising of Lazarus (John 11:1-46), are in the context of *family life*, and both are declared to be manifestations of *glory* (John 2:11; 11:4, 40). Any depreciation of the family has against it the witness of all Scripture.

This miracle gives us a resurrection that is not comparable to our Lord's, nor to ours at the end of the world. Lazarus arose from the grave, but, in time, he would again face death, whereas our general resurrection is to eternal life. But Lazarus knew that Jesus Christ was and is all-powerful, and in his resurrection we have a sign of the total power of Jesus Christ over all things. We see how staggering unbelief is when we realize that the religious leaders actually believed they could kill Jesus. For them, the universe was one of brute or meaningless factuality, and there was no causality at work. They were substituting their will for God's and saying, in effect, As I will, so must it be, the ancient proverb of occultism. But the Lord God reigns, and He uses men's evil to accomplish His purpose.

Chapter Thirty-Six

The Council and the Decision
(*John 11:47-57*)

47. Then gathered the chief priests and the Pharisees a council, and said, What do we? for this man doeth many miracles.
48. If we let him thus alone, all men will believe on him: and the Romans shall come and take away both our place and nation.
49. And one of them, named Caiaphas, being the high priest that same year, said unto them, Ye know nothing at all,
50. Nor consider that it is expedient for us, that one man should die for the people, and that the whole nation perish not.
51. And this spake he not of himself: but being high priest that year, he prophesied that Jesus should die for that nation;
52. And not for that nation only, but that also he should gather together in one the children of God that were scattered abroad.
53. Then from that day forth they took counsel together for to put him to death.
54. Jesus therefore walked no more openly among the Jews; but went thence unto a country near to the wilderness, into a city called Ephraim, and there continued with his disciples.
55. And the Jews' passover was nigh at hand: and many went out of the country up to Jerusalem before the passover, to purify themselves.
56. Then sought they for Jesus, and spake among themselves, as they stood in the temple, What think ye, that he will not come to the feast?
57. Now both the chief priests and the Pharisees had given a commandment, that, if any man knew where he were, he should shew it, that they might take him. (John 11:47-57)

We are told in v. 47 that the chief priests and the Pharisees held a council meeting. It would have been led by the controlling Sadduceean party, whose power depended on their cooperation with Rome. The Temple and its presiding priests were Sadducees. The question raised was, "What do we do?" We are faced with a great crisis, and we cannot sit back and await its outcome: we must act. Now, it was not a question of who Jesus was: He was a threat to their power and had to be dealt with as such.

The summation was this: "If we let him thus alone, all men will believe on him, and the Romans shall come and take away both our place and nation" (v. 48). A man who can raise someone dead and buried four days will have all men believe on him. Without mentioning Lazarus, the leaders were referring to his resurrection as an open and obvious fact: *they never questioned it.* The consequence they feared, or said they feared, was that the Romans would come to take over Judaea and displace the Jews. This was a very remote possibility. True, the people would try to make Jesus their Messiah-King, but this had already been attempted (John 6:15), and it had been rejected by Jesus. What the religious leaders were actually afraid of was that Jesus would destroy their power and somehow replace them. Since they were the tools of Roman power, the Sadducees at this point openly assumed the leadership in opposing Jesus.

In that particular year, the Roman appointee as high priest was Caiaphas. Since the office gave great power and wealth to the office-holder, Rome allowed no man to hold the office more than briefly. His statement (vv. 49-50) was addressed, not to doubters as to what the course of action should be, but to the squeamish, those who wanted Jesus dead but balked at judicial murder. The issue, said Caiaphas, is this: who should live, this man, or us and our power over the nation? Someone is going to die: either Jesus, or us and our rule over the nation. Take your choice. No moral question is raised. The issue is seen as one of power and control.

When faced with this choice, there was no longer any hesitation. "Then from that day forth they took counsel together for to put him to death" (v. 53). They were now self-consciously planning the death of the One who had revealed Himself to be God's Son and the Messiah.

John adds, ironically, that Caiaphas spoke, unknowingly, as a prophet: the death of Jesus would indeed save the *true* nation, the Kingdom of God, His elect from every tribe, tongue, and nation (v. 51-52). All would be gathered together into membership in His Kingdom.

Jesus left the area for a remote place, Ephraim, which was probably situated northeast of Jerusalem (v. 54).

Dr. Cornelius Van Til often called attention to epistemological self-consciousness, which means, roughly, knowing ourselves and what we know; it is the self-recognition of our moral and religious ground and nature. Men are prone to giving themselves noble motives and reasons even when they sin, and to credit themselves with good intentions in all things. To be epistemologically self-conscious is to be fully aware of what we are and of our often specious reasoning about it. Most men fight against epistemological self-consciousness and indulge in self-justification. They try to make even their sin into a form of nobility on their part. In prisons, a strict caste system exists. Commonly, child-molesters are at the bottom, but even they have their rationales and self-justifications: they blame the child.

The council under Caiaphas made a decision and a choice. They offered a rationale: this man, or us and the nation. All the same, their decision was clearly an evil one. They knew *better than the disciples* that Jesus had declared that, on the third day after His crucifixion, He would rise from the dead. They therefore asked Pilate to place a troop of Roman guards at the tomb (Matt. 27:62-66). They had paid better attention to Jesus' words than had the disciples, but they also trusted that Roman soldiers would be able to deal with one risen from the dead.

The festival of the Passover was nearing, and, as the pilgrims began to enter Jerusalem, their great subject of interest was Jesus. They asked one another, "What think ye, that he will not come to the feast?" (v. 55f). Their attitude was clearly not hostile: it was curious. They wanted to witness history's key event. They no doubt craved the blessed results of it, but had no wish to incur personal risk. They were devout and religious people, but their desire was to remain uninvolved.

Meanwhile, "the chief priests and the Pharisees," both the major power groups in the nation, "had given a commandment, that, if any man knew where he (Jesus) were, he should shew it, that they might take him" (v. 57). Their long animosity to one another now gave way to an alliance against Jesus. The Sadducees and the Pharisees alike wanted Jesus crucified.

To understand the enormity of their evil, remember their words, "What do we? for this man doeth many miracles" (v. 47). Their denial of His claims was thus in opposition to their own knowledge. They knew that Jesus was right in stating that His miracles were God's work in and through Him. They were therefore not only rejecting Jesus, but they were also rejecting God. Their choice was the nation and their own power, rather than God and Jesus Christ. Here again we see epistemological self-consciousness. Like all sinners, only more so, they were without excuse. They had sentenced Jesus to death because He was God's Messiah *and not theirs*.

Chapter Thirty-Seven
In the Name of the Poor
(*John 12:1-8*)

1. Then Jesus six days before the passover came to Bethany, where Lazarus was which had been dead, whom he raised from the dead.
2. There they made him a supper; and Martha served: but Lazarus was one of them that sat at the table with him.
3. Then took Mary a pound of ointment of spikenard, very costly, and anointed the feet of Jesus, and wiped his feet with her hair: and the house was filled with the odour of the ointment.
4. Then saith one of his disciples, Judas Iscariot, Simon's son, which should betray him,
5. Why was not this ointment sold for three hundred pence, and given to the poor?
6. This he said, not that he cared for the poor; but because he was a thief, and had the bag, and bare what was put therein.
7. Then said Jesus, Let her alone: against the day of my burying hath she kept this.
8. For the poor always ye have with you; but me ye have not always. (John 12:1-8)

This episode is often confused with a similar incident reported in Matthew 26:6-13 and Mark 14:3-9. A woman appeared with a costly ointment and poured it over Jesus' *head*. The place was at the home of Simon the leper, an ex-leper apparently healed at some time by Jesus. The ointment was in an alabaster box, and it was spikenard. In this instance, at the home of Lazarus, Mary used a pound of spikenard, very costly, to anoint Jesus' *feet*. Matthew and Mark indicate that in the incident at Simon's home, several disciples protested the "waste," as they saw it. In the later episode at Lazarus' home, it is Judas who protests the "waste" (John 12:4). There are very substantial differences, as well as marked similarities. Mary obviously knew of the earlier episode and was, in gratitude, reproducing it. This was prior to Palm Sunday.

Luke tells us that Simon was a Pharisee. The woman he describes as a "sinner." She wept as she washed and anointed Jesus' feet. Simon felt that, if Jesus were a prophet, He would know the woman to be a sinner and He would therefore refuse to be touched by her (Luke 7:36-50). In Luke's account, the woman is pronounced forgiven and saved by Jesus. In John's account, Mary is a saved woman and a friend.

The group at Lazarus' house sat or reclined at the table (v. 2). The whole house was filled with the odor of the perfume. The cost of the perfume is described as 300 pence, which, in our day of inflation, might be close to $300; at that time it was enough to keep a family for a year. Judas Iscariot objected to this act, insisting, as had others with him on the earlier occasion

157

at Simon's house, "Why was not this ointment sold for three hundred pence, and given to the poor?" (v. 5). He said this because, as treasurer for the group, he was a thief (v. 6).

Over the centuries, Judas' comment has been echoed by many. People who visit medieval churches and cathedrals often comment that they are indeed beautiful, but no doubt the poor went hungry. The fact is that the congregations of those ancient churches were far more generous than are congregations of the second half of the twentieth century. Over and over again, believers who have given generously to build God's house have also been generous in charity and in missionary activities.

Our Lord rebukes Judas at once: "Let her alone: against the day of my burying hath she kept this. For the poor always ye have with you, but me ye have not always" (vv. 7-8). This is, our Lord says, an advance anointing for the day of His burial. Apparently, Mary used only part of the spikenard and reserved the rest for Jesus' forthcoming death and burial.

In Matthew 26:6, the word used by the disciples to describe the anointing of Jesus' head with the costly spikenard was *waste*. The word used in the Greek is *apoleia*, which means not only *waste*, but also *perdition*, and it is Judas whom our Lord later describes as "the son of perdition" (John 17:12), as Joseph Parker has somewhere noted. In John 13:29, we see in passing that Jesus was regularly given to caring for the poor, so that, when Jesus at the Last Supper dismissed Judas, the other disciples assumed that Jesus commanded Judas to care for the poor (John 13:26-30).

This incident is closely related to the raising of Lazarus. Both episodes have death in focus. Lazarus died, and Jesus raised him from the dead. It was generally known that the religious leaders were preparing to arrest and execute Jesus. For resurrecting Lazarus from the dead, Jesus had to die.

Anointing the feet was at the least unusual; wiping the feet with hair (the feet may have been freshly washed, as was the custom) was unseemly, because women did not loosen their hair in public. The whole attitude of Mary was one of humility, and she evinced a full awareness of what was being plotted against Jesus. Of the woman who washed His feet in Simon's house, our Lord said that she would be remembered for her action to the end of time. Here, Mary is named, and there is no need to speak of her being remembered, because her closeness to Lazarus as well as Jesus made her unforgettable.

Some believe that this supper may have included more than Lazarus, Jesus, and the disciples, since we are not told who "made him a supper" (v. 2). This is possible, but not important: what does stand out is that Jesus, normally very mindful of the poor, says plainly, "The poor ye have always with you: but me ye have not always" (v. 8). From beginning to end, the Bible emphasizes the importance of charity, but it does not permit a man-centered perspective. The priority of God the Son over the poor is very bluntly stated. Apart from being a thief, Judas was man-centered in his perspective. He saw the use of the spikenard as a *waste*, as *perdition*, and humanists in our time view all Christian worship and action as *perdition*, as contrary to human welfare. What came into focus at the supper in Bethany, as before in the house of Simon the leper, was a conflict between two alien faiths. What is most important, God's requirements or human need? If priority is given to the *poor*, it must be denied to the *Kingdom of God*. John tells us that to give priority to the poor is a pretext for theft in too many cases. In our century, we see the systematic looting of the public treasuries in the name of the poor, the earth, and other like reasons.

Chapter Thirty-Eight
The Triumphal Entry
(John 12:9-19)

9. Much people of the Jews therefore knew that he was there: and they came not for Jesus' sake only, but that they might see Lazarus also, whom he had raised from the dead.

10. But the chief priests consulted that they might put Lazarus also to death;

11. Because that by reason of him many of the Jews went away, and believed on Jesus.

12. On the next day much people that were come to the feast, when they heard that Jesus was coming to Jerusalem,

13. Took branches of palm trees, and went forth to meet him, and cried, Hosanna: Blessed is the King of Israel that cometh in the name of the Lord.

14. And Jesus, when he had found a young ass, sat thereon; as it is written,

15. Fear not, daughter of Sion: behold, thy King cometh, sitting on an ass's colt.

16. These things understood not his disciples at the first: but when Jesus was glorified, then remembered they that these things were written of him, and that they had done these things unto him.

17. The people therefore that was with him when he called Lazarus out of his grave, and raised him from the dead, bare record.

18. For this cause the people also met him, for that they heard that he had done this miracle.

19. The Pharisees therefore said among themselves, Perceive ye how ye prevail nothing? behold, the world is gone after him. (John 12:9-19)

This Passover brought out many people: they wanted to see Jesus; was He the Messiah? He had raised Lazarus from the dead, and this miracle had become so widely known that the chief priests considered executing Lazarus also (vv. 9-10). Many came to the Passover to see Lazarus, a man who had returned from the realm of the dead. Because of Lazarus, many Judaeans believed on Jesus (v. 11). The news of Lazarus' resurrection had raced across the country, and there was an air of expectation. The statement in v. 11 that "many of the Jews went away, and believed on Jesus," means that they withdrew from their previous associations to become believers in Jesus. A polarization of belief had begun.

On the next day, as many were entering into Jerusalem for the Passover week, the news raced about that Jesus was coming to the city (v. 12). These pilgrims took palm branches and went out to meet Him. As they saw Him, they shouted words from Psalm 118:25-26: "Hosanna: Blessed is the King of Israel that cometh in the name of the Lord" (v. 13). Their doubt was gone: they believed He was the Messiah.

Meanwhile, Jesus had found a young ass and mounted it, as Zechariah 9:9-10 had prophesied:

> 9. Rejoice greatly, O daughter of Zion: shout, O daughter of Jerusalem: behold, thy King cometh unto thee: he is just, and having salvation: lowly, and riding upon an ass, and upon a colt the foal of an ass.
> 10. And I will cut off the chariot from Ephraim, and the horse from Jerusalem, and the battle bow shall be cut off: and he shall speak peace unto the heathen: and his dominion shall be from sea even to sea, and from the river even to the ends of the earth.

The donkey is emphatically not an animal for military use. Thus, for the Messiah to enter Jerusalem riding the colt of an ass meant that the reign would be one of peace, of conquest, not by over-powering military might, but by conversion. As His Kingdom advances, so too peace advances. His Kingdom will in time conquer all nations and govern all the earth. The triumphal entry on Palm Sunday was thus an open declaration of the non-political nature of Christ's Kingdom. This in itself was an offense to the religious leaders. Fallen men have all through history seen the road to world transformation as one of power: by power and statist control, the true new world order will be established. Part of this power strategy involves compulsory education into some form of humanism.

The disciples at this point did not understand what Jesus meant or why the cross was necessary. They failed to see the necessity for the atonement. The Pharisees and Sadducees understood the purpose of Jesus better than the disciples did, and they hated it with all their being. Although the disciples lacked understanding, they did not lack faith in their Lord, a faulty faith, but one with a capacity for growth. *Both* understanding and faith are necessary for life in Christ. When "Jesus was glorified," the disciples remembered all that Jesus had said, and they then understood Him. The hatred of the religious leaders only intensified. Old Testament prophesies became an open book to the disciples after the ascension.

The great crowd on Palm Sunday was in large part due to the raising of Lazarus, a most public event. Those who had been present had borne witness to the event far and wide (v. 17). We are told in v. 18, "For this cause the people also met him, for they had heard that he had done this miracle." John stresses the public nature of our Lord's life and works, as do Matthew, Mark, and Luke. The notion that these three gospels do not is a myth. Matthew, for example, tells us at the conclusion of the Sermon on the Mount that the people were astonished, "for he taught them as one having authority, and not as the scribes" (Matt. 7:28f). Exactly. Jesus spoke as *the Lord*, saying, *I say unto you.* There was never any hesitation on His part to speak of the Lord God; as the Lord, He taught them the meaning of the Kingdom.

The entry into Jerusalem made clear to the religious leaders that action was necessary if they were to survive; they said one to another, "Perceive ye how ye prevail nothing? behold, the world is gone after him" (v. 19). They despaired of any hope except from drastic action, a legalized murder. In John 4:42, even the Samaritans declared their faith, saying to the woman at the well, "Now we believe, not because of thy saying: for we have heard him ourselves, and know that this is indeed the Christ, the Saviour of the world."

Given the great throngs that met Jesus on Palm Sunday, we may well wonder how many truly believed. No doubt many did, because from the Day of Pentecost on, the number of believers grew rapidly.

But both the disciples and the crowds had their faith tested, as every faith is, often in ways invisible to those around them.

It is common to speak of the trials of faith. Perhaps we should also speak of the trials of unbelief, the vast emptiness and total meaninglessness of all things, and the progressive inability to make moral distinctions. The outer circumstances of the ungodly may be very good, but their lives are lived in the suburbs of hell. The Greek and Hebrew words for hell refer to the city dump, a place where everything is broken, disconnected, and meaningless. Without faith, a society becomes less a society and more a hell. The randomness of life outside of God places fallen man in the suburbs of hell.

Chapter Thirty-Nine
The Rejection
(John 12:20-36)

20. And there were certain Greeks among them that came up to worship at the feast:
21. The same came therefore to Philip, which was of Bethsaida of Galilee, and desired him, saying, Sir, we would see Jesus.
22. Philip cometh and telleth Andrew: and again Andrew and Philip tell Jesus.
23. And Jesus answered them, saying, The hour is come, that the Son of man should be glorified.
24. Verily, verily, I say unto you, Except a corn of wheat fall into the ground and die, it abideth alone: but if it die, it bringeth forth much fruit.
25. He that loveth his life shall lose it; and he that hateth his life in this world shall keep it unto life eternal.
26. If any man serve me, let him follow me; and where I am, there shall also my servant be: if any man serve me, him will my Father honour.
27. Now is my soul troubled; and what shall I say? Father, save me from this hour: but for this cause came I unto this hour.
28. Father, glorify thy name. Then came there a voice from heaven, saying, I have both glorified it, and will glorify it again.
29. The people therefore, that stood by, and heard it, said that it thundered: others said, An angel spake to him.
30. Jesus answered and said, This voice came not because of me, but for your sakes.
31. Now is the judgment of this world: now shall the prince of this world be cast out.
32. And I, if I be lifted up from the earth, will draw all men unto me.
33. This he said, signifying what death he should die.
34. The people answered him, We have heard out of the law that Christ abideth for ever: and how sayest thou, The Son of man must be lifted up? who is this Son of man?
35. Then Jesus said unto them, Yet a little while is the light with you. Walk while ye have the light, lest darkness come upon you: for he that walketh in darkness knoweth not whither he goeth.
36. While ye have light, believe in the light, that ye may be the children of light. These things spake Jesus, and departed, and did hide himself from them. (John 12:20-36)

There were at Jerusalem some Greeks, converts to Judaism, who had come for the Passover. They were faithful worshippers who took seriously the need to go to Jerusalem for the feast, and they had also heard about Jesus. They went therefore to the disciple Philip, saying, "Sir, we would see Jesus" (vv. 20-21). Philip, being hesitant, went to Andrew, who had brought Nathanael to Jesus (1:41), and whose practical nature we see in John 6:8-9. Both Philip and Andrew had Greek names.

165

We are not told of what the Greeks asked, only the substance of what Jesus said to them (vv. 27-28). Plummer's comment is very much to the point:

> These men from the West at the close of Christ's life set forth the same truth as the men from the East at the beginning of it — that the Gentiles are to be gathered in. The wise men came to the cradle, these to His cross, of which their coming reminds Him; for only by His death could "the nations" be saved.[1]

This was a momentous event because, in Westcott's words, "The extension of the Gospel to the world rests on the death of Christ, on His rejection by His own people."[2] Israel's rejection of Christ as a people and as a "church," i.e., as an established faith, prevented the church from becoming dominated by national or ethnic loyalties. The church had to be *Christian* rather than Jewish. Not a few countries so closely identify their church with their nation that they are very near to the error of Israel.

Our Lord's answer to Andrew, Philip, and the Greeks is simple and direct: "The hour is come that the Son of man should be glorified" (v. 23). His death and His resurrection were His glorification. By His atonement, He would become the world's Savior. The coming of the Greeks was for Him the sign of His world mission, and this He tells them to remember. Death, He said, is the way to world conquest. A grain of wheat cannot bear fruit until it falls into the ground and dies; "but if it die, it bringeth forth much fruit" (v. 24). We grow as we die to the old man and develop in the new.

Verse 25 tells us plainly that self-centeredness is death, whereas to be God-centered is life. To "hate" one's "life in the world" means to reject a humanistic, man-centered life in favor of one obedient to the Lord and faithful to His purposes. In v. 26, Jesus says, "If any man serve me, let him follow me." The reference is to *any man*, Jew, or Greek, or other. With the atonement, the faith is now fully internationalized. In too many cases, churches are too nationalistic and are identified with the state rather than the Kingdom of God. *Any man* means that the Kingdom of God is above and beyond any nation or people.

As our Lord says all this, He also recognizes that the way to the Kingdom of God requires the cross. Therefore, "Now is my soul troubled; and what shall I say? Father, save me from this hour: but for this cause came I unto this hour" (v. 27). Jesus knows what agony and torture the cross will hold. Who would want it? Yet He cannot ask to be spared the cross, because it is the purpose of His incarnation, and the only hope of this world.

---

[1] A. Plummer, *The Gospel According to St. John* (Cambridge, England: Cambridge University Press, 1880, 1906), 252.

[2] B. F. Westcott, *The Gospel According to St. John* (Grand Rapids, MI: Eerdmans (1881) 1954), 180.

Jesus then asks boldly, "Father, glorify thy name" (v. 28). Reveal Thyself in what I am about to undergo. "Then came there a voice from heaven, saying, I have both glorified it, and will glorify it again" (v. 28). In everything from the incarnation until this moment, and in Christ's death, resurrection, and ascension, God had revealed His glory in the Son. Now He again revealed to all in an audible voice from heaven. The people heard a sound; some thought it was thunder, others, the voice of an angel (v. 29). Jesus told them that the voice was for their sakes (v. 30). It seemed to be addressed to Jesus, but it was for them, to make plain that the heart of all history was to be revealed in the atonement and the resurrection, in the creation of a new human race culminating in a new creation and the resurrection of God's people.

Jesus says also, "Now is the judgment of this world: now shall the prince of this world be cast out" (v. 31). There are many judgments in history. Certainly the Fall was one, and the Flood another; there have been many less devastating judgments as well. The two great judgments are the Cross and the Last Judgment. Satan has ruled the unbelieving world of the Fall. Now his power is broken; it continues, but it is in essence crushed.

"And I, if I be lifted up from the earth, will draw all men unto me. This he said, signifying what death he should die" (v. 32-33), i.e., by crucifixion.

There were others present besides the disciples and the Greeks, and they asked, how can you say that the Son of Man must die, when we are taught that He lives forever? Who is this Son of Man of whom you speak? (v. 34). Jesus' idea of the Messiah is repulsive to them.

Jesus then warned them, I, as the Light of the world, am still with you. Use My Light, or else you shall walk in darkness. Become children of the Light, lest you perish walking in the darkness of sin (vv. 35-36). With that, Jesus left them to remain in seclusion preparatory to the Passover.

The multitude objected because the Messiah as set forth by Jesus was not to their taste. This should not surprise us. Despite the plain statements of Scripture, very many churchmen *refuse* to believe that God can send anyone to hell, or predestine anyone, or reject a prayer for healing by a good man, and so on. In all cases, it is held that God cannot do what man believes is wrong. In this view, man is the judge and determiner of both good and evil, which is precisely the argument of the tempter (Gen. 3:5). How ironic that the tempter's program is now that which churchmen want to foist on God!

A flagrant example of this was reported in *The San Joaquin Record*. Steve Kindle, pastor of the First Christian Church, held that neither the Old nor the New Testaments "offers a definitive position on the morality of homosexuality." He once believed that homosexuality was a sin. "But now I say, if that's true, shame on God...That's not the God I know" (13 August

1995: B16). But there is no other God, and the gods of our imagination are idols all.

The people recognized the supernatural power of Jesus Christ, but they rejected Him because He did not conform to what they believed the Messiah should be. The same kind of rejection continues.

Chapter Forty

His Commandment as Life
(*John 12:37-50*)

37. But though he had done so many miracles before them, yet they believed not on him:
38. That the saying of Esaias the prophet might be fulfilled, which he spake, Lord, who hath believed our report? and to whom hath the arm of the Lord been revealed?
39. Therefore they could not believe, because that Esaias said again,
40. He hath blinded their eyes, and hardened their heart; that they should not see with their eyes, nor understand with their heart, and be converted, and I should heal them.
41. These things said Esaias, when he saw his glory, and spake of him.
42. Nevertheless among the chief rulers also many believed on him; but because of the Pharisees they did not confess him, lest they should be put out of the synagogue:
43. For they loved the praise of men more than the praise of God.
44. Jesus cried and said, He that believeth on me, believeth not on me, but on him that sent me.
45. And he that seeth me seeth him that sent me.
46. I am come a light into the world, that whosoever believeth on me should not abide in darkness.
47. And if any man hear my words, and believe not, I judge him not: for I came not to judge the world, but to save the world.
48. He that rejecteth me, and receiveth not my words, hath one that judgeth him: the word that I have spoken, the same shall judge him in the last day.
49. For I have not spoken of myself; but the Father which sent me, he gave me a commandment, what I should say, and what I should speak.
50. And I know that his commandment is life everlasting: whatsoever I speak therefore, even as the Father said unto me, so I speak. (John 12:37-50)

In John 12:37-43, John comments on the implications of what had happened. *First*, although Jesus had done so many remarkable miracles before their eyes, yet they refused to believe on Him (v. 37). They rejected the obvious conclusion about Jesus because His presence threatened their way of life.

Second, the rejection of Jesus was a second fulfillment of Isaiah's prophecy in Isaiah 53:1ff. and 6:9-11. Isaiah foretold the coming of the Lamb of God, but his prophecy was neither accepted then, nor in our Lord's day. For the Servant of God to become the atonement was not acceptable in Isaiah's day, nor in John's. They were judicially blinded by God, so that, in the face of all evidence, they denied the Christ and plotted His death (vv. 38-42).

169

Their blinding is basic to this text and its understanding. It was both a self-blinding and a blinding by God, for God's predestination works in the context of man's will. Since Eden, all men as fallen creatures have seen their salvation in their own will, and they see the meaning of their salvation in terms of Genesis 3:5, every man as his own god and savior. Some churchmen insist that God enables man to make all the ultimate decisions; Eastern Orthodox churches have a doctrine of *theosis*, man's salvation as deification. Antinomianism transfers the essential lawmaking prerogative of God to man, and so on and on. The denunciation of Jesus at His trial and crucifixion was marked by a self-righteous fury. For His enemies, Jesus was evil, an enemy of religion and order. Since His day, more than a few Christians have in some degree suffered a like animosity. For example, Cornelius Van Til was the target of venomous hostilities, and some of his enemies were moved to pornographic language occasionally. In the volume edited by E. R. Geehan, *Jerusalem and Athens, Critical Discussions on the Philosophy and Apologetics of Cornelius Van Til* (1971), some of the contributors, while controlled in their language, still speak of Van Til with rage and hatred. Their temper is superficially scholarly, but in reality it gives expression to religious division and moral confusion.

Third, Isaiah wrote as he did because he saw Christ' *glory* (v. 41). Thus, what the religious leaders rejected, the atonement by the death of the Messiah, Isaiah saw as Christ's *glory*.

John then adds that there were rulers, or members of the Sanhedrin, "who believed on him" (v. 42), but at this time they gave no open expression to their beliefs. They were careful to make no confession of such a faith lest they be excommunicated. They preferred to see Christ excommunicated (v. 42). And they preferred, as Westcott noted, the praise or glory of men to the praise or glory of God (v. 43).[1]

In vv. 44-50, Jesus speaks again with finality, in a voice of judgment, because His words bring judgment upon all who reject Him.

First, Jesus makes clear that this is no localized issue. A judgment on Him is a judgment on God. To reject Him is to reject God (v. 44). To *see* Jesus is to see God (v. 45). The connection between God the Father and God the Son is an inseparable one, and to deny one is to deny the other. A little later, Jesus tells His disciples, "no man cometh unto the Father, but by me" (14:6). The inseparableness of the Father and the Son, and the exclusiveness of approach to the Father by the Son, are so basic that their denial is a denial of Christianity.

Second, our Lord tells the people that the world is in *darkness*, the darkness of the Fall and of sin. He is the Light of the world who alone can

[1]. B. F. Westcott. *The Gospel According to St. John* (Grand Rapids, MI: Eerdmans, 1881, 1954), 186.

disperse the darkness. He is not "a light," as the King James suggests, but *the Light* in His person (v. 46). Man being fallen, his normal state is darkness.

Third, Jesus makes clear that the rejection of Him means judgment, but He also says, "I judge him not," because He has come to save the world, not to condemn it (v. 47). This statement in no way diminishes the fact of judgment but rather expands it. Jesus says that His words on judgment cannot be reduced to the local opinion of a controversial figure: they are a part of God's eternal order. "He that rejecteth me, and receiveth not my words, hath one that judgeth him: the word I have spoken, the same shall judge him in the last day" (v. 48). The premise of God's great judgment on the Last Day is Jesus Christ. In Him they were confronted in Judaea with the final judgment over all men and nations. It was not therefore simply the words of Jesus which confronted them, but *God's total order*.

In the phrase, "the word that I have spoken, the same shall judge him in the last day" (v. 49), we have a legal premise. When a man goes to court, the judge *presides*, but the law *judges* him. The law states the offense, and the man is judged guilty or not guilty in terms of the law. This means that, at the Last Judgment, men shall be judged by God's every word, with Jesus Christ as the presiding Judge. Men will reveal whether or not they are truly in Christ and cleansed by His atoning blood by their faithfulness to the law-word of the Redeemer-King. "Faith without works is dead" (see James 2:17-26).

Because Jesus Christ is life (John 14:6), "His commandment is life everlasting" (v. 50); there is no contradiction or opposition between the members of the Trinity, nor between them and their enscriptured Word, the Bible. All are life to those who by God's grace are the redeemed.

These are our Lord's final words to the people before the Last Supper. He not only identifies Himself fully with the Father, but also with His every word. When we speak, we hope there is no contradiction between ourselves and our words, but, being sinners, we achieve at best a clear similarity. The Father speaks through the Son, and every word is without any contradiction to their being. There is a perfect identity of person, word, and act. Our Lord here makes any separation untenable.

In v. 49, our Lord says that "I have not spoken of myself." The Father Himself has commanded Him, "what I should say, and what I should speak." The words of Jesus are all the words of God. The words come through the mouth of Jesus, but their origin is the Father; no other conclusion can be derived from these words.

In v. 50, our Lord says of the Father, "And I know that his commandment is life everlasting." The word translated as *commandment* is *entole* in the Greek, and it refers to an authoritative precept or charge. It is a word of no small importance: in the Septuagint, *law*, God's law, is the translation of *entolai*, as in Psalm 119:86. The purpose of every word and commandment of God is *life everlasting*. Salvation is by Christ's atoning sacrifice, and the redeemed of God therefore know that Life Himself (John 14:6) speaks in Scripture's law and precepts. Westcott commented:

> The word may find acceptance or rejection, but this remains sure. The commandment of the Father, His will manifested in my commission, is eternal life. The Father's commandment not only is directed towards life, to quicken or to support it. It is life. Truth realised is that by which we live. The commandment of God is the expression of the absolute Truth.[2]

It is evil to set God's grace against His law, or His commandments against life. There are no contradictions in the Being of God.

God's purpose for us is life; His atonement redeems us for life; His commandment is life. As the redeemed of God, we are the people of life.

---

2. *ibid.*, 187

Chapter Forty-One

Foot Washing
(*John 13:1-11*)

1. Now before the feast of the passover, when Jesus knew that his hour was come that he should depart out of this world unto the Father, having loved his own which were in the world, he loved them unto the end.
2. And supper being ended, the devil having now put into the heart of Judas Iscariot, Simon's son, to betray him;
3. Jesus knowing that the Father had given all things into his hands, and that he was come from God, and went to God;
4. He riseth from supper, and laid aside his garments; and took a towel, and girded himself.
5. After that he poureth water into a bason, and began to wash the disciples' feet, and to wipe them with the towel wherewith he was girded.
6. Then cometh he to Simon Peter: and Peter saith unto him, Lord, dost thou wash my feet?
7. Jesus answered and said unto him, What I do thou knowest not now; but thou shalt know hereafter.
8. Peter saith unto him, Thou shalt never wash my feet. Jesus answered him, If I wash thee not, thou hast no part with me.
9. Simon Peter saith unto him, Lord, not my feet only, but also my hands and my head.
10. Jesus saith to him, He that is washed needeth not save to wash his feet, but is clean every whit: and ye are clean, but not all.
11. For he knew who should betray him; therefore said he, Ye are not all clean. (John 13:1-11)

John's account of the Last Supper differs from that of Matthew, Mark, and Luke. Instead of an account of the actual supper and its sacramental nature, we have instead our Lord's teaching on that occasion.

The time was "before the feast," (v. 1) on the evening prior to it. Jesus knew that His time had come, and soon He would rise from the dead and ascend into heaven. He loved His disciples, despite their obtuseness, while He walked with them. Now His love for them and for us meant His willingness to die for us.

Judas Iscariot had already determined to betray Jesus and enable the religious leaders to make a night arrest. This would avoid a problem with the people, confronting them with an accomplished fact before they could react. Jesus knew that the devil had led Judas to this decision to betray Him (v. 2).

Jesus knew also that the Father had given all things, i.e., the atonement, the resurrection, the Kingdom of God, the judgment of all creation, and more, into His hands. He had come from the Father and would soon return to Him (v. 3).

173

Knowing Himself to be God incarnate, He arose, took off His outer tunic, and began to wash the feet of the disciples (v. 4). Normally, on arriving at a home, someone, commonly a servant in many homes, would wash and dry the feet of all the visitors. But Jesus and the disciples had arranged the temporary use of an upper room for their Last Supper. They had no servant to care for them. The meal had been arranged, but nothing more.

Jesus faced an abashed silence as He went from one disciple to another, washing and drying their feet (v. 5). Earlier in His ministry, He had said,

> 42. ...Ye know that they which are accounted to rule over the Gentiles exercise lordship over them; and their great ones exercise authority upon them.
> 43. But so shall it not be among you: but whosoever will be great among you, shall be your minister:
> 44. And whosoever of you will be the chiefest, shall be servant of all.
> 45. For even the Son of man came not to be ministered unto, but to minister, and to give his life a ransom for many. (Mark 10:42-45)

He was now demonstrating the meaning of this in very realistic terms.

When Jesus came to Simon Peter, Peter protested, "Lord, dost thou wash my feet?" (v. 6). We have no way of knowing in what order the disciples' feet were washed. We do know that Peter did protest it. Jesus answered, "What I do thou knowest not now: but thou shalt know hereafter" (v. 7). With the crucifixion, resurrection, and ascension, Peter would know better who Jesus was and is. He would understand the love and the humility of all our Lord's life from His incarnation on. He would understand the love of God (John 3:16). Paul tells us, in Romans 5:6-10:

> 6. For when we were yet without strength, in due time Christ died for the ungodly.
> 7. For scarcely for a righteous man will one die: yet peradventure for a good man some would even dare to die.
> 8. But God commendeth his love toward us, in that, while we were yet sinners, Christ died for us
> 9. Much more then, being now justified by his blood, we shall be saved from wrath through him.
> 10. For if, when we were enemies, we were reconciled to God by the death of his Son, much more, being reconciled, we shall be saved by his life.

The New Testament Greek word for God's love is *agape*, meaning unmerited favor, a love that is pure grace. God the Son in this foot-washing episode demonstrates the meaning of this ministry of grace and love.

But Peter, ashamed at his own lack of a ministering spirit, said to Jesus, "Thou shalt never wash my feet." Our Lord's answer is a devastating one: "If I wash thee not, thou hast no part with me" (v. 8). The great cleansing for Peter, as for us, was just ahead, the cross and Christ's atonement for our sin. He washed and regenerated us by His atoning blood. The foot-washing was nothing compared to the crucifixion and the atonement.

Foot-washing became a ritual later on in some churches. Often high churchmen washed the feet of the poor; kings sometimes took part in such ceremonies in their courts, acting as Christ's vicegerunts. It is of interest to note that, however formalized, and in some cases with the feet pre-washed to make it less offensive, this rite was still a reminder that church and state are ministries under Christ and will be so judged. This does not mean that this ritual is Biblically required.

Peter's response to Jesus' statement, "If I wash thee not, thou hast no part with me" (v. 8), was, "Lord, not my feet only, but also my hands and my head" (v. 9). Peter as a Jew knew the relationship between baptism and the covenant. He recognized it as a sign of covenant membership and regeneration.

Our Lord then said that all who were cleansed and redeemed by Him were *washed*, i.e., bathed or cleansed, and He was thus dealing with the dust on their feet. "Ye are clean, but not all," referring to the unclean or unatoned one, Judas (v. 10-11).

Returning to v. 1, we are told that Jesus loved His disciples, and "he loved them unto the end." Of this last phrase, Morgan observed, "The words, 'unto the end,' *eis telos*, means to completion. It has been rendered beautifully, 'to the uttermost.'"[1] This can mean that His love was dying for them, and it also refers to the completion of their lives in Him.

Peter later in life made, perhaps, an oblique reference to this episode in 1 Peter 5:2-5:

> 2. Feed the flock of God which is among you, taking the oversight thereof, not by constraint, but willingly; not for filthy lucre, but of a ready mind;
> 3. Neither as being lords over God's heritage, but being ensamples to the flock.
> 4. And when the chief Shepherd shall appear, ye shall receive a crown of glory that fadeth not away.
> 5. Likewise, ye younger, submit yourselves to the elder. Yea, all of you be subject one to another, and be clothed with humility: for God resisteth the proud, and giveth grace to the humble.

Peter makes clear that all Christ's people must be ready to serve one another, be subject one to another, and be clothed with humility. The believer is not a spectator to the works of the clergy and its associates: we are all laborers in the vineyard.

---

[1] G. Campbell Morgan, *The Gospel According to John* (New York, NY: Fleming H. Revell, n.d.), 231.

Chapter Forty-Two

"Know Ye What I Have Done to You?"
(John 13:12-20)

12. So after he had washed their feet, and had taken his garments, and was set down again, he said unto them, Know ye what I have done to you?

13. Ye call me Master and Lord: and ye say well; for so I am.

14. If I then, your Lord and Master, have washed your feet; ye also ought to wash one another's feet.

15. For I have given you an example, that ye should do as I have done to you.

16. Verily, verily, I say unto you, The servant is not greater than his lord; neither he that is sent greater than he that sent him.

17. If ye know these things, happy are ye if ye do them.

18. I speak not of you all: I know whom I have chosen: but that the scripture may be fulfilled, He that eateth bread with me hath lifted up his heel against me.

19. Now I tell you before it come, that, when it is come to pass, ye may believe that I am he.

20. Verily, verily, I say unto you, He that receiveth whomsoever I send receiveth me; and he that receiveth me receiveth him that sent me. (John 13:12-20)

After washing the disciples' feet, and re-clothing Himself with His outer tunic, our Lord resumed His place at the dinner table. He asked the disciples a searching question: "Know ye what I have done to you?" (v. 12). Knowing that He would leave them shortly, He was challenging them to understand the meaning of His ministry and theirs. The difference between what He and His Kingdom represent and the kingdoms of this world is *power* versus *service*. Twenty centuries of Christianity have left their marks on the world. The modern power-state seeks to gain credit as a service state by means of welfarism and like strategies. These concerns for the poor and the needy are devices to gain and maintain power, so that the modern state is still pagan at heart.

A state can be either *ministerial*, administering God's law-word to the people as God's servant or His ministry of justice, or it can be *legislative*, creating its own ideas of law and justice. The modern state is openly legislative; it has usurped God's prerogatives of determining law and justice.

Our Lord's question of the twelve disciples who are the patriarchs of God's new Israel requires them to see the meaning of the Gospel. *First*, the necessity for the atonement had already been stressed. A new humanity was to be created in and for the Christ. *Second*, this new humanity would not follow the tempter's plan (Gen. 3:5), but would serve God, and, under God, it would also serve man. This means a faithfulness to every jot and tittle of God's law-word (Matt. 5:17-20).

Our Lord continues, saying, "Ye call me Master and Lord: and ye say well; for so I am" (v. 13). *Master* is Teacher, and is better read as *The Master*, and again, *The Lord*. If I am the Lord and Master, Jesus said in effect, then you are my servants.

"If I then, your Lord and Master, have washed your feet; ye also ought to wash one another's feet" (v. 14). Service to one another is a debt and a duty in Christ. In 1 Timothy 5:10, the qualifications for a member of the order of widows include a reputation for good works, rearing her children ably, lodging strangers, washing the feet of the saints, relieving the afflicted, and following "every good work." Foot washing is no longer a literal need, but the concept of humble service remains. Here it is a requirement of the leaders of the church and kingdom.

Jesus then declares, "For I have given you an example, that ye should do as I have done to you" (v. 15). It is not the literal reproduction of Jesus' action that is commanded, because He does not command us to do "*what* I have done to you," but "*even as* I have done."[1] Not ritual, but Christian service in humility is required.

"Verily, verily, I say unto you, The servant is not greater than his lord; neither he that is sent greater than he that sent him" (v. 16). As Plummer noted:

> This saying occurs four times in the Gospels, each time in a different connexion: (1) to shew that the disciples must expect no better treatment than their Master (Matt. x. 24); (2) to impress the Apostles with their responsibilities as teachers, for their disciples will be as they are (Luke vi. 40); (3) here; (4) with the same purpose as in Matt. x. 24, but on another occasion (xv. 20).[2]

Our Lord redefined authority so that, instead of raw power and prestige, it meant the union of moral authority with status.

"If ye know these things, happy are ye if ye do them" (v. 17). Earlier, the disciples had been arguing about who should have the highest positions in Christ's Kingdom, which they expected Him to establish in Judaea. The mother of Zebedee's children boldly made a request for power and position for her sons, which angered the other disciples. Our Lord then stated plainly that ministry and service establish status in His Kingdom (Matt. 20:20-28). The issue was thus not a new one. Our Lord's foot-washing simply illustrated what He had already taught them.

This statement is a beatitude: "happy (or, blessed) are ye if ye do them" (v. 17). As in the Sermon on the Mount, happiness or blessedness is defined in terms of God's Kingdom, not man's.

---

[1] A. Plummer, *The Gospel According to St. John* (Cambridge, England: Cambridge University Press (1880) 1906), 265.
[2] *ibid.*, 265.

We are then told that this does not apply to all: "I speak not of you all" (v. 18). One of you, who has eaten bread with Me, lived in communion with Me, "hath lifted up his heel against me" (v. 18). To lift up the heel means lawless, intemperate, and hateful violence. "Eaten bread with me" can be rendered *eaten my bread.*[3] Jesus as Lord provides for those of His royal household. To eat His bread, as a member of His family, and then to betray Him, is treason.

But, our Lord says, "I know whom I have chosen," whether for service or for perdition, so that what Judas was about to do came as no surprise to Him, however much the disciples may have been shocked. All this was in fulfillment of the Scriptures (Ps. 41:9).

"Now I tell you before it come, that when it is come, ye may believe that I am he" (v. 19). Jesus tells them of the treachery before the event, so that the disciples would realize that He knew Judas from the beginning. It would be a witness to the total knowledge and power of their Lord: all things come from Him, are ordained by Him and are a part of His sovereign purpose.

"Verily, verily, I say unto you, He that receiveth whomsoever I send receiveth me; and he that receiveth me receiveth him that sent me" (v. 20). Our Lord had made this same statement earlier when He sent the disciples out to heal and to preach (Matt. 10:40). To receive His faithful apostles is to receive, not the men who go out, but the messengers of Christ the King. If they faithfully proclaim His Gospel, to receive them is to receive Jesus Christ, whose emissaries they are. In v. 18, our Lord declares, "I know whom I have chosen": His predestination covers all men, the Judas as well as the faithful saint. It is He who upholds us, so to look to our own resources when we are under attack is to trust in the frailest of straws.

To receive Christ's messenger is to receive Him, and to receive Christ is to receive the Father (v. 20).

In v. 19, Jesus states that He has told the disciples these things so that, when they come to pass, the disciples may believe that "I am he," or more accurately, that "*I am.*" I am the God revealed in the Scriptures. He is the Lord, and yet now He is also the sacrifice, the Lamb of God, come to make atonement for the sins of the world (John 1:20), and yet King over all kings, and Lord over all lords (1 Tim. 6:15), very God of very God.

"Know ye what I have done to you?" I have placed you in a position of service whereby you will reveal who you are by what you do.

[3.] *ibid.*, 266.

Chapter Forty-Three
The Betrayal
(John 13:21-30)

21. When Jesus had thus said, he was troubled in spirit, and testified, and said, Verily, verily, I say unto you, that one of you shall betray me.
22. Then the disciples looked one on another, doubting of whom he spake.
23. Now there was leaning on Jesus' bosom one of his disciples, whom Jesus loved.
24. Simon Peter therefore beckoned to him, that he should ask who it should be of whom he spake.
25. He then lying on Jesus' breast saith unto him, Lord, who is it?
26. Jesus answered, He it is, to whom I shall give a sop, when I have dipped it. And when he had dipped the sop, he gave it to Judas Iscariot, the son of Simon.
27. And after the sop Satan entered into him. Then said Jesus unto him, That thou doest, do quickly.
28. Now no man at the table knew for what intent he spake this unto him.
29. For some of them thought, because Judas had the bag, that Jesus had said unto him, Buy those things that we have need of against the feast; or, that he should give something to the poor.
30. He then having received the sop went immediately out: and it was night. (John 13:21-30)

This is a difficult text, not because it is hard to understand, but because it is so startling in its vision of the enormity of evil. *Betrayal* is something most people are familiar with, and it is a painful fact. It always comes as a shock, although, in our Lord's case, His foreknowledge was clear. Betrayal is a deep hurt, because it means that a part of our life, work, and trust is despised and trampled upon. The betrayal of the sinless Son of God especially reveals the enormity of evil. All sin, all evil, is anti-God in its motive. A world without God, an impossibility, is imagined a better world, and therefore God and His people must be betrayed. Man wants an *exception* made to God's law in his case, so that man's will can be done, and he resents the inflexibility of God and His law. As one man said, "I don't see why a minor exception cannot be made in my case!" Those who want exceptions want the privilege of playing god.

Judas apparently shared the popular expectations concerning the Messiah, which conceived of him as a savior with a nationalistic and political agenda. Those who recognized that Jesus in some sense came from God saw Him as *betraying* the people's hope. They shared Caiaphas' belief that "it is expedient for us, that one man should die for the people, and that the whole nation perish not" (John 11:50). There are many today who single out aspects of Scripture as "not practical." One able and likeable man, a powerful industrialist, once told me that the Biblical laws concerning debt were "impractical" for modern society and would destroy the economy.

In v. 21, we are told that Jesus, troubled in spirit, said, "Verily, verily, I say unto you, that one of you shall betray me." Matthew and Mark tell us that the disciples sorrowfully began to ask, "Is it I, Lord?" (Matt. 26:22; Mark 14:19). Luke tells us that "they began to question among themselves, which of them it was that should do this thing" (Luke 22:23). The question, "Is it I, Lord?", is a revealing one. Apparently all were troubled by our Lord's decision to return to Jerusalem and face death. They wondered if they were capable of betraying Him; their hearts already were troubled with thoughts that were a betrayal. They looked at one another, unsure of whom He spoke (v. 22).

They were at the table, and the Jews had adopted the contemporary Western custom of reclining at the table. This meant resting on the left elbow and eating with the right hand. Good friends rested their body against the person to their left. In v. 23, John indirectly identifies himself as the one who was leaning against Jesus. Next to John was Simon Peter, who beckoned to John to ask Jesus who the traitor was (v. 24). It was obvious that Jesus was not about to make a public denunciation; perhaps He would quietly tell John. John therefore asked, "Lord, who is it?" (v. 25). While all the others were questioning one another as to what they knew, "Jesus answered, He it is to whom I shall give a sop, when I have dipped it. And when he had dipped the sop, he gave it to Judas Iscariot, the son of Simon" (v. 26). The "sop" was a piece of bread broken off the loaf and dipped in wine. Sharing a sop was comparable to toasting a person with wine. It was a mark of friendship, not ill will. No one other than John knew at the moment that Jesus was identifying the traitor, because no one else heard Him. Jesus was not trying to shame Judas nor to impede him. It is an error to see in this act any evidence of Christ's love for Judas. Rather, He thereby reminded Judas, that he had received nothing but privilege at his Master's hands. Disagreeing, Judas could have simply left the company of the disciples. Instead, he chose to betray Jesus. Our Lord's act was intended to shame Judas into an awareness of what he was and what he was doing.

At that moment, John tells us, Satan entered into Judas (v. 27). Luke tells us that, earlier, Satan had also entered into Judas and had led him to the chief priests and captains to betray Jesus for a sum of money (Luke 22:1-6). Judas' every inclination was betrayal; as a result, at least twice Satan entered him to unite his will with that of Judas.

Then Jesus said to Judas, "That thou doest, do quickly," or, more quickly (v. 27). Get it over with, and stop rehearsing your betrayal. No man at the table understood the meaning of this remark, apparently not even John (v. 28). Our Lord had no intention of creating a scene of denunciation against Judas: with or without Judas, our Lord's arrest and execution would occur.

As a result, with the sop, He gave a mixed and confusing signal to all. Some of the disciples assumed that Jesus asked Judas to take care of the expenses of the feast, or to give something to the poor (v. 29). The human inclination would have been some kind of confrontation, useless and emotional, whereas our Lord knew the futility of words where evil and betrayal were concerned. As a result, He turned a potentially pointless confrontation into a means of revealing knowledge. Judas was made aware that Jesus knew of his betrayal, and he was thereby shamed and confounded. Precisely because Jesus' action was so contrary to the usual reaction, not even John understood what was happening at the time.

Judas, having taken the sop, left immediately. We are told that it was night (v. 30). When our Lord said that one of the disciples would betray Him, it must have shattered Judas to know that Jesus was aware of his treachery. The sop and the instruction to proceed with his chosen way added to Judas' confusion. To Jesus' miraculous powers was now added His knowledge of Judas' secret activity. Clearly, Jesus was more than man, and yet this did not deter Judas, no matter how it shook him. Being evil and having chosen evil, he persisted in his evil. Later, Judas "repented himself" and sought to cancel out his betrayal by returning the thirty pieces of silver, the price of a slave, to the chief priests and elders (Matt. 27:3-10). This was not repentance unto life, because all he did was to try to separate himself from the crime, not to work against it. His confession of sin was only to the chief priests and elders, not to God, nor to Jesus Christ. He confessed to those in whom he believed, except he now knew their evil, and so he committed suicide. His betrayal of Jesus was the betrayal of his own life and future.

Chapter Forty-Four
The Glory of God
(*John 13:31-38*)

31. Therefore, when he was gone out, Jesus said, Now is the Son of man glorified, and God is glorified in him.
32. If God be glorified in him, God shall also glorify him in himself, and shall straightway glorify him.
33. Little children, yet a little while I am with you. Ye shall seek me: and as I said unto the Jews, Whither I go, ye cannot come; so now I say to you.
34. A new commandment I give unto you, That ye love one another; as I have loved you, that ye also love one another.
35. By this shall all men know that ye are my disciples, if ye have love one to another.
36. Simon Peter said unto him, Lord, whither goest thou? Jesus answered him, Whither I go, thou canst not follow me now; but thou shalt follow me afterwards.
37. Peter said unto him, Lord, why cannot I follow thee now? I will lay down my life for thy sake.
38. Jesus answered him, Wilt thou lay down thy life for my sake? Verily, verily, I say unto thee, The cock shall not crow, till thou hast denied me thrice. (John 13:31-38)

After Judas left, our Lord, in vv. 31-32, spoke of His glory. The glory of God means His presence among men in power and in fulness of His justice. He speaks of the glory in a four-fold sense. *First*, "Now is the Son of man glorified." The time has come for my glorification on the cross. This is the great manifestation of God's grace and mercy toward fallen man and the world. The Creator is also the Redeemer. The glory of God means a revelation of His presence in power, and God reveals His glory and power in the atonement, so that we see in the cross a supreme revelation of God's being. The glory sought by fallen men is the power to break and to crush people. In George Orwell's *1984*, the glory of the humanistic socialist state is sought through total control and oppression, "a boot stomping on a human face forever." For us as Christians, the glory of God is manifested by the cross.

Second, "God is glorified in him," in the Son and His atoning sacrifice. The power of God is far greater than man's imagination can ever fathom, and His power and glory are revealed in the cross, in Christ's atoning sacrifice. This is in direct contradiction to man's dreams of glory; such dreams exalt man at the cost of human lives and seek man's power for the sake of power. It leads to the disillusion and cynicism that marked the 1920s and was expressed in the play title, "What Price Glory, Now?" God is glorified in Christ's work, which gives us a revelation of God's glory (v. 31).

185

Third, "If God be glorified in him, God shall also glorify him in himself." Jesus Christ, by His obedience to the cross, thereby glorified the Father. God reveals His glory in the incarnation and the cross. Jesus Christ is glorified by the Father, so that, in some way beyond our imagination, the Son is magnified and glorified in the Triune Godhead. Because the incarnation and the cross are the revelation of the very being of God, the revelor, Jesus Christ, is glorified within the Trinity and in His Kingship.

Fourth, the Father "shall straightway glorify him." The cross is the glory of Jesus, and God then glorifies Him (v. 32). Jesus Christ is the way, the truth, and the life, the exclusive link to God (John 14:6), so that no man comes to the Father except through Him.[1]

In v. 33, Jesus addresses the disciples as "little children." As truly God, and from all eternity in His deity, He looks upon their incomprehension and confusion with compassion. Like children they are unable to understand. I shall be with you only a little time longer. As I told the religious leaders, I am going where you cannot now come. I tell you this in order to prepare you for your calling.

"A new commandment I give unto you, that ye love one another; as I have loved you, that ye also love one another" (v. 34). As Plummer noted, love is not a new commandment. What is new is the motive, that we love one another as Christ loves us.[2] *New* in "new commandment" is one of two Greek words for *new*. One is *young* as opposed to *aged*, and the other is *fresh* as opposed to *aged*. It is this latter meaning and word that applies here.[3] The commandment of love in Leviticus 19:18 now has its focus on our love as a response to Christ's love.

All men will recognize Christ's disciples by the reality of their love for one another (v. 35).

It had become obvious to the disciples that Jesus was giving them some parting counsel. Peter, distressed by this fact, had been preoccupied with that thought and had to some extent ignored our Lord's words. Now he interrupts to ask, "Whither goest thou?" Our Lord's answer is that Peter cannot follow Him where He now goes, "but thou shalt follow me afterwards" (v. 36).

But Peter is persistent: "Why cannot I follow thee now? I will lay down my life for thy sake" (v. 37). Jesus questions this resolution: "Wilt thou lay down thy life for my sake? Verily, verily, I say unto you, the cock shall not crow till thou hast denied me thrice" (v. 38). And so it happened.

---

[1] William Barclay: *The Gospel of John*, vol. 2 (Philadelphia, PA: Westminster Press, 1955, 1975), 148f.

[2] A. Plummer: *The Gospel According to St. John* (Cambridge, England: Cambridge University Press, 1880, 1906), 270.

[3] *ibid.*

What our Lord says about His glory is closely and essentially tied to the foot washing episode. Fallen man seeks glory by playing god. Jesus tells us that redeemed man finds glory by being God's man to the world, by being the visible presence of God's grace and mercy.

The disciples had hoped to see Jesus crowned as the Messianic King. The triumphal entry into Jerusalem probably revived their hopes. Earlier, they had quarreled over gaining high places in Christ's Kingdom (Matt. 20:20f; Luke 22:24). Now Jesus was pointing to a radically different glorification.[4]

It was imperative that the disciples learn the meaning of Christ's glorification. As Hoskyns noted, "the glorification of the Son of man involves separation from His disciples."[5] In time, their recollection of His words would lead to a recognition of the meaning of His glory.

Our Lord speaks first of the relationship of His coming death to His glory. He then speaks of its relationship to His disciples.[6]

The cross was at that time the epitome of shame and dishonor. For God the Father to decree that this ugly fact, crucifixion, should set forth the glory of God the Son in His revelation of the Godhead's glory was rather startling. The incomprehension of the disciples is understandable. As John records these events, it becomes apparent to him that "the whole story was the glorification of the Son of man."[7] According to Paul E. Kretzmann,

> It is the Son of Man, the God-man, that has been glorified through all the miracles of His life, and who is now to be glorified through the greatest miracle of all, following His death and burial. And God is glorified in the Son. It is God's salvation; God was in Christ; God would be the Cause and the Promoter of His glorification, which was thus bound to result in the Father's glorification as well. The Son having accomplished the work of salvation, the Father would receive the honor and glory for the resultant benefit for the whole world. But so close is the union between the Father and the Son that there is a mutual exchange of honor and glory between the two.[8]

What is said by our Lord concerning God's glory is very important because it is in radical contradiction to all man's ideas about glory. God's glory is the manifestation of His divine nature. God, who in His greatness is beyond our imagination and conception, is revealed to us in the fulness of His glory through His atonement effected by Christ's death and

---

[4.] Lyman Abbott: *The Gospel According to John* (New York, NY: A. S. Barnes, 1876, 1888), 170.

[5.] Edwyn Clement Hoskyns: *The Fourth Gospel* (London, England: Faber and Faber, 1947), 450.

[6.] Alvah Hovey: *Commentary on the Gospel of John* (Philadelphia, PA: American Baptist Publication Society, 1888), 277.

[7.] John Marsh: *Saint John*, (Hammondsworth, Middlesex, England: Penguin Books, 1968, 1977), 495.

[8.] Paul E. Kretzmann: *Popular Commentary of the Bible, The New Testament*, vol. I (St. Louis, MO: Concordia Publishing House, 1921), 487.

resurrection. Intellectually, man's reason cannot comprehend God, but, in our salvation, His glory is manifested to us in a marvellous way.

As once-fallen creatures our minds are still in this life darkened, and thus we neither see His glory in all its fulness, nor are we fully aware of its greatness. All the same, we know that the Lord of all glory is so mindful of us that He has given His only begotten Son for our redemption (John 3:16), and we are now prepared by Him to reverse the fallen values of this world in terms of the regeneration of our Redeemer-King.

Chapter Forty-Five

The King Commands Petition
(John 14:1-14)

1. Let not your heart be troubled: ye believe in God, believe also in me.
2. In my Father's house are many mansions: if it were not so, I would have told you. I go to prepare a place for you.
3. And if I go and prepare a place for you, I will come again, and receive you unto myself; that where I am, there ye may be also.
4. And whither I go ye know, and the way ye know.
5. Thomas saith unto him, Lord, we know not whither thou goest; and how can we know the way?
6. Jesus saith unto him, I am the way, the truth, and the life: no man cometh unto the Father, but by me.
7. If ye had known me, ye should have known my Father also: and from henceforth ye know him, and have seen him.
8. Philip saith unto him, Lord, shew us the Father, and it sufficeth us.
9. Jesus saith unto him, Have I been so long time with you, and yet hast thou not known me, Philip? he that hath seen me hath seen the Father; and how sayest thou then, Shew us the Father?
10. Believest thou not that I am in the Father, and the Father in me? the words that I speak unto you I speak not of myself: but the Father that dwelleth in me, he doeth the works.
11. Believe me that I am in the Father, and the Father in me: or else believe me for the very works' sake.
12. Verily, verily, I say unto you, He that believeth on me, the works that I do shall he do also; and greater works than these shall he do; because I go unto my Father.
13. And whatsoever ye shall ask in my name, that will I do, that the Father may be glorified in the Son.
14. If ye shall ask any thing in my name, I will do it. (John 14:1-14)

Just before our Lord commanded the disciples to be untroubled at heart, unworried, He told Peter that Peter would deny Him three times before the cock crowed the next morning (13:38). This shook all the disciples: if Peter denied Christ, would they do so as well? Our Lord's answer was to reassure them. He did *not* say, ten of your number will not deny Me; He gave them no reassurance whatsoever that they would stand firm. Instead, He grounded their future in His grace. Believe or trust in God, and also in Me, *not* in your own capacity to stand. The future of the disciples was not in their works, but in Christ's grace and mercy.

"In my Father's house are many mansions: if it were not so, I would have told you. I go to prepare a place for you" (v. 2). Clearly, our Lord refers to heaven. He looks beyond time, beyond the disciples' confusion and scattering, beyond Pentecost and their apostolic ministries, to their place in heaven. They are not Judases, by His grace, and any fear of betrayal like

Peter's would be forgiven. Jesus Christ Himself confidently goes ahead to prepare a place for them.

Moreover, "if I go and prepare a place for you, I will come again, and receive you unto myself, that where I am, there ye may be also" (v. 3). "I will come again," can be interpreted in several ways: 1) I will return with My resurrection; or 2) I will return with the gift of the Spirit; or 3) when you die, I will meet you; or 4) My presence will be with you in the Church or 5) I will meet you at My coming at the end of the world. Since the reference is not specific, it certainly refers to the resurrection and the second coming, but it refers perhaps equally to the time of death. The closer in time, the more likely it is the primary reference.

Then Jesus says, "Whither I go ye know, and the way ye know" (v. 4). But the disciples at this point are too confused to know or to remember the simple things. Thomas is not afraid to expose his ignorance, and he says, "Lord, we know not whither thou goest; and how can we know the way?" (v. 5). Behind his question there still lurks the expectation of an earthly kingdom.

"Jesus saith unto him, I am the way, the truth, and the life: no man cometh unto the Father but by me" (v. 6). "I am the way" means that no other route to God exists, because to reject the incarnate One is to reject God the Son. "*Ego sum Via, Veritas, Vita.*" His incarnation provides us with the Way: He is our Mediator, our Great High Priest, and our atoning sacrifice that reestablishes us as righteous before God. He is the Truth, so that for us Truth is not an abstract concept but God the Son, the great heart of all reality and the Meaning behind all meaning. He is the Life, the great Creator of all life, and the only source of all life. To know Him is to have everlasting life.

Therefore there is no access to God apart from Jesus Christ: "no man cometh unto the Father, but by me" (v. 6). To separate the Son from the Father is to deny the Father.

"If ye had known me, ye should have known my Father also: and from henceforth ye know him, and have seen him" (v. 7). To know Jesus Christ is to know the Father. As a result, as the early church studied Christology, it studied theology, and the great statements of faith in the early councils of the Church were implicit in the knowledge of Christ: the knowledge of Christ meant the knowledge of God.

Philip asks a question, his fourth appearance in this gospel (he appears previously in John 1:44-49; 6:5-7; and 12:22). Philip says now, "Lord, shew us the Father, and it sufficeth us" (v. 8). Philip wants a theophany, a miraculous appearance of God like that witnessed by Moses and others. He fails to see God present in the person of Jesus. He wants a vision to confirm his hope, a special experience or a revelation to mark the Father's reality and presence.

Our Lord's answer is very blunt: "Have I been so long time with you, and yet hast thou not known me, Philip? he that hath seen me hath seen the Father; and how sayest thou then, Shew us the Father?" (v. 9). The disciples were so set on their own thinking about the Messiah that they could only think in terms of their expectations. Three of the disciples had been with Jesus on the Mount of Transfiguration (Matt. 17:1-9), but that event had not made clear to them that Jesus was God incarnate.

Jesus continued, "Believest thou not that I am in the Father, and the Father in Me? the words that I speak unto you, I speak not of myself: but the Father that dwelleth in me, he doeth the works" (v. 10). Our Lord makes clear here, once again, that He is a member of the Godhead, and that His word and works are not self-originated, but have their expression from the very Being of the Godhead. He does not speak as a person, but as one of the Persons of the Godhead. The word and works of the Members of the Godhead cannot be separated.

Jesus continues, "Believe me that I am in the Father, and the Father in me: or else believe me for the very works' sake" (v. 11). Start with either My word or My works, Jesus says, and you will see that they are of God. Implied, then, is this: My Person is of God and is God.

"Verily, verily, I say unto you, He that believeth on me, the works that I do shall he do also; and greater works than these shall he do; because I go unto my Father" (v. 12). Jesus declares that He is going to rejoin His Father. The work of the Kingdom of God is now their work — and ours. These works shall be *greater works*. The church's temptation has been to see this as many greater healing works, greater miracles, whereas the meaning is that the Kingdom will see greater works of evangelism at the hands of the apostles and us (Matt. 6:33).

"And whatsoever ye shall ask in my name, that will I do, that the Father may be glorified in the Son" (v. 13). This promise has a Kingdom orientation, not a personal one. "In my Name," means in terms of My Kingdom and My victory. There are personal promises in Scripture, but this is a Kingdom promise.

"If ye ask anything in my name, I will do it" (v. 14). Some ancient texts read, "If ye ask *me* anything in my name, I will do it." But this is already implicit in the text. We are to ask Jesus as our King, Priest, and Prophet, as God made flesh for us: we ask for the sake of His Kingdom and reign, and because He commands it. The King commands petitions.

Chapter Forty-Six

The Strengthener Promised
(John 14:15-31)

15. If ye love me, keep my commandments.

16. And I will pray the Father, and he shall give you another Comforter, that he may abide with you for ever;

17. Even the Spirit of truth; whom the world cannot receive, because it seeth him not, neither knoweth him: but ye know him; for he dwelleth with you, and shall be in you.

18. I will not leave you comfortless: I will come to you.

19. Yet a little while, and the world seeth me no more; but ye see me: because I live, ye shall live also.

20. At that day ye shall know that I am in my Father, and ye in me, and I in you.

21. He that hath my commandments, and keepeth them, he it is that loveth me: and he that loveth me shall be loved of my Father, and I will love him, and will manifest myself to him.

22. Judas saith unto him, not Iscariot, Lord, how is it that thou wilt manifest thyself unto us, and not unto the world?

23. Jesus answered and said unto him, If a man love me, he will keep my words: and my Father will love him, and we will come unto him, and make our abode with him.

24. He that loveth me not keepeth not my sayings: and the word which ye hear is not mine, but the Father's which sent me.

25. These things have I spoken unto you, being yet present with you.

26. But the Comforter, which is the Holy Ghost, whom the Father will send in my name, he shall teach you all things, and bring all things to your remembrance, whatsoever I have said unto you.

27. Peace I leave with you, my peace I give unto you: not as the world giveth, give I unto you. Let not your heart be troubled, neither let it be afraid.

28. Ye have heard how I said unto you, I go away, and come again unto you. If ye loved me, ye would rejoice, because I said, I go unto the Father: for my Father is greater than I.

29. And now I have told you before it come to pass, that, when it is come to pass, ye might believe.

30. Hereafter I will not talk much with you: for the prince of this world cometh, and hath nothing in me.

31. But that the world may know that I love the Father; and as the Father gave me commandment, even so I do. Arise, let us go hence. (John 14:15-31)

In v. 15, we have an emphatic statement: "If ye love me, keep my commandments." Many attempts have been made to alter the force of these words, and to weaken them by implying that the *commandments* refer only to what Jesus said, and not to the Law. But, since Jesus was God incarnate, the I AM, every word of Scripture is His Word. In reality, our text is forceful, in that our Lord says, "If you love me, *you* keep my

commandments": the test of love is obedience. The modern mind especially
has reduced love to a generalized feeling, whereas our Lord declares it to be
obedience. In marriage, family life, and in religion, our era has tried to
break the connection of obedience to love, but our Lord is a witness against
this.

To those who obey Him, our Lord promises, "And I will pray the Father,
and He shall give you another Comforter, that he may abide with you
forever: Even the Spirit of truth; whom the world cannot receive, because
it seeth him not, neither knoweth him; but ye know him; for he dwelleth
with you, and shall be in you" (vv. 16-17). It is noteworthy that our Lord
calls the Holy Spirit *another* Comforter, or *Advocate*. The original
Comforter for the disciples is Jesus Himself. Because He will soon leave the
disciples, He sends them the Spirit to *comfort*, or, in its older meaning, to
strengthen. They are not bystanders, and they will soon become the pillars
of God's Kingdom on earth. As such, they will need strengthening for their
work.

The Comforter or Advocate is the Holy Spirit; He is our Intercessor
with the Father. We want the world to strengthen us, but the source of our
reinvigoration must be the Holy Spirit, the third Person of the Trinity. He
is the Spirit of Truth who battles the spirit of error. In 1 John 5:6 we are
told, "the Spirit is truth." Because the fallen humanity of Adam rejects God,
it rejects truth. Having submitted to the tempter's premises, fallen men
believe that the essential element in truth is man's autonomy and man's
power to determine for himself what is good and evil, law and morality,
true and false (Gen. 3:5).

Jesus Christ must leave them, but the other Strengthener will never leave
them (v. 17) He *dwelleth* or *abideth* with you. In the Holy Spirit, we have a
strengthener and a legal counsel who is with us forever.

"I will not leave you comfortless: I will come to you" (v. 18). Our Lord
did not leave His disciples without an Advocate to strengthen them.
Moreover, He promises to come to their aid, to be with them, although not
in the flesh. If we are not aware of His strengthening Presence, it is because
we do not choose to know it, because we want His Presence, in our own
way and on our own terms.

"Yet a little while, and the world seeth me no more; but ye see me:
because I live, ye shall live also" (v. 19). After the ascension, Christ's *visible*
Presence would be gone. His *invisible* Presence will be seen by His faithful
followers. Because He, as the last Adam (1 Cor. 15:45-49), has destroyed the
power of sin and death, we share in His victory, and we have everlasting
life.

"At that day ye shall know that I am in my Father, and ye in me, and I
in you" (v. 20). From Pentecost to the second coming, you shall know that

I and the Father are one. The Father is in Me, and I am in the Father. You are in me as members of My new human race, one born again into righteousness, justice, and life. I am in you as your new federal Head, your greater Adam, as your new and redeemed humanity.

"He that hath my commandments, and keepeth them, he it is that loveth me: and he that loveth me shall be loved of my Father, and I will love him, and will manifest myself to him" (v. 21). As B. F. Westcott noted:

> The verse is in part the converse of v. 15. There active obedience is seen to be consequence of love. Here active obedience is the sign of the presence of love. [1]

It is a very serious error to separate Jesus from the Old Testament. All three Persons of the Trinity are the sources of the whole of Scripture. To limit Jesus Christ's words to those in red, in red-letter editions, is in effect to present another canon or rule within the canon of Scripture, and this is heresy. We see again, very emphatically, that love and obedience can no more be separated than can faith and works (Matt. 7:15-20; Jam. 2:15-26; Rom. 3:31). It is suicidal for the church to separate love and obedience, or faith and works.

In v. 22, we have Judas, not Iscariot, ask, "Lord, how is it that thou wilt manifest thyself unto us, and not unto the world?" There are six men in the New Testament bearing the name Judas. This one is a disciple, "Judas, the brother of James" (Luke 6:16); he was apparently known also as "Lebaeus, whose surname was Thaddaeus" (Matt. 10:3; Mark 3:18). In bilingual countries, having more than one name was commonplace; Thomas was also known as Didymus.

This Judas was baffled. Like the other disciples, He expected Jesus to become Israel's messianic king; how could He avoid revealing His kingship to all peoples? Given his presupposition, his question was valid.

Jesus answered, "If a man love me, he will keep my words; and my Father will love him, and we will come unto him, and make our abode with him" (v. 23). My Kingdom, our Lord makes clear, is not of this world; it does not mean external power and coercion, but regeneration and a submission of life and works. My Kingdom is not of coercion but conversion, not revolution but regeneration.

"He that loveth me not keepeth not my sayings; and the word which ye hear is not mine, but the Father's which sent me" (v. 24). Our Lord forbids any distinction between His word and the Father's word, His commandments and the Father's. Dividing the Old and New Testaments, the law and the gospel, love and obedience, faith and works, and so on, is contrary to the word of God. God is One, perfect and entire, and His being

---

[1.] B. F. Westcott: *The Gospel According to St. John* (Grand Rapids, MI: Eerdmans, 1881, 1954), 207.

and works cannot be divided. In our lives, there can be a great gap between our profession of love and our obedience, but it is sinful to project such a gap onto Scripture and its world of thought.

In vv. 25-26, our Lord makes clear to his disciples that they shall soon have the supernatural help of the Holy Spirit in remembering what He has taught them and in being taught all that is needful. The Holy Spirit will then be their teacher. This will not be an independent or a further revelation. Even as the Son teaches only what the Father chooses, so too does the Spirit teach, so that all three Persons of the Trinity speak the same word. The Father sends the Spirit, and the Spirit confirms the word given by the Son, who received it from the Father.

Verse 27 is one of Scripture's greatest statements: "Peace I leave with you, my peace I give unto you: not as the world giveth, give I unto you. Let not your heart be troubled, neither let it be afraid." The promised peace is one with God; it is Christ's peace, and it is He who gives it. Therefore, we should be neither troubled nor afraid.

Verse 28 begins with a rebuke to the disciples because they are troubled that He is leaving them. "If ye loved me, ye would rejoice, because I said, I go unto my Father." They are more concerned with losing Him than in His gain. Then our Lord added, "for my Father is greater than I." The Arians used this statement often, while neglecting or undermining those words wherein our Lord identified His oneness with the Father. There is an economical subordination in the Trinity, but not an essential one, one of function, not of being. Moreover, in His incarnation, the Son was both God and man, and thus the Father was the greater, in that He was God and God alone. In substance, God the Father, God the Son, and God the Holy Spirit are one.

In v. 29, our Lord tells them that His instructions concerning His departure have been given to prepare them for the event and to increase their faith by this foreknowledge.

"Hereafter I will not talk much with you: for the prince of this world cometh, and hath nothing in me" (v. 30). The prince or ruler of this world is Satan. This does not mean that he is earth's king, simply the ruler over fallen men. Because our Lord is the second Adam, sinless, and King of the universe in His own right, there is nothing in Jesus' person, history, life, acts, or thoughts over which Satan has an iota of control. His servants in the church of that day may crucify the Christ, but they cannot control Him or limit His absolute power.

"But that the world may know that I love the Father; and as the Father gave me commandment, even so I do. Arise, let us go hence" (v. 31). The evidence indicates that they did not leave at this point; the material of chapters 15-17 follows. They may have ended the meal, or their time at the table. What is important is what He said. What He said in v. 31 is that He is obedient to the Father's commandment, specifically, the cross, demonstrating to those who *would* know how totally the Son loved the Father. It was God's love for His creation (John 3:16) that governed the Trinity's redemptive work.

Chapter Forty-Seven

The Vine and the Branches
(*John 15:1-8*)

1. I am the true vine, and my Father is the husbandman.
2. Every branch in me that beareth not fruit he taketh away: and every branch that beareth fruit, he purgeth it, that it may bring forth more fruit.
3. Now ye are clean through the word which I have spoken unto you.
4. Abide in me, and I in you. As the branch cannot bear fruit of itself, except it abide in the vine; no more can ye, except ye abide in me.
5. I am the vine, ye are the branches: He that abideth in me, and I in him, the same bringeth forth much fruit: for without me ye can do nothing.
6. If a man abide not in me, he is cast forth as a branch, and is withered; and men gather them, and cast them into the fire, and they are burned.
7. If ye abide in me, and my words abide in you, ye shall ask what ye will, and it shall be done unto you.
8. Herein is my Father glorified, that ye bear much fruit; so shall ye be my disciples. (John 15:1-8)

In John 15:1-8, we have a comparison of Jesus to a vine, and His disciples and us to branches. Israel was often compared to either an olive tree or a fig tree. The olive tree was regarded as the king of trees (Judges 9:8) because its fruit and oil were so basic to life and health. In the Old Testament, Israel is often compared to a vine, but the references are normally negative, i.e., they speak of a degenerate Israel (Ps. 80:8-13; 19:10; Isa. 5:1; Jer. 2:21; Ezek. 15:2; Hosea 10:1). However, the coins of the Maccabees depicted Israel as a vine. The vine produces grapes, raisins, and wine. The True Vine, Jesus Christ, is here shown as the new Israel of God.[1]

The use of the vine by our Lord points to both its *productivity* and its *relationship* to the vineyardist. For a small "tree," the vine is very fertile, and its grapes can be so plentiful that their bulk in comparison to the size of the vine is amazing. Moreover, the productivity of the vine is maintained by the vineyardist's annual pruning. The vine that grows wild produces little, whereas the vine that is pruned is highly productive. This means that the continual discipline of pruning is essential to a producing vine.

Jesus identifies Himself as the true vine, and His Father as "the husbandman" or vineyardist (v. 1). The dead branches are removed, and every healthy, productive branch is pruned back so that it will bear more fruit (v. 2). The disciples are "clean" through Christ's words, which have separated them from evil and from apostasy (v. 3). The disciples may not

---

[1.] J. H. Bernard, A.H. McNeile: *The Gospel According to St. John*, vol. II, (Edinburgh: T. & T. Clark, 1928, 1972), 477f.

199

have immediately understood all that Jesus taught but they would understand later.

The branch is dead apart from the vine, and so, too, are they lifeless unless they abide in Him (v. 4). "Churches" and "Christians" who separate themselves from Jesus Christ are soon dead.

This is because Christ is the vine, our source of life (John 14:6), and only if we abide in Him can we bear fruit. "Without me ye can do nothing" (v. 5). Dead branches can bear no fruit. All men and churches that separate themselves from Christ are dead. They are fit only for burning, for destruction (v. 6).

As against this, our Lord says, "If ye abide in me, and my words abide in you, ye shall ask what ye will, and it shall be done unto you" (v. 7). This is a remarkable statement. The first conditional clause is, "If ye abide in me..." It means that we must live in Christ, as a member of His new human race and as His life-bearing, fruit-giving branch. The second conditional clause is, *if* "my words abide in you." Three living powers are cited in these two clauses: Christ, us, and *His words.* His words are presented as life-giving forces of divine power. If we meet these conditions, *then* "ye shall ask what ye will, and it shall be done unto you." At this point, too much thinking in the church has centered on *the believer* and *his* wishes, as though the believer were the vine and not a branch. There are particular promises to the believer, but this is a promise to a branch of the true vine, to someone seeking to bear fruit to Jesus Christ. To generalize unduly can mean to dissipate the meaning of the text.

"Herein is my Father glorified, that ye bear much fruit; so shall ye be my disciples" (v. 8). Here is the focus: it is on being Christ's disciple by bearing much fruit for Him. We *become* His disciples as we are productive for Him. But we are productive only as we are fully dedicated to His word. G. Campbell Morgan translated v. 7 thus: "If ye abide in Me, and My words abide in you, you shall demand as your due whatever you are inclined to, and it shall be generated unto you."[2]

Pruning is a form of discipline exercised on the vine by the vineyardist. God as our Keeper continually exercises His pruning power in our lives to prepare us to bear more fruit, both in time and in eternity. Westcott observed that, while a Christian *is* a Christian, "A Christian never 'is,' but always 'is becoming' a Christian."[3] Modern existentialism gives Westcott's wording a new meaning, but, as Westcott meant it, the Christian's life is

[2] G. Campbell Morgan: *The Gospel According to John* (New York, NY: Fleming H. Revell, n.d.), 254.
[3] B. F. Westcott: *The Gospel According to St. John* (Grand Rapids, MI: Eerdmans, 1881, 1954), 219.

one of growth. In Leon Morris' words, "Always the true disciple is becoming more fully a disciple."[4]

These words are spoken to the disciples, and they now apply to *all* within the church. Our lives must either have results for Christ and His Kingdom, or we are cut off. What is here said has no reference to the world at large.

Verse 4 specifies that no branch can bear fruit of itself. If separated from the vine, Jesus Christ, it is dead and worthless, fit only for destruction. The comparison of God to a vineyardist is very important. It does not allow us to think of God as an absentee landlord: He is the very present Keeper who carefully watches our growth and productivity, "pruning" us when we need it.

Jesus in v. 1 declares, "I am the true (or, the real) vine, and my Father is the husbandman." This means Christ is in us as our life, and God is over us as the one judging our productivity. This means that the purpose of our lives is not *our* salvation, but our *productivity* for Christ's Kingdom. It means that each of us brings his or her particular domain under the dominion and into the service of His Kingdom. Just as the vineyardist prunes the vine, we prune our sphere of life to serve God's Kingdom.

A common and serious error limits fruit-bearing to "spiritual" exercises and to faithfulness of a pietistic kind. The analogy to fruit-bearing in these verses is to *actual results*. The branches do not simply grow and bear beautiful leaves: they produce grapes. This means that our faith must bear fruit by commanding the way we live, what we do, and the practical consequences for our sphere of life.

[4.] Leon Morris: *The Gospel According to John* (Grand Rapids, MI: Eerdmans, 1971, 1977), 673.

Chapter Forty-Eight

The Meaning of Biblical Love
(John 15:9-17)

9. As the Father hath loved me, so have I loved you: continue ye in my love.
10. If ye keep my commandments, ye shall abide in my love; even as I have kept my Father's commandments, and abide in his love.
11. These things have I spoken unto you, that my joy might remain in you, and that your joy might be full.
12. This is my commandment, That ye love one another, as I have loved you.
13. Greater love hath no man than this, that a man lay down his life for his friends.
14. Ye are my friends, if ye do whatsoever I command you.
15. Henceforth I call you not servants; for the servant knoweth not what his lord doeth: but I have called you friends; for all things that I have heard of my Father I have made known unto you.
16. Ye have not chosen me, but I have chosen you, and ordained you, that ye should go and bring forth fruit, and that your fruit should remain: that whatsoever ye shall ask of the Father in my name, he may give it you.
17. These things I command you, that ye love one another.
(John 15:9-17)

Our text speaks of love, but not in the pagan and modern antinomian sense. Love is tied to obedience. Obedience is the test of love and essential to it.

Our Lord begins by declaring, "As the Father hath loved me, so have I loved you: continue ye in my love" (v. 9). This has been variously phrased. Plummer rendered it, "Even as the Father loved Me, I also loved you; abide in My love." Westcott's wording is somewhat similar: "Even as the Father loved me and I loved you, abide in my love."[1] The pattern of our obedience and love is established by God the Father and by the Son. We do not define obedience: it has been done for us. The redemptive and gracious love of God does not have us as the end; it must be revealed to others through us.

In v. 10, we see the essential and inseparable relationship between love and obedience: "If ye keep my commandments, ye shall abide in my love; even as I have kept my Father's commandments, and abide in his love." There is only one way to abide in the love of the Triune God: by keeping His commandments. Jesus Christ abides in God's love because He kept God's commandments. This statement again makes untenable the common view that *commandments* refers only to Jesus' words, as highlighted in the

---

[1] A. Plummer: *The Gospel According to St. John* (Cambridge, England: Cambridge University Press, 1880, 1906), 289; B. F. Westcott: *The Gospel According to St. John* (Grand Rapids, MI: Eerdmans, 1881, 1954), 219.

red-letter editions of the Bible. The standard is "my Father's commandments." Antinomianism is condemned by John's Gospel and the whole of the Bible. Westcott rightly observed, "Obedience and love are perfectly correlative."[2] Again, Leon Morris said of love, "This is not some mystical experience. It is simple obedience." Morris fully associates obedience with love.[3]

In v. 11, our Lord continues, "These things have I spoken unto you, that my joy might remain in you, and that your joy might be full." Our Lord describes His frame of mind as one of *joy*. This was a rather strange description, coming as it did before the agony of the cross. It did, however, well describe His awareness of the cosmic victory for all time and eternity that He was about to accomplish. He prepares his disciples to share that joy in the atonement, resurrection, and ascension. His purpose in speaking to the disciples and to us is so that we understand what is being accomplished, and so that we become filled with joy.

In v. 12, He proceeds, "This is my commandment, that ye love one another, as I have loved you." The commandment that is Mine, the commandment that is a revelation of My nature, is that, even as I have loved you, so you must love one another. This means an obedient, self-sacrificing love, a ministering love, not a struggle for power. It is therefore not an emotional love, but it is action based on obedience to God's law in sacrificial terms. The standard and test of our love is Christ's love.

"Greater love hath no man than this, that a man lay down his life for his friends" (v. 13). This is a text of great importance. The word translated as *friends* is in the Greek text *philos*; the same word is translated in the Septuagint version of Esther 1:18 as *princes*. In antiquity, there were no hereditary titles of nobility. A king's friends, who had access to his table, were fed and clothed by him and were *princes of grace*. Their status was due to the king's love and grace. The meaning here is that all faithful, obedient Christians are *princes of grace*. "Ye are my friends (my princes of grace) if ye do whatsoever I command you" (v. 14).

Then in v. 15 we have a further definition: "Henceforth I call you not servants; for the servant knoweth not what his lord doeth: but I have called you friends; for all things that I have heard of my Father I have made known unto you" (v. 15). Our Lord speaks of several kinds of men in relation to His flock or people. In John 10:12, He refers to the hireling, or the hired servant. In John 10:1, He speaks of the thief and the robber. We have thus the thief on the outside, who seeks to rob and to kill. The hireling works for wages only. The household servant, a permanent part of the

2. *ibid.*, 219.
3. Leon Morris: *The Gospel According to John* (Grand Rapids, MI: Eerdmans, 1971, 1977), 673.

family, is faithful, but he is ignorant of the master's thinking. The *friend,* the prince of grace, knows His Lord's mind, and he obeys Him beyond normal duties.

Then, in v. 16, our Lord declares:

> Ye have not chosen me, but I have chosen you, and ordained you, that ye should go and bring forth fruit, and that your fruit should remain: that whatsoever ye shall ask of the Father in my name, he may give it you.

Here as elsewhere in John's Gospel, as in all of Scripture, predestination is assumed, not argued. It is Christ who chooses us, not we, Christ. The premise of Arminian revivalism, that man can choose Christ, is thus entirely wrong and theologically and morally untenable. Moreover, Christ declares that He has ordained, appointed, or chosen us for a particular post or calling. He has done this that we should go to work "and bring forth fruit," a very practical concern. There is nothing here of the pietistic spirituality. Rather, the concern is Kingdom growth and dominion. Not only does He ordain our productivity, but also that our "fruit should remain." This is a very practical concern with results.

Next, we are told, "whatsoever ye shall ask of the Father in my name, he may give it you." This is a general promise. "Whatsoever" includes anything we can legitimately ask for in Christ's name.

In v. 17, our Lord says, "These things I command you, that ye love one another." This is a commandment to the Christian community, not to the world.[4] The Christian community must manifest love, i.e., care, protection, charity, and a loving discipline in dealing with one another. But love requires obedience to God's every word, and the application of God's law-word to all our relationships. Love and obedience have been defined for us by the word of God. There must be this obedient love in Christian community, but the goal is greater than the community: it is the Kingdom of God and His righteousness (Matt. 6:33).

[4.] J. H. Bernard, A. H. McNeile: *Gospel According to St. John,* vol. II (Edinburgh, Scotland: T. & T. Clark, 1928, 1972), 490.

Chapter Forty-Nine
The World's Hatred
(John 15:18-27)

18. If the world hate you, ye know that it hated me before it hated you.
19. If ye were of the world, the world would love his own: but because ye are not of the world, but I have chosen you out of the world, therefore the world hateth you.
20. Remember the word that I said unto you, The servant is not greater than his lord. If they have persecuted me, they will also persecute you; if they have kept my saying, they will keep yours also.
21. But all these things will they do unto you for my name's sake, because they know not him that sent me.
22. If I had not come and spoken unto them, they had not had sin: but now they have no cloke for their sin.
23. He that hateth me hateth my Father also.
24. If I had not done among them the works which none other man did, they had not had sin: but now have they both seen and hated both me and my Father.
25. But this cometh to pass, that the word might be fulfilled that is written in their law, They hated me without a cause.
26. But when the Comforter is come, whom I will send unto you from the Father, even the Spirit of truth, which proceedeth from the Father, he shall testify of me:
27. And ye also shall bear witness, because ye have been with me from the beginning. (John 15:18-27)

We come now to our Lord's comments on *hatred*. Hatred in and of itself is without a moral qualification unless we know what is hated. To hate murder, rape, theft, and false witness is morally sound, but to hate justice, morality, and Christianity is a mark of evil. The same is true of love: if a man loves evil and revells in it, his love is evil. It is simplistic and morally unsound to condemn or approve of love and hate without knowing the object of either.

Soon, with their Lord gone, the disciples would bear the brunt of the world's hatred, but this would be because of fallen man's prior hatred for Jesus Christ (v. 18).

We are known by what we love and hate. To idealize love as a universally desirable trait is to indulge in nonsense, because the love of evil is no virtue. It is moral idiocy to insist on universal love of everything, as too many do, because too often it is an acceptance of evil. The objects of the Marquis de Sade's loves cannot be ours.

"If ye were of the world, the world would love his own: but because ye are not of the world, but I have chosen you out of the world, therefore the world hateth you" (v. 19). The word "world" is used five times in this sentence. There is a stress on the difference between Christ's chosen ones and *the world*. This emphasis is strong in character, because we are not allowed to blur the dividing line, as too many in the world *and* in the church strive to do. There is an inescapable alignment of men in terms of what they are and who they follow. It is true that both sides have persons who want a blurred line, but God does not long permit this.

"Remember the word that I said unto you, The servant is not greater than his lord. If they have persecuted me, they will also persecute you; if they have kept my saying, they will keep yours also" (v. 20). The reference is to His earlier statement (John 13:16), "Verily, verily, I say unto you, The servant is not greater than his lord; neither he that is sent greater than he that sent him." "The saying reminds them that the treatment given the Master determines that accorded to the servant."[1] Jesus Christ was crucified by this world order; at the least, that same order will reject us. Our Lord's words here refer not only to John 13:16, but also to Matthew 10:24-25:

> 24. The disciple is not above his master, nor the servant above his lord.
> 25. It is enough for the disciple that he be as his master, and the servant as his lord. If they have called the master of the house, Beelzebub, how much more shall they call them of his household?

Jesus was often called a *devil*; it they say this of Jesus, whom they feared, how much more readily will they not be ready to say this of us? We are as nothing to them, and their vicious abuse comes readily.

"But all these things will they do unto you for my name's sake, because they know not him that sent me" (v. 21). They are wilfully ignorant of God; they hate God, and, not knowing Him as their Lord and Judge, they hate Christ, who speaks of God's claims on all of us, and they hate us because they hate Christ.

"The true knowledge of God carries with it the knowledge of Christ."[2] This means that the religious leaders did not know Christ because they did not know God. Persecution, abuse, and martyrdom can thus become the lot of Christians at the hands of evil men.

"If I had not come and spoken unto them, they had not had sin: but now they have no cloke for their sin" (v. 22). The reference here is to the religious leaders: they lived in the confidence that they truly represented the remote God whose earthly agents they claimed to be. Christ's coming exposed their unbelief. Now they were conscious of their sin as they had not been before. The cloke of self-satisfied ignorance had been stripped from them.

---

1. Leon Morris: *The Gospel According to John* (Grand Rapids, MI: Eerdmans, 1971,1977), 679.
2. B. F. Westcott: *The Gospel According to St. John* (Grand Rapids, MI: Eerdmans, 1881, 1954), 223.

"He that hateth me hateth my Father also" (v. 23). God cannot be separated from Jesus Christ. To hate the one is to hate the other. There can be no true religion claiming to worship the God of Scripture while rejecting Jesus Christ. When Unitarianism rejected Jesus Christ, it was not long before it rejected God also.

"If I had not done among them the works which none other man did, they had not had sin: but now have they both seen and hated both me and my Father" (v. 24). The sins of the religious leaders included these: *first*, they rejected the works of Jesus; *second*, they separated His works from His person (John 9:24-28); *third*, when they were compelled to admit a miracle, the raising of Lazarus, they saw it as a good reason to kill Him (John 11:50). Expediency, not faith, governed them. Their knowledge of Jesus Christ led to the hatred of Him *and the Father.*

"But this cometh to pass, that the word might be fulfilled that is written in their law, They hated me without a cause" (v. 25). The reference is to Psalms 35:19 and 69:4. *This reference is to the psalms, but our Lord calls it "law," because every word of God is binding and true.* It is "their law" because the religious leaders claimed it to be so, and they held that they were the valid interpreters. This word is "fulfilled," become reality in all its fulness.

"But when the Comforter is come, whom I will send unto you from the Father, even the Spirit of truth, which proceedeth from the Father, he shall testify of me" (v. 26). The phrase, "which proceedeth from the Father," is used by the Eastern Orthodox churches to deny the procession of the Spirit from the Son. Since other texts imply a procession from both the Father and the Son, it is hardly valid to invalidate them. The Spirit is our advocate, comforter, or strengthener. He is the Spirit of truth, and the truth is Jesus Christ (John 14:6). His testimony will support Jesus Christ.

"And ye also (shall) bear witness, because ye have been with me from the beginning" (v. 27). The Holy Spirit and Christ's disciples bear witness together. They are God's testimony to a fallen world. Failure to hear and heed this witness is a sin against truth. It is marked by a hatred of truth. Revelation 22:15 speaks of "whosoever loveth and maketh a lie." There is a clear line of division which, however blurred by some, cannot be erased. The lie and the truth stand forever separate. Precisely because the line cannot be erased, the hatred of the world is intense. Our Lord here prepares His followers for that hatred by the world.

Chapter Fifty

The Avenging Spirit
(John 16:1-11)

1. These things have I spoken unto you, that ye should not be offended.
2. They shall put you out of the synagogues: yea, the time cometh, that whosoever killeth you will think that he doeth God service.
3. And these things will they do unto you, because they have not known the Father, nor me.
4. But these things have I told you, that when the time shall come, ye may remember that I told you of them. And these things I said not unto you at the beginning, because I was with you.
5. But now I go my way to him that sent me; and none of you asketh me, Whither goest thou?
6. But because I have said these things unto you, sorrow hath filled your heart.
7. Nevertheless I tell you the truth; It is expedient for you that I go away: for if I go not away, the Comforter will not come unto you; but if I depart, I will send him unto you.
8. And when he is come, he will reprove the world of sin, and of righteousness, and of judgment:
9. Of sin, because they believe not on me;
10. Of righteousness, because I go to my Father, and ye see me no more;
11. Of judgment, because the prince of this world is judged.
(John 16:1-11)

Our Lord tells the disciples, "These things have I spoken unto you, that ye should not be offended" (v. 1), or, in A. Plummer's rendering, that ye "should not be made to stumble."[1] The savage hostility they would face would tend to shake any man. They are therefore in need of strength to face this attack. Christ plans to arm them 1)through His words, and 2) by means of the Holy Spirit, the Strengthener.

Verses 1-11 thus deal with the Holy Spirit. It is a mistake to assume that the Spirit's work is only with Christ's people. In vv. 8 ff., the Holy Spirit *reproves* the world. The word *reprove (elenche,* here *elenchei)* means to convict, rebuke, or expose. Thus, while the Holy Spirit strengthens us, He weakens the enemies of Christ. While this can inflame them all the more, it means also that they will be weakened by the inner knowledge of their guilt and evil. The Holy Spirit is thus the Strengthener of Christ's new human race and also the Weakener of fallen man, of Christ's enemies. The Holy Spirit is thus a Warrior in the Wars of the Lord.

[1.] A. Plummer: *The Gospel According to St. John* (Cambridge, England: Cambridge University Press, 1880, 1988), 296.

The enemies of Christ will strike at His people to gain revenge. "They shall put you out of the synagogues: yea, the time cometh, that whosoever killeth you will think that he doeth God service" (v. 2), or, "offereth service to God."[2] Tacitus (*Ann.* xv. 44), a pagan Roman, saw the persecution of Christians as morally justified, and this is true of the enemies of Christ today. It is a bitter hostility because it deals with life's basic issues.

"And these things will they do unto you, because they have not known the Father, nor me" (v. 3). They cannot know Jesus Christ because they do not know God the Father. This is not ignorance due to lack of knowledge of the facts, but a willful, moral self-blinding because they are determined to be their own gods (Gen. 3:5). Because of this, they refuse to know God, except on their own terms. The ungodly hate God while sometimes giving Him lip service. In their enmity to God, they strike at His people.

"But these things have I told you, that when the time shall come, ye may remember that I told you of them. And these things I said not unto you at the beginning, because I was with you" (v. 4). Up to this point, Jesus had been the target of hostility, malice, and misrepresentation. Now, because He would soon be leaving them, they would become the object of the evil will of ungodly men. Jesus had delayed telling them of this earlier because He had been with them, and He had taken upon Himself the malice of men.

"But now I go my way to him that sent me; and none of you asketh me, Whither goest thou?" (v. 5). The disciples were so wrapped up in their own expectations that none had yet asked, Whither goest thou? Peter, in John 13:36, and Thomas, in John 14:5, had both asked such a question, but not even remotely in the sense that Jesus meant it. Their own expectations prevented them from hearing Jesus as He intended to be heard. They comprehended Him only as the subject of their faith and hope, not as He Himself was and is. They loved the Lord, but they remade Him in the image of their faith and hope.

"But because I have said these things unto you, sorrow hath filled your heart" (v. 6). Their sorrow was grounded in their failed expectations, not in the reality of Christ's enthronement as King, Priest, and Prophet in the days ahead. He could not console them because their own grief had so captured them. Jesus was soon to be crucified, and yet the disciples were more absorbed in their grief than in His coming passion, death, and resurrection.

"Nevertheless, I tell you the truth: It is expedient for you that I go away: for if I go not away, the Comforter will not come unto you; but if I depart, I will send him unto you" (v. 7). Christ's departure is necessary. The responsibility for conquest of all men and nations is on the believers'

[2.] *ibid.*, 296.

shoulders. The Comforter, or Strengthener, will come when Christ departs. "But if I depart, I will send him unto you." This statement clearly speaks of the procession of the Spirit from the Son.

"And when he is come, he will reprove the world of sin, and of righteousness, and of judgment" (v. 8). This is a very important text. It tells us that the Holy Spirit keeps fallen man mindful of his condition. Fallen men are willfully ignorant of their sin; they refuse to acknowledge that God's justice is alone righteous because they prefer their law to God's law. They refuse to admit that God's judgment, already written on the tablets of their hearts, is true and altogether just. The Holy Spirit is thus very active in the hearts of the ungodly.

"Of sin, because they believe not on me" (v. 9). The rejection of Jesus Christ is at the basis of all sin. Such a rejection means that self-righteous men refuse to acknowledge Christ's atoning work. The fallen man wants God to be, *at best*, his helper, not his sovereign. Too much theology is disguised anthropology, and man too often plays the ventriloquist, talking for God.

"Of righteousness, because I go to my Father, and ye see me no more" (v. 10). The Holy Spirit would force onto the minds of the ungodly a new recognition of the meaning of righteousness or justice. In spite of men's rejection of Jesus Christ, the Holy Spirit would compel the ungodly to an unwilling awareness of God's justice in Christ.

"Of judgment, because the prince of this world is judged" (v. 11). The meaning of judgment is revealed in the reality itself: there is a chasm between good and evil, and between God and Satan. *Judgment* prevents men from obliterating the difference. The goal of fallen men is to eliminate the antithesis between good and evil and to reduce moral choice to a question of personal taste.

In present-day thinking, an absolute moral law is denied. Moral matters are purely personal preferences, not universal concerns. Again and again, men have reduced God's moral law to a question of custom, private tastes, and irrelevant tyrannies, but the law remains to judge all men.

The Holy Spirit thus works in all men, but in different ways. To Christ's new human race, He is the Advocate, Comforter, and Strengthener. To the ungodly, He is a Prosecutor, a Terror, and a Weakener.

To reduce the work of the Holy Spirit to the inner life of Christians is to severely limit Him. We need to pray that He convicts Christ's enemies of their sins, and brings them down, if not to their knees.

Our Lord tells the disciples, and us, that, in sending the Spirit, He is turning loose on the world an unrivaled force that brings terror and weakness to Christ's enemies.

The prevalence of psychiatrists, psychologists, and psychoanalysts in our rebellious era is evidence enough of the devastation wrought upon Christ's enemies by the Holy Spirit.

What we have written about the Spirit may seem strange to modern man, including those familiar with this text. Our minds have been darkened by ancient heresies, most notably the Joachimite heresy. The medieval Abbott Joachim divided history into three stages. *First*, there is the age of the Father, the age of wrath, *law*, and justice. *Second* comes the age of the Son, the age of grace. *Third*, there is the age of the Spirit, the age of love. From Hegel on, we have secular versions of third-age thinking.

Joachim's ideas are heresy because they imply three gods of differing natures. God the Father is indeed love, justice, law, wrath, and much, much more, and the same is true of the Son and the Spirit. Those who reduce the Holy Spirit to love and pious gushing do not know the Spirit, nor the Son, nor the Father. John 16:1-11 is in all Bibles: how do they read it? Blindly?

Chapter Fifty-One

The Undivided Trinity
(John 16:12-15)

12. I have yet many things to say unto you, but ye cannot bear them now.
13. Howbeit when he, the Spirit of truth, is come, he will guide you into all truth: for he shall not speak of himself; but whatsoever he shall hear, that shall he speak: and he will shew you things to come.
14. He shall glorify me: for he shall receive of mine, and shall shew it unto you.
15. All things that the Father hath are mine: therefore said I, that he shall take of mine, and shall shew it unto you. (John 16:12-15)

As we have seen, the doctrine of the Holy Spirit appears in its fullness in John. The notion that the filioque controversy first introduced the idea of the procession of the Spirit from the Son as well as the Father is nonsense. It takes much time for the church to catch up with the Bible, if it ever can. It is also false to separate the Spirit from the doctrine of judgment. Just as the idea of "gentle Jesus, meek and mild," is a myth, so too is the concept of the Holy Spirit as One concerned solely with loving and ecstatic manifestations wrong. In vv. 11-15, our Lord speaks again of the Spirit, as in vv. 7-11. J.H. Bernard and A.H. McNeile said of v. 11:

> There is nothing arbitrary in the Divine judgment; it is the inevitable result of moral laws. Good is not the same as evil, and the sharpness of the distinction is revealed by the Spirit in His assurance of *krisis*, i.e. separation or judgment. He will convince the world at once of the *justice* and the *righteousness* of God's judgments.[1]

The Holy Spirit is the Comforter, but He is much more. The tendency to reduce Him to the level of a mere comforter falsifies the doctrine because it neglects His part in judgment. In Ephesians 4:30 we are told, "Grieve not the Holy Spirit of God, by whom you were sealed for the day of redemption." Some take *grieve* to mean bringing sadness to the Holy Spirit; the word translated so means to burden or to bring heaviness. In Ephesians 4: 20-29 we are told to abandon the course of life which marked us in Adam and to become a new man, clothed in Christ's new humanity. Instead of exploiting one another, we are members one of another. To behave otherwise is disruptive of the new humanity of which we are members, and of the Holy Spirit, our Strengthener and Advocate: how can He be the Advocate of sin? Rather, He then becomes our reprover and chastiser.

[1.] J.H. Bernard, and A. H. McNeile: *A Critical and Exegetical Commentary on the Gospel According to St. John*, Vol. II (Edinburgh, Scotland: T.T. Clark, 1928, 1972), 508.

215

A heresy which recurs at times portrays the Holy Spirit as the feminine component of the Trinity, and *feminine* is used in the sense of tender, soft, and weepy. It is difficult to have anything but disgust for those who hold such an opinion, which is disrespectful of both the Holy Spirit and of women.

In v. 12, our Lord says, "I have yet many things to say unto you, but ye cannot hear them now." This is a text of importance in that it tells us about God's mercy. Paul tells us much the same in 1 Corinthians 10:13:

> There hath no temptation taken you but such as is common to man: but God is faithful, who will not suffer you to be tempted above that ye are able; but will with the temptation also make a way to escape, that ye may be able to bear it.

In a fallen world, trials and temptations are routine, but where our faith is concerned, God does not allow us to be overwhelmed. As a result, our Lord waited until the time between the resurrection and the ascension to tell them more about these events and their meaning.

"Howbeit when he, the Spirit of truth, is come, he will guide you into all truth: for he shall not speak of himself; but whatsoever he shall hear, that shall he speak: and he will show you things to come" (v. 13). This verse is also very important to the doctrine of the Holy Spirit, because our Lord says emphatically, "he shall not speak of himself." Some, like the medieval Joachimites and their modern followers, have understood the coming of the Spirit as the "third age," as the age of the Spirit and love; the first age was of the Father and law, and the second age, of the Son and grace, making for three essentially different religions. This scheme uses Biblical materials for anti-Biblical conclusions. The relative ignorance of the Spirit is *in part* God-intended. We cannot replace the centrality of Son who redeems us.

Jesus Christ is identified as the *truth* in John 14:6; here, the Spirit is described as "the Spirit of truth." In 1 Timothy 3:15, God the Father is the "pillar and ground" of truth.

The Holy Spirit, as Truth, will guide us into all truth, or, more literally, "into all the Truth." The guiding is not simply intellectual, although it is that as well. We are led, tested, tried, and taught *the Truth* in many ways.

The Spirit does not give us a truth exclusively His own. He does not speak for Himself but for the Trinity, Father, Son, and Spirit. He speaks what He hears; He speaks for the Triune Godhead.

"He will shew you things to come." This does not mean specific events, but rather the direction and goal of all events, the triumph of the Kingdom of God.

Our Lord then says, "He shall glorify me: for he shall receive of mine, and shall shew it unto you" (v. 14). The Trinity's three persons are one in being, without any subordination of function. The Father's place in function *precedes* the Son, and the Spirit *proceeds* from the Father and the Son, but they are equal in being and nature. The work of the Spirit is Christ-centered: "he shall receive of mine, and shall shew it unto you." It does not go a step beyond Jesus Christ, but the work of the Spirit centers on Christ.

In v. 15, our Lord says, "All things that the Father hath are mine...and shall shew it unto you." In John 17:10, our Lord says, "And all mine are thine, and thine are mine; and I am glorified in them." There is full and perfect communion between the Father and the Son, and among the Father, Son, and Spirit.

Truth is one, and the Trinity is one, so that the Father, the Son and the Spirit have one being and one purpose. There is no division in the Godhead.

Our text and the verses preceding and following it very plainly set forth the doctrine of the Trinity. The church did not invent it, and modernists, when told this, insist on seeing John as one who contributed to the invention of this doctrine. If told that Paul held the same doctrine, they insist on seeing Paul as an inventor of tales, like John and others. Like Caiaphas, they will not believe.

Again, we have another problem in the sentimentalization of the doctrine of the Holy Spirit. But it is clear that He is as much the Judge as are the Father and the Son. What we have in many doctrines of the Holy Spirit is a Joachimite type of adaptation. The three ages idea is Hellenic and evolutionary; supposedly, a progression takes place, an evolutionary development, from the Father through the Son to the Spirit. Such thinking is Biblically illiterate. Its approach to the Bible is of the smorgasbord variety, with the freedom to pick and choose and thereby build a religion acceptable to the modern mind. Acceptable it may be, but not true.

The Godhead is one and undivided in its being, and united in its works of creation and redemption.

Chapter Fifty-Two

Jesus is Lord
(John 16:16-24)

16. A little while, and ye shall not see me: and again, a little while, and ye shall see me, because I go to the Father.
17. Then said some of his disciples among themselves, What is this that he saith unto us, A little while, and ye shall not see me: and again, a little while, and ye shall see me: and, Because I go to the Father?
18. They said therefore, What is this that he saith, A little while? we cannot tell what he saith.
19. Now Jesus knew that they were desirous to ask him, and said unto them, Do ye enquire among yourselves of that I said, A little while, and ye shall not see me: and again, a little while, and ye shall see me?
20. Verily, verily, I say unto you, That ye shall weep and lament, but the world shall rejoice: and ye shall be sorrowful, but your sorrow shall be turned into joy.
21. A woman when she is in travail hath sorrow, because her hour is come: but as soon as she is delivered of the child, she remembereth no more the anguish, for joy that a man is born into the world.
22. And ye now therefore have sorrow: but I will see you again, and your heart shall rejoice, and your joy no man taketh from you.
23. And in that day ye shall ask me nothing. Verily, verily, I say unto you, Whatsoever ye shall ask the Father in my name, he will give it you.
24. Hitherto have ye asked nothing in my name: ask, and ye shall receive, that your joy may be full. (John 16:16-24)

Our Lord here makes a statement which was enigmatic to the disciples, but clear in terms of history. In v. 16, He declares, "A little while, and ye shall not see me: and again, a little while, and ye shall see me, because I go to the Father" (v. 16). Soon, after His crucifixion, resurrection, and ascension, they would no longer see Him. He will ascend to the Father, and then they will see and understand Him as never before. The two words translated as *see* are different; the second *see* (*theoreo*) means to see the meaning of something. They would then see more than the incarnate Jesus; they would understand who He was and is. They would not only see Jesus Christ but also Christology. The baptismal creeds of the early church saw the doctrine of Christ as essential. In Philippians 2:9-11 we have the basic baptismal affirmation of the early church, "Jesus Christ is Lord." Here the Jesus of history affirms the Jesus of doctrine, and the modernists, confounded by this unity, can only deny its historicity. But this finally means the denial of all history, because the alternative to the triune God is chance and meaninglessness. Hegel's neo-pantheism could only use Christ as a facade for an alien faith which could only self-destruct.

219

The disciples, after Jesus' ascension, would then understand what they now only saw physically. Thus, Jesus' departure would enable them to understand who He was, God made flesh.

"Then said some of his disciples among themselves, What is this that he saith unto us, A little while, and ye shall not see me; and again, a little while, and ye shall see me; and, Because I go to my Father?" (v. 17). They understood what He said, but they rejected it. Their statement shows a firm grasp of His meaning. *Understanding* is a religious fact. It means comprehension of the presupposition and implications of what is said. But the disciples were rejecting the *meaning* of our Lord's words. "They said therefore, What is this that he saith, A little while? we cannot tell what he saith" (v. 18). There is a petulance in this statement. The disciples are in effect saying, Say it isn't so! Their frame of reference was a Jewish messianic kingdom. Given this presupposition, nothing Jesus said made sense. Our Lord had prepared them for His cross (Matt. 16: 21-23), and they had rejected His words. Their failure to understand was due to their intense desire that He should be what they wanted Him to be.

In v. 19, we are told, "Now Jesus knew that they were desirous to ask Him, and said unto them, Do ye inquire among yourselves of that I said, A little while and ye shall not see me: and again a little while, and ye shall see me?" They did understand that later they would see or know who and what He was, but they were, at the least, unhappy at the thought that, at present, they did not truly know Him.

Our Lord said that, in a short time, they would truly know Him, but they *feared* that knowledge. They wanted the Messiah of their imaginations. Today, many people cling to a favorite verse, which is well and good, except that too often God and Christ are reinterpreted in terms of that text and a purely personal application. This means making ourselves the principle of interpretation. In v. 20, our Lord continues, "Verily, verily, I say unto you, that ye shall weep and lament, but your sorrow shall be turned into joy." The world, i.e., fallen men, shall rejoice at my crucifixion, while you are sorrowful, but, with my resurrection, there will be a reversal, and the joy will be yours.

This verse describes the reaction in our Lord's day to His seeming defeat. It also describes the attitudes of our time. The world wants to rejoice at every apparent defeat that Christ and His people suffer, and it works to ensure that defeat. But our God is in the resurrection business, and every seeming defeat becomes a triumph.

"A woman when she is in travail hath sorrow, because her hour is come; but as soon as she is delivered of the child, she remembereth no more the anguish, for joy that a man is born into the world" (v. 21). Delivery is painful for a woman, but the birth of a child brings joy. What is specified here is a male child. Feminists resent such texts, but the plain meaning is that the birth of a male child meant both safety and dominion: safety, because the future care and protection of the family was the prerogative of the a male, and dominion, because the male's calling to exercise dominion would advance God's Kingdom. The word translated as *child* is *paideon*, and it means strictly a *child*, but then *anthropos*, *man*, is used, fixing the meaning.

"And ye now therefore have sorrow; but I will see you again, and your heart shall rejoice, and your joy no man taketh from you" (v. 22). The resurrection will end their sorrow, and the knowledge that their risen Lord is King over all creation and their Redeemer will give them a lasting joy.

In v. 23, our Lord says, "And in that day ye shall ask me nothing. Verily, verily, I say unto ye, Whatsoever ye shall ask the Father in my name, he will give you." To "ask me nothing" means that they will ask no questions and have no doubts. Ignorance and doubt will be replaced with faith and trust. Doubting questions will be replaced by the prayers of faith.

"Hitherto ye have asked nothing in my name; ask, and ye shall receive, that your joy may be full" (v. 24). This echoes Matthew 7:7. Because they did not know Him in the fullness of His office and being, they had not yet prayed to Jesus, or in Jesus' Name. Now they are to pray to God through Him, the Intercessor, and they shall be answered, "that your joy may be full," i.e. completed.

The meaning of these verses is that the disciples will soon know clearly who Jesus is; they will understand His relationship to God the Father, and mankind, and to history. Then their joy will be full, because they will see Christ's Kingship and His Kingdom as the goal of history, and Jesus as Lord over all.

Chapter Fifty-Three
Faith and Knowledge
(John 16:25-33)

25. These things have I spoken unto you in proverbs: but the time cometh, when I shall no more speak unto you in proverbs, but I shall shew you plainly of the Father.
26. At that day ye shall ask in my name: and I say not unto you, that I will pray the Father for you:
27. For the Father himself loveth you, because ye have loved me, and have believed that I came out from God.
28. I came forth from the Father, and am come into the world: again, I leave the world, and go to the Father.
29. His disciples said unto him, Lo, now speakest thou plainly, and speakest no proverb.
30. Now are we sure that thou knowest all things, and needest not that any man should ask thee: by this we believe that thou camest forth from God.
31. Jesus answered them, Do ye now believe?
32. Behold, the hour cometh, yea, is now come, that ye shall be scattered, every man to his own, and shall leave me alone: and yet I am not alone, because the Father is with me.
33. These things I have spoken unto you, that in me ye might have peace. In the world ye shall have tribulation: but be of good cheer; I have overcome the world. (John 16:25-33)

In vv. 25 and 29 our Lord uses a word translated as "proverbs." It can also be translated as "parable" and the word refers to something which is both concealed and revealed, a "by the way" statement for the wise and discerning. Our Lord's statement in v. 25 tells us that He would, after the resurrection, speak "plainly," i.e., more openly and directly. This does not mean that parabolic sayings are not plain, but that they must be studied with dedication. The parables are simple and direct, but their subtle implications are not grasped by those who will not hear. We are not always ready for a fullness of understanding. Knowledge is more than information, more than facts or data; it is a moral perception. Those who view knowledge merely as data can be very learned yet unwise.

Our Lord continues, "At that day ye shall ask in my name; and I say not unto you, that I will pray the Father for you: For the Father himself loveth you, because ye have loved me, and have believed that I came out from God" (vv. 26-27). The frame of reference is the knowledge of God, Father, Son, and Holy Spirit. The disciples are at the moment bewildered and unable to understand the meaning of what is happening to their Lord. From the resurrection through Pentecost, the Father will grant them understanding hearts, so that the present bewilderment will be replaced with knowledge. There are many statements about prayer in John's Gospel, and some, like this, have a specific reference.

Because the disciples, however bewildered by the turn of events, truly loved their Lord, the Father, who loved them, would give them the grace of knowledge. Christ's intercession here ordained their status and their belief in Jesus Christ as the Son of God.

In v. 28, our Lord declares, "I came forth from the Father, and am come into the world: again, I leave the world, and go to the Father." That mission will shortly be accomplished, and so I will leave you and return to the Father.

Our Lord most emphatically rules: ours is not a world of chance. All things move in terms of the design of the Father, and not a leaf falls, nor a hair, apart from Him. The disciples are deeply troubled by the turn of events; they do not meet human expectations. Our Lord assures them that all things are moving totally in terms of the Father's will:

> 29. His disciples said unto him, Lo, now speakest thou plainly, and speakest no proverbs.
> 30. Now are we sure that thou knowest all things, and needest not that any man should ask thee: by this we believe that thou camest forth from God. (John 16:29-30)

The total assurance of our Lord enabled the disciples to more clearly perceive His divine nature. As a result, they felt that they had moved beyond parables and into plain knowledge. Jesus certainly had the power to answer unasked questions; He need not wait for any man to ask Him questions. As truly divine, a Member of the Godhead, He knew what was in men's hearts.

But the disciples were assuming that information is knowledge, and that learning and knowledge are identical. Modern man believes that "knowledge is power," by which he means that information or learning is the same as knowledge. Solomon tells us, "The fear of the LORD is the beginning (or, principal part) of knowledge" (Prov. 1:7). True knowledge is wisdom. "Wisdom is the principal thing; therefore get wisdom: and with all thy getting get understanding" (Prov. 4:7). The disciples too readily equated being informed with knowledge and faith. Our Lord therefore asks, "Do ye now believe?" (v. 31). The word *pisteuo*, a verb, is used by John ninety-eight times; the word *pistis*, a noun, is never used. John makes a very important distinction. Faith or belief is not a thing but an action, not a noun but a verb. Our Lord does not say, you do not believe, but rather, you do not yet know what it is to believe. You have not yet been tested and tried, not yet paid a price for your faith. Faith is the gift of God, but it is tried in the fire to refine and purify us. Only so can faith become, not merely a set of beliefs but our very life. Every faith will be tested, and no man can expect faith to be other than a gift of testing.

Our Lord continues, v. 32 and 33:

> 32. Behold, the hour cometh, yea, is now come, that ye shall be scattered, every man to his own, and shall leave me alone: and yet I am not alone, because the Father is with me.
> 33. These things I have spoken unto you, that in me, ye might have peace. In the world ye shall have tribulation: but be of good cheer; I have overcome the world.

As we have seen, knowledge is a moral fact. The testing of the disciples would shortly begin with Jesus' arrest, trial, crucifixion, and death. The disciples would scatter in fear, though later they would face death bravely. Their faith was not yet refined by fire, and they would desert Jesus. Yet Jesus was not alone, "because the Father is with me." In spite of this, on the cross, Jesus would cry out, "My God, my God, why hast thou forsaken me?" (Mark 15:34), because in our trials by fire, however much God be with us, we alone undergo the testing.

Events would scatter them, and they would experience tribulation in and from the world, because the world hates God the Father and God the Son, and does not know God the Spirit. In spite of this, they would have peace in Christ. For moral reasons, the ungodly neither know nor want to know the Trinity, but those who do know God shall have peace.

Therefore, they should "be of good cheer; I have overcome the world." The world was and is trying to overcome, destroy, and obliterate Jesus Christ. Yet, by His victory, His atoning death and resurrection, He is overcoming the world, creating a new human race, and empowering them to disciple all nations and make the world the Kingdom of God.

The knowledge they must seek is a religious and moral knowledge, and the victory that shall come is also religious and moral.

But the fallen world insists on separating morality from knowledge, and it denies all validity to morality, which is reduced to purely personal values. Knowledge is therefore falsified and denied.

In commenting on the use of the verb *believe*, we saw that John tells us that *knowledge* and *faith* go hand in hand. True faith gives moral perception to our understanding, so that, instead of more information, we have knowledge. It is subtle nuances like this that make John's Gospel so telling. To strip morality from knowledge is to deny and renounce it. This is a moral universe, and we can never truly know anything apart from that awareness.

Elsewhere in the New Testament, *faith* is used as a noun. It describes various related things, such as trust, an aspect of God's grace to us, and a deposit of doctrinal premises (Jude 3: "...the faith which was once delivered unto the saints"). For John, it is an action based upon knowledge, of which Christ is the Alpha and the Omega.

Chapter Fifty-Four

The Father and the Son
(John 17:1-5)

1. These words spake Jesus, and lifted up his eyes to heaven, and said, Father, the hour is come; glorify thy Son, that thy Son also may glorify thee:
2. As thou hast given him power over all flesh, that he should give eternal life to as many as thou hast given him.
3. And this is life eternal, that they might know thee the only true God, and Jesus Christ, whom thou hast sent.
4. I have glorified thee on the earth: I have finished the work which thou gavest me to do.
5. And now, O Father, glorify thou me with thine own self with the glory which I had with thee before the world was. (John 17:1-5)

Chapter 17 of John's Gospel is often called the high priestly prayer by Jesus, or, the prayer of consecration. As Westcott pointed out, there are three main sections to this prayer. *First* in vv. 1-5, the subject is the Son and the Father. *Second*, vv. 6-19 concerns the Son and His immediate disciples, while, *third*, vv. 20-26 centers on the Son and the Church.[1]

Jesus faces the cross, but the prayer is not that of a victim, but rather a victor, not the response of one who is being moved and governed by events, but of one who determines them. Soon after this prayer, in the Garden of Gethsemane, our Lord prayed, as He faced the agony of the cross, "Father, if thou be willing, remove this cup from me: nevertheless not my will, but thine, be done" (Luke 22:42). As truly man, Jesus knew the horror of crucifixion, but He also knew the will of God.

The prayer was spoken aloud (v. 1), and the Father heard it. It was a prayer to God, but it was also a statement about the Father and the Son which the disciples needed to hear to arm them for their own calling in the days ahead.

In v. 1, our Lord says, "Father, the hour is come; glorify thy Son, that thy Son also may glorify thee." The statement, "The hour is come," like so much else in Scripture, presupposes God's absolute predestination. As James said in Acts 15:18, "Known unto God are all his works from the beginning of the world." Paul in Ephesians 1:4 tells us that God "hath chosen us in Him before the foundation of the world, that we should be holy and without blame before Him in love." The fact that God ordained the cross did not eliminate its pain and agony, but it made an integral part of a glorious plan.

[1.] B.F. Westcott: *The Gospel According to St. John* (Grand Rapids, MI: Eerdmans, 1881, 1954), 237.

227

"Glorify thy Son, that thy Son may glorify thee" means, as Leon Morris pointed out, that the cross was the glory of Jesus Christ. God was glorified by Christ's work because they are one God. [2]As Plummer noted, "To make God known is to glorify Him."[3] The cross was a revelation of who and what God is, and a glorification of His majesty and grace.

In v. 2, our Lord continues, "As thou hast given Him power (or, authority) over all flesh, that he should give eternal life to as many as thou hast given Him." In Jesus Christ, the power and the authority of the Godhead are one and the same. All fallen mankind is subject to Christ's royal power. Those who are *given* to Christ by God's predestinational power are *given* eternal life with Him.

In v. 3, we are told, "And this is life eternal, that they might know thee the only true God, and Jesus Christ, whom thou hast sent." Eternal life is defined as knowing Jesus Christ as our Redeemer and Lord. Not to know Him is implicitly eternal death. Because Jesus Christ is the way, the truth, and the *life* (John 14:6), not to know Him *is* a form of death. "The only true God" is an important statement. In antiquity, and around the world since, most cultures are syncretistic in religious faith. They insist on regarding all religions as essentially one, and hence their assimilation of the practices of other religions is easily undertaken.

As we have previously seen, knowledge is a moral fact, and to know God as the only true God means to know Jesus as the One sent by the Father. The word *sent* again refers to God's absolute determination of all things.

In v. 4, Jesus says, "I have glorified thee on earth: I have finished the work which thou gavest me to do." By speaking of all His life, ministry, death, and resurrection as one *work*, our Lord makes clear that His existence has a common pattern, the glorification of God. The glory of God is seen in all His works, notably in creation, redemption, and providence. By our salvation, we enter into the Lord's Kingdom and the realm of His glory, whereas the ungodly go from shame to shame and into eternal reprobation. Jesus glorified God on earth by revealing the majestic grace of God: He accomplished what He was sent to do. We likewise glorify God when we do the task we are called to do by His grace and Spirit.

In v. 5, our Lord prays, "And now, O Father, glorify thou me with thine own self with the glory which I had with thee before the world was." When my work is done, as it shortly will be, glorify Me in heaven as I have glorified Thee on earth. According to Plummer, we have in vv. 4 and 5 two great declarations, namely,

---

[2] Leon Morris: *The Gospel According to John* (Grand Rapids, MI: Eerdmans, 1971, 1977), 718.
[3] A. Plummer: *The Gospel According to St. John* (Cambridge, England: Cambridge University Press, 1880, 1906), 307.

(1) that the Son is in Person distinct from the Father; (2) that the Son, existing in glory with the Father from all eternity, working in obedience to the Father on earth, existing in glory with the Father now, is in Person one and the same. [4]

The doctrine of Christology was not an invention of the church in a later age; rather, it took time for the church to begin to understand the Scriptures.

Our Lord here makes a distinction, but not a separation, between Himself as God the Son from all eternity, and His life as an incarnate being, both God and man. He speaks of His status "before the world was." In Philippians 2:9-11, Paul refers to this and speaks of the exaltation of Jesus Christ in heaven.

Morris, in his commentary, says of Jesus the Christ, "He looks for glory in the last place that men would seek it, namely, in the cross."[5]

The preexistence of the Son is presupposed in these verses, especially v. 5. The consciousness of this by Jesus, the incarnate one, is clearly apparent.

> The High Priestly Prayer is *high-priestly* not merely because of its being the *intercession* of Christ for His entire kingdom of God, but also on account of its consummation of the sacrifice of Christ, His offering up of Himself, vv. 5, 13, and especially v. 19. At the same time, however it is also *prophetic* prayer, in that, seizing up the principal periods and stages, it sketches and announces with divine certitude the entire progress of the kingdom of God in development. None the less it is *kingly* conscious of His internal victory over the world, and believing in the *consequences* of this victory, Christ transports Himself, not to the standpoint of the Last Day or of the *Ascension-Day*, but to that of the deliverance upon Golgotha: *It is finished.*[6]

Our words reveal us. How much more is this true of the word of Jesus Christ. Modernists have tried to excise from history as much of the Gospels as possible, but, even in the fragments they allow as history, the deity of Jesus Christ comes through powerfully. The pitiful absurdities of unbelief cannot stand against the Light.

[4] *ibid.*, 309.
[5] Morris, *op. cit.*, 721.
[6] John Peter Lange: *Commentary on the Holy Scriptures, John* (Grand Rapids, MI: Zondervan, reprint, n.d.), 524f.

Chapter Fifty-Five

Truth
(John 17:6-19)

6. I have manifested thy name unto the men which thou gavest me out of the world: thine they were, and thou gavest them me; and they have kept thy word.

7. Now they have known that all things whatsoever thou hast given me are of thee.

8. For I have given unto them the words which thou gavest me; and they have received them, and have known surely that I came out from thee, and they have believed that thou didst send me.

9. I pray for them: I pray not for the world, but for them which thou hast given me; for they are thine.

10. And all mine are thine, and thine are mine; and I am glorified in them.

11. And now I am no more in the world, but these are in the world, and I come to thee. Holy father, keep through thine own name those whom thou hast given me, that they may be one, as we are.

12. While I was with them in the world, I kept them in thy name: those that thou gavest me I have kept, and none of them is lost, but the son of perdition; that the scripture might be fulfilled.

13. And now come I to thee; and these things I speak in the world, that they might have my joy fulfilled in themselves.

14. I have given them thy word; and the world hath hated them, because they are not of the world, even as I am not of the world.

15. I pray not that thou shouldest take them out of the world, but that thou shouldest keep them from the evil.

16. They are not of the world, even as I am not of the world.

17. Sanctify them through thy truth: thy word is truth.

18. As thou hast sent me into the world, even so have I also sent them into the world.

19. And for their sakes I sanctify myself, that they also might be sanctified through the truth. (John 17:6-19)

In vv. 6-19, our Lord prays for His disciples. He knows that His trial and crucifixion will have a shattering effect on them, and, while personally facing the supreme agony of the cross, He prays for them.

His first statement in this prayer is, "I have manifested thy name unto the men which thou gavest me out of the world" (v. 6). The *name* of God is really a non-name, Jehovah, or Jahweh, meaning *I am that I am*, or He who is (Ex. 3:14). Names are limitations, and God is beyond limits. He is the eternally existent One.

Jesus manifested the meaning of that Name: He had made clear that God's purpose could not be equated with man's, nor could God's concerns be reduced to man-centered ones. It is man's obligation to believe, serve, and obey God, not God, man. The religious leaders understood this clearly, and they rejected Him. The disciples had not understood this, but they were ready to die with Him (John 11:16).

Our Lord continues in His prayer, "Thine they were, and thou gavest them me; and they have kept thy word" (v. 6). The disciples came to know Jesus as Lord because God had ordained their coming and their believing. They had been faithful to God's word while not fully understanding it.

In v. 7, our Lord proceeds, "Now they have know that all things whatsoever thou hast given me are of thee." Although there was much that the disciples did not understand, they did recognize that Jesus came from God and that, in some way, He and God were one.

Verse 8 stresses this fact:

> For I have given unto them the words which thou gavest me; and they have received them, and have known surely that I came out from thee, and they have believed that thou didst send me.

The disciples had received the specific utterances of Jesus Christ as the very words of God. Whatever their failings in grasping the meaning of Christ's coming, they knew that He came from God. On this, they were steadfast. Our Lord emphasizes the fact that the disciples knew that Jesus came "out from God and had been sent by God."

In v. 9, our Lord says, "I pray for them. I pray not for the world, but for them which thou hast given me; for they are thine." *First*, our Lord tells us that He prays for His disciples, not for the fallen and hostile world around them. The world is at war with God, and it needs converting. This will be the disciples task later on. *Second*, the disciples are God-given, and they are God's property. They belong to God who made them and redeemed them.

Verse 10, "And all mine are thine, and thine are mine; and I am glorified in them." Because the disciples are God's possession, they are also Christ's, and, with Pentecost, they are also the Spirit's. The disciples are told of the unity of the Godhead and their relationship to the triune God. They are His possession. They are not in the position of command: God is. It is God the Son who, before His ascension, tells them, "Go ye into all the world" (Matt. 28:18-20). We are God's possession, and therefore He can command us freely.

In vv. 10-11, we read:

> 10. And all mine are thine, and thine are mine; and I am glorified in them.
> 11. And now I am no more in the world, but these are in the world, and I come to thee. Holy Father, keep through thine own name those whom thou hast given me, that they may be one, as we are.

Our Lord's prayer here calls for the unity of the disciples. The prayer for the church follows, beginning in v. 20. Now it is the unity of His immediate followers which is our Lord's concern. We know that, despite some differences, great unity prevailed. Some scholars, often with a will to create false divisions, have posited centers of apostolic disharmony around Peter, Paul, James, and others. We have instead a readiness to come to a common understanding.

Our Lord looks forward to going to the Father. He commits the disciples into the hands of the Father. They are the property of both Father and Son. Moreover, Christ says, "I am glorified in them." Their faithfulness will soon bring wisdom and understanding, and then their witness will glorify the Son, even as their faith glorifies Him now.

Jesus Christ's departure from the world is imminent. He will soon go to the Father, and He asks the Father to "Keep through thine own name those whom thou hast given me, that they may be one, as we are." Jesus Christ is the revelation of the Name of God: history and time cannot comprehend Him, for He is their Maker. To keep the disciples in the Name means to keep them centered in all their being on the transcendent Trinity, on the nature of God as the focus of their lives and their work. It meant going beyond a messianic hope of a Jewish world-order to the Kingdom of God; it required moving from a man-centered to a God-centered faith. Theology must replace anthropology. To be *kept* in the Name of God is to be preserved from an anthropocentric perspective. Only so could the disciples be one as God is one.

> 12. While I was with them in the world, I kept them in thy name; those that thou gavest me I have kept, and none of them is lost, but the son of perdition; that the scripture might be fulfilled.
> 13. And now come I to thee, and those things I speak in the world, that they might have my joy fulfilled in themselves. (John 17:12-13)

Our Lord declares that He had kept the disciples in God's *Name*, in the reality of God's being, nature, and power. They had understood Him less *with respect to His mission,* less than the religious leaders did, but they had known Him to be God's presence on earth. Their knowledge was faulty, but it was morally sound. Only Judas, "the son of perdition," was lost, as he was predestined to be. Now, as the Lord faces the end, He rejoices at the prospect of soon being in heaven with the Father.

> 14. I have given them thy word; and the world hath hated them, because they are not of the world, even as I am not of the world.
> 15. I pray not that thou shouldest take them out of the world, but that thou shouldest keep them from the evil. (John 17:14-15)

Our Lord had given to the disciples the necessary revelation of Himself and of His message. The fallen humanity of Adam recognized our Lord's followers as their enemies, despite their limited understanding of Him. The followers were obviously not members of this fallen humanity, and hence were resented and hated, even as Jesus Christ was and is. Our Lord does not pray for the removal of His followers from this world because their calling is to conquer it and make it God's Kingdom. He therefore prays that God will keep them from "the evil," or, literally, "the evil one." Evil in abstraction does not exist. Murder, adultery, theft, and other sins are things people do. Evil is a personal act; sin is an offense committed by sinners, by fallen man. The reference is thus to Satan, who first set forth the premise of sin, every man as his own god, determining for himself what is good and what is evil, becoming his own source of law and morality (Gen. 3:5). Greek philosophy reduced everything to abstractions, to forms or ideas, whereas Biblical revelation declares the absolute Person, God, and mankind as made in His image, as persons.

Our Lord then says, "They are not of the World, even as I am not of the world. Sanctify them through thy truth; thy word is truth" (vv. 16-17). God is truth: Father, Son, and Holy Spirit together. The word of God is truth. It is God who is truth because He is reality. "I am God, and there is none else" (Isa. 46:9). To forsake God is to forsake reality, to deny the Truth. Our Lord prays that His followers be separated to the reality of God, for there is no other Truth. Various cultures have differently defined truths, and, currently, *truth* itself is denied as a valid concept. Reality is seen by many as meaningless, as a surd, so that truth is impossible in such a scheme of things.

Then, in vv. 18 and 19, our Lord ends the section of His prayer that is for His immediate disciples:

> 18. As thou hast sent me into the world, even so have I sent them into the world.
> 19. And for their sakes I sanctify myself, that they also might be sanctified through the truth.

Our Lord sets forth a remarkable doctrine of sanctification, i.e., of separation to holiness. God the Father sent the Son into the world to redeem fallen mankind and to create a new human race. The Kingdom of God is to be created out of the members of the Kingdom of Man. Our Lord became man to redeem and sanctify us. This requires His disciples to carry on the Lord's work by sanctifying themselves to the task of bringing in all peoples and nations. They are to be "sanctified through the truth." Sin is rebellion against God; it is madness and death. The truth, the reality of God, separates Christ's disciples from the world of lies, from the madness and unreality of sin, from acting as though God the Lord did not exist. It delivers them from the suicidal blindness of sin (Prov. 8:36) into the light and reality of God, into salvation. The more the truth of God, the reality of His being and the truth of His word, possesses us, the more we are strong and effective in His service.

Chapter Fifty-Six

Unity in Christ
(John 17:20-26)

20. Neither pray I for these alone, but for them also which shall believe on me through their word;
21. That they all may be one; as thou, Father, art in me, and I in thee, that they also may be one in us: that the world may believe that thou hast sent me.
22. And the glory which thou gavest me I have given them; that they may be one, even as we are one:
23. I in them, and thou in me, that they may be made perfect in one; and that the world may know that thou hast sent me, and hast loved them, as thou hast loved me.
24. Father, I will that they also, whom thou hast given me, be with me where I am; that they may behold my glory, which thou hast given me: for thou lovedst me before the foundation of the world.
25. O righteous Father, the world hath not known thee: but I have known thee, and these have known that thou hast sent me.
26. And I have declared unto them thy name, and will declare it: that the love wherewith thou hast loved me may be in them, and I in them.(John 17:20-26)

We have here Christ's prayer for the whole church of all time and in all places. The prayer begins, in vv. 20-21, with a goal of oneness, unity:

20. Neither pray I for these alone, but for them also which shall believe on me through their word;
21. That they all may be one; as thou, Father, art in me, and I in thee, that they also may be one in us; that the world may believe that thou hast sent me.

The opening words of v. 21 are commonly used by modernist ecumenical groups, "That they all may be one." Their goal is an organic, institutional union of bureaucracies, not the unity of faith. Such men assume the non-historicity of John and the other Gospels, but they do believe in the union of all churches.

Our Lord begins by looking beyond the disciples to the believers of all times. He is *not* speaking of nominal church members, but of the redeemed of all ages. There can be no unity with the unredeemed. He prays that believers in all ages may be as united by faith as are the Father and the Son. This goal can only be *fully* attained in heaven, but it must be an objective on earth, one we seek to approximate all the days of our lives. The unity of believers will be a mighty witness both to and against the world, to convict them and to bring them to Christ. Our unity must reflect that of the Father and the Son.

In v. 22, our Lord stresses this unity with the Father: "And the glory which thou gavest me, I have given them; that they may be one, even as we are one." The word *glory* in Scripture refers to many things associated with God in Himself, the reality of His Being, His absolute power and majesty, His royal and sovereign Person and rule, and much, much more. Christ here says that the glory He received, as the incarnate One, from the Father, He now gives to His redeemed peoples. The true Christians are alone "more than conquerors" in Christ because they live in the reality of His Being and in its power. The goal of their new lives is that they become one, even as the Father and the Son are One. The Spirit is not mentioned here because He will soon come and lead them into all truth.

In v. 23, our Lord says,

> I in them, and thou in me, that they may be made perfect in me; and that the world may know that thou hast sent me, and hast loved them, as thou hast loved me.

We have again a procession of grace and power, from God the Father, through God the Son, to the believer and to one another among Christians. This procession, as we have seen, is to come through the Spirit. But, above all, the procession from the Trinity to the believer and through the Christian is one of love; the word for *love* is the verbal form of *agape*, used here and in v. 26. It means the uncaused love, i.e., not grounded in man's merit or his deserved love, but in the grace of God. The believer, having received grace, manifests grace.

Our Lord continues, in v. 24:

> Father, I will that they also, whom thou hast given me, be with me where I am; that they may behold my glory, which thou hast given me; for thou lovedst me before the foundation of the world.

Our Lord here prays for the vindication of the believer's faith. His redeemed people will undergo hostility, hatred, and even death. If Christ's elect can see in heaven the fullness of Christ's glory with the Father, they will be fully vindicated in their faith. There will then be a joyful and triumphant exuberance in the reality of the unity of the Godhead and grace from the Throne. All the redeemed were ordained to be Christ's from all eternity, even as from all eternity God the Father loved Jesus Christ, the incarnate One. Eternity, like infinity, is too vast for the mind of man to grasp, and to comprehend the greatness of God's love for us is beyond our capabilities, but we are able to show our gratitude for all that God is and does.

The prayer concludes, in vv. 25-26, with these words:

> 25. O righteous Father, the world hath not know thee; but I have known thee, and these have known that thou hast sent me.

26. And I have declared unto them thy name, and will declare it; that the love wherewith thou hast loved me may be in them, and I in them.

The name of God may be used by the world, and the idea of God invoked, but the world does not know God, our Lord says. "But I have known thee," and the redeemed know that Jesus Christ was sent from God. Jesus has *declared* the Name of God to the world: He has made known God, He has revealed God to all who will hear Him, and He will continue to declare it through His followers. The goal of this declaration is that God's love for Jesus Christ, His last Adam (1 Cor. 15:45ff), may be known to this new human race. The purpose of this knowledge is that the love of God for Jesus Christ, His new Adam, may be in them, and that Christ Himself might indwell in them.

The goal is unity in faith and in knowledge. Its ground is truth, the reality of God and the glory of His grace and purpose. This unity is not a matter of feeling, but of nature. It exists because we belong, as members of Jesus Christ's new humanity, to the Kingdom of God. We are a new creation with an eternal destiny. Ours is a unity of nature, our new nature in Christ. As we grow in grace, we grow in unity with the Father and His redeemed people. At the same time, this growth separates us from the fallen humanity around us, because we are to them an alien people.

The world's idea of unity is union, a one-world, one-church order. We have those who argue for salvation by any religion and hold that there are many roads to God. Our unity with God by His grace will make for our disunity with the world. To be in agreement with everything and every person and faith is a form of death, for the dead alone are passive towards all things. The premise of Christian unity is Jesus Christ and our faithfulness to God's every word.

Unity itself is not necessarily good, if we are in union with evil, or with criminal groups. Unless we begin with God and His word, we will assume man and his word as our premise.

Our humanistic age rejects God as its starting point because its scientific views demand "hard facts." "Seeing is believing," we are told. But, as Joseph Parker said, "Who has seen life? Where does life reside in the body? Put a finger on the residence of life, saying, Here you will find it, and nowhere else. No man has seen life."[1] No man has seen God, but Jesus Christ is the exegesis, the declaration of God.

---

[1]. Joseph Parker: *The People's Bible,* Vol. XXII, *John* (New York, NY: Funk & Wagnalls, n.d., reprint), 378.

Chapter Fifty-Seven
Malchus' Ear
(John 18:1-11)

1. When Jesus had spoken these words, he went forth with his disciples over the brook Cedron, where was a garden, into the which he entered, and his disciples.
2. And Judas also, which betrayed him, knew the place: for Jesus ofttimes resorted thither with his disciples.
3. Judas then, having received a band of men and officers from the chief priests and Pharisees, cometh thither with lanterns and torches and weapons.
4. Jesus therefore, knowing all things that should come upon him, went forth, and said unto them, Whom seek ye?
5. They answered him, Jesus of Nazareth. Jesus saith unto them, I am he. And Judas also, which betrayed him, stood with them.
6. As soon then as he had said unto them, I am he, they went backward, and fell to the ground.
7. Then asked he them again, Whom seek ye? and they said, Jesus of Nazareth.
8. Jesus answered, I have told you that I am he: if therefore ye seek me, let these go their way:
9. That the saying might be fulfilled, which he spake, Of them which thou gavest me have I lost none.
10. Then Simon Peter having a sword drew it, and smote the high priest's servant, and cut off his right ear. the servant's name was Malchus.
11. Then said Jesus unto Peter, put up thy sword into the sheath: the cup which my Father hath given me, shall I not drink it? (John 18:1-11)

These verses are properly titled by many "The Betrayal," but John stresses Christ's status, not as a victim, but as the Messiah in His glorification. Until this moment, Christ's conflict has been with the religious leaders. Now, as Rudolf Bultmann pointed out, another phenomenon advances against Jesus, *the Roman State.*[1] The world at its best, in its religious and civil forms, was now arrayed against the Christ, man's greatest means against God incarnate.

The disciples and Jesus crossed the brook Kedron. When the Passover lambs were killed at the Temple, their blood was poured on the altar as an offering to God. Many lambs were sacrificed; thirty years later, a census counted 256,000 lambs offered. This tells us how many *families* of Judeans and pilgrims were in Jerusalem. From the altar, a channel led to the brook Kedron, and the blood flowed into it. When Jesus crossed the brook, it probably still ran red from the blood of the Passover lambs, a grim

---

[1.] Rudolf Bultmann: *The Gospels of John, A Commentary* (Philadelphia, PA: Westminster Press, 1971), 633.

239

reminder to Jesus Christ that He Himself would be the true Passover Lamb.[2]

His destination was the garden of Gethsemane. It was not open to the general public, but some wealthy citizen had apparently given a key to Jesus and the disciples, who found there a quiet retreat when in Jerusalem.[3]

Judas knew this, and so he came there with a band of soldiers sent by the chief priests and Pharisees to arrest Him. The *officers* mentioned in v. 3 were Temple police; the band or *speira*, a Greek word, could mean, 1) a Roman cohort of 600 men; 2) a cohort of auxiliary soldiers consisting of 1,000 men; or 3) a *maniple*, a detachment of 200 men.[4] For even 200 men to be sent out to arrest a lone man meant that they feared He would have a vast throng of supporters surrounding Him. They came with torches, lanterns, and weapons.

Jesus went forward to meet them, asking, "Whom seek ye?" (v. 4). The answer was, "Jesus of Nazareth." Jesus answered, "I am he." Judas was with the crowd (v. 5). When Jesus identified Himself, the crowd stepped back, and, in so doing, stepped on those crowding behind them; they all stumbled and fell to the ground (v. 6). Again our Lord asked, "Whom seek ye?," and they said, "Jesus of Nazareth" (v. 7). Jesus answered, "I have told you that I am he: if therefore ye seek me, let these go their way," meaning his disciples (v. 8). He had earlier declared that none would be lost in this coming trial (John 17:12).

At this point, Simon Peter, seeing the fearfulness of the arresting men, drew his sword against the high priest's servant (Matt. 26:51; Mark 14:47, Luke 22:50-52), which was a blow the man ducked. His ear, however, was cut off; our Lord then healed the wound (Luke 22:51). Our Lord's act here is not recorded by John, for whom the necessary details are only those which tell us of His Person and task. John does tell us that the man's name was Malchus (v. 10).

Our Lord's word to Peter, and to any other disciple about to pull out his sword, was, "Put up thy sword into the sheath: the cup which my Father hath given me, shall I not drink it?" (v. 11). The future of mankind depended on His atoning work. It was inconceivable that He would avoid that calling.

The presence of Malchus, the high priest's servant, has an irony to it. The word in the Greek text is *doulon*, a form of *doulas*, a bondservant. In effect, Malchus stood between two high priests, Caiaphas (John 11:49) and Jesus Christ (Hebrews 7:22-28). Caiaphas could regenerate no man; Jesus Christ

---

2. William Barclay: *The Gospel of John, vol. 2* (Philadelphia, PA: Westminster Press, 1955, 1975), 221.
3. *ibid.*, 222.
4. *ibid.*

could raise the dead and make a man a new creation. To his dying day, Malchus was an unwitting testimony, a witness to the power of Jesus Christ as against Caiaphas.

The healing of Malchus' ear was Christ's last miracle, His last ministry to human suffering and need. All His miracles testified to the fact that He was God incarnate. Now the glory of the atonement would replace miracles. For a time, Christ continued to work miracles through His apostles, but these eventually gave way to the glory of the atonement and the resurrection. The promise was now more than healing: it was eternal life in Him and personal and cosmic resurrection and renewal.

A key statement in our text is in v. 6: literally, Jesus does not say, "I am he," but *"I am."* In other words, He declared Himself to be God, *I AM*, declared in Exodus 3:14, the eternal Being, the Lord, Creator, and Governor over all things. It was the combination of His boldness in stepping forward and this statement of self-identification that made the throng of soldiers and Temple officers fall down in confusion. They were badly shaken in finding One who was not a victim, One Who confronted them as their Lord. The soldiers, even as they arrested Him, were a disturbed lot, because they had been confronted by a statement implying deity which was followed by a miraculous act of healing, a cut off ear restored.

Verse 12, properly a part of the next section, is naturally related to vv. 1-11. We are told that the arresting officers *bound* Jesus; they tied Him up for delivery to the high priest's kangaroo court. They had seen the miracle of Malchus' ear and had heard Jesus declare Himself to be one with God, but they still felt that their bonds could hold Him.

Too many scholars and theologians place bands on Jesus, assuming that they can contain Him. It would be easier to chain the universe than to chain God the Son, God incarnate.

John writes with a fine irony, as do the other evangelists, Matthew, Mark, and Luke. The blindness of sin is a radical one, and it leads to blindness in the most deadly form, an inability to recognize God's truth and Person.

Chapter Fifty-Eight

The Ecclesiastical or Church Trial
(John 18:12-27)

12. Then the band and the captain and officers of the Jews took Jesus, and bound him,

13. And led him away to Annas first; for he was father in law to Caiaphas, which was the high priest that same year.

14. Now Caiaphas was he, which gave counsel to the Jews, that it was expedient that one man should die for the people.

15. And Simon Peter followed Jesus, and so did another disciple: that disciple was known unto the high priest, and went in with Jesus into the palace of the high priest.

16. But Peter stood at the door without. Then went out that other disciple, which was known unto the high priest, and spake unto her that kept the door, and brought in Peter.

17. Then saith the damsel that kept the door unto Peter, Art not thou also one of this man's disciples? He saith, I am not.

18. And the servants and officers stood there, who had made a fire of coals; for it was cold: and they warmed themselves: and Peter stood with them, and warmed himself.

19. The high priest then asked Jesus of his disciples, and of his doctrine.

20. Jesus answered him, I spake openly to the world; I ever taught in the synagogue, and in the temple, whither the Jews always resort; and in secret have I said nothing.

21. Why askest thou me? ask them which heard me, what I have said unto them: behold, they know what I said.

22. And when he had thus spoken, one of the officers which stood by struck Jesus with the palm of his hand, saying, Answerest thou the high priest so?

23. Jesus answered him, If I have spoken evil, bear witness of the evil: but if well, why smitest thou me?

24. Now Annas had sent him bound unto Caiaphas the high priest.

25. And Simon Peter stood and warmed himself. They said therefore unto him, Art not thou also one of his disciples? He denied it, and said, I am not.

26. One of the servants of the high priest, being his kinsman whose ear Peter cut off, saith, Did not I see thee in the garden with him?

27. Peter then denied again: and immediately the cock crew. (John 18:12-27)

Jesus was tried twice. The first trial was by the Sanhedrin, the second by the Roman civil authority.

The arresting officers bound Jesus. He was arrested on capital charges, with execution likely, and hence steps were taken to prevent escape. Also, given Jesus' popularity, the arrest was at night for fear of the crowds who normally followed Him (v. 12).

243

Jesus was led to Annas, a very powerful ex-high priest whose ties to Rome were so strong that he was able to secure the same office for five of his sons, and also for his son-in-law, Caiaphas. The name Annas in other forms is Ananius, Ananus, and Hanan. The family dominated the high priestly office from Annas' term, A.D. 7-14, on. The critical, primary examination was before Caiaphas, who then held office, but Annas was so important that Jesus was first led to him (v. 13).

Caiaphas was the man who had said that it was better for one man to die than for a nation to perish (v. 14; John 11:50-52).

John gives less space to the trial than we would expect, and he concentrates on Peter's denial of Christ. John was with Peter at the time. Both had indicated their readiness to die with Jesus, as had all the disciples. They were outside the examination room, but the open door enabled them to see and hear what happened and what was said. John was related to the ruling families and was able to gain entrance for them. He was inside much of the time but no doubt went back and forth and kept in touch with Peter. A serving girl at the door seemed to recognize Peter as a disciple, and she questioned him. Peter denied that he was a follower of Jesus (vv. 15-17). There was a fire in that area where various servants and officers warmed themselves, as did Peter. Again Peter was asked if he were not a disciple, and again he denied it (v. 25). A third time, a kinsman of Malchus, whose ear Peter had severed, asked the same question. This man had been one of the arresting party. Because of the darkness, identification was not certain. Again Peter denied Christ, "and immediately the cock crew" (vv. 26-27).

No man gained credit for standing faithfully for Jesus Christ. All had to acknowledge that they stood only by His grace, not by their merit. This gave them no ground for presumption, but only served as a motive for grateful and faithful service. Peter in his betrayal was not unique. Here he serves as a representative of all the disciples.

The trial of Jesus began with a demand that He give an accounting of His disciples and of His doctrine. Apparently some consideration had been given to arresting and trying all the disciples if any disturbances should erupt. Furthermore, they demanded an accounting of His teachings. They were insisting that Jesus give them what they wanted for His prosecution. The evidence in hand was highly favorable to Jesus, and included His healing miracles and more. The evidence against Him was miracles performed on the Sabbath. What was avoided was His messiahship, a touchy subject. What they had already found reprehensible in Him was that He declared Himself to be the Son of God. The religious leaders, in their statement to Pilate, said, "We have a law, and by our law he ought to die, because he made himself the Son of God" (John 19:7). Then as now, religious leaders find this offensive.

Jesus' response was direct. He said, "I spoke openly to the world; I ever taught in the synagogue, and in the temple" (v. 20). Ask of those who heard me, and you will get the truth if you want it (v. 21). Our Lord clearly states that the truth is no concern of the religious leaders: they seek only His condemnation. His ministry had been a very public one. They were avoiding the critical issues of His messiahship and deity. When Pilate did ask Him, "Art thou the King of the Jews?" (Matt. 27:11), the question was obviously uppermost in Pilate's mind. The religious leaders were not so direct.

On His refusal to answer Annas, an officer of the Sanhedrin slapped Jesus, saying, "Answerest thou the high priest so?" (v. 22). Annas was given this title, although no longer holding office, as a courtesy, even as ex-governors are now still called "Governor."

Jesus answered, again very pointedly, "If I have spoken evil, bear witness of the evil: but if well, why smitest thou me?" (v. 23). His answer was fearless and concise. They had no evidence against Him of any wrongdoing. As to who He was, they had more than enough evidence, and they wanted no part of it.

The only "evidence" admissible to this fraudulent court was "evidence" to convict. The rules of many a court then and now are opposed to the truth because men are evil, and, in our time, evil is too often both behind and before the bench. For an innocent man to be subject to an evil court is a travesty.

Jesus was then sent, still bound, to the court of the high priest, Caiaphas (v. 24). His challenge, "If I have spoken evil, bear witness of the evil" (v. 23), dared Annas to bring forth any evil word or deed in His life and ministry whereby they could rightfully try and convict Him. In effect, He said, Produce your evidence; you know there is none. This impossible task Annas passed on to Caiaphas.

Every attempt was made to give a semblance of legality to an illegal trial. According to the Bible, a man was a high priest for life. The Romans ended that. With the money-changing and the sale of sacrificial animals, a high priest at this time could become a millionaire within a year, and would be a powerful and dangerous man. As a result, frequent rotations were made mandatory by the Romans. Legally, in terms of Biblical law, Annas was still the high priest. Thus, in trying Jesus before Annas first and then Caiaphas, the sticklers for the details of the law would be satisfied. This was the spirit of Phariseeism, which infected the Sadducees as well.

In a fallen world, the last thing men want is the truth.

I have called this text "The Ecclesiastical or *Church* Trial," and with reason. Whenever the church, explicitly or implicitly, departs from Christ and the holy and inscriptured Word of God, the Bible, it departs from the truth and attempts to put Christ and His true church on trial.

Chapter Fifty-Nine

The Civil Trial, I
(John 18:28-40)

28. Then led they Jesus from Caiaphas unto the hall of judgment: and it was early; and they themselves went not into the judgment hall, lest they should be defiled; but that they might eat the passover.
29. Pilate then went out unto them, and said, What accusation bring ye against this man?
30. They answered and said unto him, If he were not a malefactor, we would not have delivered him up unto thee.
31. Then said Pilate unto them, Take ye him, and judge him according to your law. The Jews therefore said unto him, It is not lawful for us to put any man to death:
32. That the saying of Jesus might be fulfilled, which he spake, signifying what death he should die.
33. Then Pilate entered into the judgment hall again, and called Jesus, and said unto him, Art thou the king of the Jews?
34. Jesus answered him, Sayest thou this thing of thyself, or did others tell it thee of me?
35. Pilate answered, Am I a Jew? Thine own nation and the chief priests have delivered thee unto me: what hast thou done?
36. Jesus answered, My kingdom is not of this world: if my kingdom were of this world, then would my servants fight, that I should not be delivered to the Jews: but now is my kingdom not from hence.
37. Pilate therefore said unto him, Art thou a king then? Jesus answered, Thou sayest that I am a king. To this end was I born, and for this cause came I into the world, that I should bear witness unto the truth. Every one that is of the truth heareth my voice.
38. Pilate saith unto him, What is truth? and when he had said this, he went out again unto the Jews, and saith unto them, I find in him no fault at all.
39. But ye have a custom, that I should release unto you one at the passover: will ye therefore that I release unto you the King of the Jews?
40. Then cried they all again, saying, Not this man, but Barabbas. Now Barabbas was a robber. (John 18:28-40)

Night trials were illegal in Jewish law because all proceedings of a court had to be open and public. The illegal trial before Annas was during the night. Mark 15:1 tells us that the trial before the high priest Caiaphas was early in the morning, since 6 a.m. would have qualified as daytime. This trial was brief, and John tells us that at an early hour Jesus was led to the Roman hall of justice, which was also the legal place of residence for the Roman governor. The Praetorium commonly opened early, so the presence of the religious leaders would be no surprise. The early hour would prevent public awareness of what was happening until it was too late. We are told by John that the religious leaders refused to enter lest they be defiled, and thereby unable to take part in the Passover meal (v. 28). Gentile houses were regarded as unclean because it was believed that they routinely practiced abortions and threw the dead children down the drain. This meant a week's uncleanness for any Jew who entered.[1] Also, the Praetorium would not have been cleansed of leaven (Ex. 12:15).

Pilate was familiar with Jewish law. Roman governors could not afford to violate local customs without cause, so Pilate went out to them. Pilate is not introduced to us. John wrote while Jerusalem was still standing, so that the city and its rulers were familiar to all who chose to know. Proper procedure required that Pilate ask, What are the charges? (v. 29). Again, the religious leaders had a problem: what charges could they file? They chose to replace the truth with indignation: "If he were not a malefactor, we would not have delivered him up unto thee" (v. 30). With this, Pilate, who no doubt already knew much about the case, knew that he was in trouble. These men wanted an execution, not a fair trial. While they later accused Jesus of blasphemy (19:7), this was not an offense against Roman law: it was a Jewish form of offense. Later on, Jesus was charged with 1) seditious agitation, 2) forbidding the payment of taxes to Caesar, and 3) assuming the title, "King of the Jews" (Luke 23:3).[2] For the present, the charge of blasphemy was irrelevant, so Pilate tried to dismiss them, saying, "Take ye him, and judge him according to your law." To this they answered, "It is not lawful for us to put any man to death" (v. 31). (John reminds us again that things are moving in terms of Jesus' prediction, v. 32.)

At this point, Pilate reentered the judgment hall and had Jesus brought in, in order to question Him in private. During this episode, Matthew 27:19 tells us, Pilate's wife sent word to Pilate, saying, "Have thou nothing to do with that just man: for I have suffered many things this day in a dream because of him." Political considerations were more important to Pilate, however, than either justice or his wife.

Pilate now asked Jesus, since the charge had been made that He claimed to be a king, "Art thou the King of the Jews?" (v. 33). This accusation was necessary if Jesus were to be convicted in a Roman court. It was also an indirect admission that this was the Messiah. In the Jewish court, such a charge depend on the religious nature of the evidence. In a Roman court, the charge was *political*, because it controverted Caesar's claims to sovereignty.

Jesus answered, "Sayest thou this thing of thyself, or did others tell it of me?" (v. 34). A Roman governor would have spies reporting to him on all aspects of the life of a restless and rebellious nation. Pilate would be well informed of Jesus' life and teaching. But Pilate refused to admit what he

---

[1.] Leon Morris: *The Gospel According to John* (Grand Rapids, MI: Eerdmans, 1971, 1977), 763n.
[2.] A. Plummer: *The Gospel According to St. John* (Cambridge, England: Cambridge University Press, 1881, 1906), 330.

knew. He was supposed to be in charge, and Jesus had taken the initiative. So "Pilate answered, Am I a Jew? Thine own nation and the chief priests have delivered thee unto me: what hast thou done?" (v. 35). Pilate was saying, you must have done something to be so charged by your own people. In effect, Pilate asked, How can you be right and all your nation and its leaders be wrong? Numbers counted with Rome and Pilate, *not truth*.

Jesus answered Pilate clearly and directly: "My kingdom is not of this world: if my kingdom were of this world, then would my servants fight, that I should not be delivered to the Jews: but now is my kingdom not from hence" (v. 36). This is a statement commonly misinterpreted. Our Lord does *not* deny that His Kingdom is *over* the world, only that its origin and authority are *from* this world: the origin is God. My way of waging war is not physical or military, because its power is not of this world. Had it been so, my men would have fought to prevent my arrest.

Pilate recognized that Jesus was declaring Himself as King, and Pilate needed, however reluctant he was, a usable charge. He therefore asked, "Art thou a king then?" Jesus answered, "Thou sayest that I am a king," or, you are right. I was born to my kingship when I came into this world. I was born to "bear witness unto the truth. Everyone that is of the truth heareth my voice" (v. 37). I am here because there is *truth*, despite men's rejection of it. As James 1:18 declared, Christ's is "the word of truth." 2 Peter 2:2 speaks of "the ways of truth," and Paul in 2 Thessalonians 2:12 speaks of the necessity for the truth, and so on and on. In the world of Roman relativism and cynicism, reference to truth struck Pilate as irrelevant. Here was a man facing death who spoke of truth, and so Pilate in irritation said, "What is truth?" He was annoyed that Jesus had no better defense. Having said that, Pilate went out to tell the religious leaders, "I find in him no fault at all" (v. 38).

Then Pilate called attention to the custom of releasing a prisoner at the Passover. Should he release Jesus, the King of the Jews? (v. 39). According to Matthew 27:17, Pilate gave them a choice, Jesus, or Barabbas, a robber (v. 40). The crowd shouted, "Not this man, but Barabbas" (v. 40). Luke 23:19 tells us that Barabbas was also guilty of sedition and murder. Mark 15:7 tells us that the murder was committed "in the insurrection."

The religious leaders acted horror-stricken at Jesus' supposed sedition, and yet they chose a murderous revolutionary over Jesus. Clearly, this showed Pilate that it was not anti-Roman sedition on Jesus' part that offended them. It was something else, His religious status and His insistence on *the truth* and His relationship to it. Fallen men hate *the truth*, most of all truth incarnate.

Chapter Sixty

The Civil Trial, Part II
(John 19:1-16)

1. Then Pilate therefore took Jesus, and scourged him.
2. And the soldiers platted a crown of thorns, and put it on his head, and they put on him a purple robe,
3. And said, Hail, King of the Jews! and they smote him with their hands.
4. Pilate therefore went forth again, and saith unto them, Behold, I bring him forth to you, that ye may know that I find no fault in him.
5. Then came Jesus forth, wearing the crown of thorns, and the purple robe. And Pilate saith unto them, Behold the man!
6. When the chief priests therefore and officers saw him, they cried out, saying, Crucify him, crucify him. Pilate saith unto them, Take ye him, and crucify him: for I find no fault in him.
7. The Jews answered him, We have a law, and by our law he ought to die, because he made himself the Son of God.
8. When Pilate therefore heard that saying, he was the more afraid;
9. And went again into the judgment hall, and saith unto Jesus, Whence art thou? But Jesus gave him no answer.
10. Then saith Pilate unto him, Speakest thou not unto me? knowest thou not that I have power to crucify thee, and have power to release thee?
11. Jesus answered, Thou couldest have no power at all against me, except it were given thee from above: therefore he that delivered me unto thee hath the greater sin.
12. And from thenceforth Pilate sought to release him: but the Jews cried out, saying, If thou let this man go, thou art not Caesar's friend: whosoever maketh himself a king speaketh against Caesar.
13. When Pilate therefore heard that saying, he brought Jesus forth, and sat down in the judgment seat in a place that is called the Pavement, but in the Hebrew, Gabbatha.
14. And it was the preparation of the passover, and about the sixth hour: and he saith unto the Jews, Behold your King!
15. But they cried out, Away with him, away with him, crucify him. Pilate saith unto them, Shall I crucify your King? The chief priests answered, We have no king but Caesar.
16. Then delivered he him therefore unto them to be crucified. And they took Jesus, and led him away. (John 19:1-16)

The religious leaders were determined to compel Pilate to crucify Jesus, however unjustly. Pilate, on the other hand, knew that Judaea was a troublesome area for the emperor, and he was determined not to be ruled by the Judaeans. The Judaean attitude was that any abuse of one of their people was offensive to them all. Pilate therefore decided to make Jesus an object of their pity, and He was turned over to the soldiers. A crown of thorns was pressed onto His head; He was covered with a purple or royal robe in mockery, and He was struck again and again by the soldiers,

251

becoming what Pilate hoped was an image of pity, with a blood-streaked face (vv. 1-3).

Jesus was then presented to the chief priests and officers by Pilate, with the statements, "I find no fault in Him" (v. 4) and "Behold the man!" (v. 5). Instead of being aroused to pity, the leaders and officers cried out, "Crucify him, crucify him." Pilate, in disgust, told them to take Jesus and crucify Him, but he himself found no fault in Him (v. 6). The answer of the Jewish leaders was, "We have a law, and by our law he ought to die, because he made himself the Son of God" (v. 7). At this point, Pilate, who knew of Jesus as a miracle worker, became "more afraid" (v. 8). Jesus was again inside, in the judgment hall, so Pilate went to Him to ask, "Whence art thou?" but Jesus did not answer (v. 9).

Pilate was irritated: he was trying to save this man's life, and yet he was given no answer. He said, angrily, "Speakest thou not unto me? Knowest thou not that I have power to crucify thee, and have power to release thee?" (v. 10). Pilate was saying, I have total power over you, so you had better answer me. Jesus knew that Pilate moved in fear of Rome's disapproval, and in fear of a negative report to Rome by the Jewish leaders; but Jesus referred neither to Rome's power nor to that of the Sanhedrin, citing God's power instead. "Thou couldest have no power at all against me, except it were given thee from above: therefore he that delivered me unto thee hath the greater sin" (v. 11). This was a startling answer because Jesus spoke of the religious leaders and Pilate as sinning in their conduct of this trial, although "the greater sin" belonged to the men of the Sanhedrin. Jesus, the one about to be executed, had put His judge and accusers in the dock instead.

Pilate knew Jesus was right, "And from thenceforth Pilate sought to release him." At this, the leaders cried out, "If thou let this man go, thou art not Caesar's friend: whosoever maketh himself a king speaketh against Caesar" (v. 12). This charge placed Pilate in a difficult position. How could he free a man whose kingship claim was possibly a threat to Caesar? Rome would not readily recognize the nature of the charge, and the life of a trouble-maker should be sacrificed by a governor to keep the Roman peace. By viewing the messianic claim as a royalist claim, the religious leaders placed a deadly twist upon the trial. It would be difficult to explain away this charge.

Pilate then had Jesus brought out and placed in a public spot for the pronouncement of the sentence. The charge that he was working against Caesar's interest satisfied Pilate. Pilate's patron was Sejanus, who was executed in A.D. 31. Pilate already had a record of troubles with the Jews, so that any further trouble could lead to his downfall and even death (v. 13).

If the reckoning of time is Roman, "the sixth hour" would be like ours, the sixth from midnight. Pilate presented Jesus to the religious leaders, saying, with anger and contempt, "Behold your King" (v. 14). The blood-stained prisoner was what they deserved, like it or not. They cried out, however, "Away with him, away with him, crucify him." Pilate asked, "Shall I (or, must I) crucify your King?" (v. 15). The religious leaders then shouted, "We have no king but Caesar." They rejected God incarnate for a pagan emperor. There was nothing more that Pilate could say. The *religious* leaders had rejected a great and good miracle worker, possibly divine, for a political leader with a reputation that diminished as he aged, according to Suetonius. So Pilate delivered Jesus to them, to be crucified by Roman officers, "And they took Jesus and led him away" (v. 16).

The culminating charge against Jesus was, "he made himself the Son of God" (v. 7). This charge was never investigated or shown to be false. The leaders called it high blasphemy, which thereby merited death. They refused to admit that it could be a true statement. The religious leaders were ready to believe in God, provided He kept far from them and allowed them to rule in His name. The nearness of God was intolerable to them.

As we have seen, truth has an inescapably moral dimension. In a fallen, sinful world, truth will be hated, most of all truth incarnate. Truth is disruptive and divisive in a fallen world, and hence truth is crucified. If truth could be intellectually affirmed without consequences, it would be popular enough, and meaningless, because truth always has consequences. The purely intellectual definitions of truth are inoffensive and lifeless.

Philosophers in an earlier era, employing Hellenic terms, reduced the Trinity to substance (the Father), structure (the Son), and act (the Spirit). Such a trinity creates no offense: it can be no more than the idea of Nature analyzed. It is essentially an intellectual concept and no more.

But God the Son is a Person, the second Person of the Godhead: He is our Creator and Judge, our Redeemer or our Prosecutor. There is no escaping Him. Psalm 139:7-12 tells us that neither hell nor the remotest places can hide us from Him, as St. Augustine, and Francis Thompson in "The Hound of Heaven," testified.

The moral dimension of truth centers on Jesus Christ. Jesus Christ was the Judge, even as He stood before Pilate, and in that trial all men and all courts were tried and found wanting. When men neglect the fact of God's invasion of history in the person of Jesus Christ, they neglect truth and justice and their own salvation.

In a fallen world, the power of a lie is real and very great. We see this in the trial of Jesus Christ. But only the Truth conquers death and is resurrected. God who made all things ordains that all things serve and glorify Him.

Chapter Sixty-One
The Crucifixion
(John 19:17-22)

17. And he bearing his cross went forth into a place called the place of a skull, which is called in the Hebrew Golgotha:
18. Where they crucified him, and two other with him, on either side one, and Jesus in the midst.
19. And Pilate wrote a title, and put it on the cross. And the writing was, JESUS OF NAZARETH THE KING OF THE JEWS.
20. This title then read many of the Jews: for the place where Jesus was crucified was nigh to the city: and it was written in Hebrew, and Greek, and Latin.
21. Then said the chief priests of the Jews to Pilate, Write not, The King of the Jews; but that he said, I am King of the Jews.
22. Pilate answered, What I have written I have written.
(John 19:17-22)

The crucifixion is briefly described by John in grim words. Jesus was required, as a condemned man, to carry his own cross, a heavy burden. In Matthew 27:32, we are told that, on the way, Simon of Cyrene was drafted by the soldiers to carry the cross. Jesus had been kept awake all night; He had been beaten, lashed perhaps to the bone by a whipping, and had suffered great loss of blood. Because of His physical exhaustion, He was unable to move ahead as rapidly as the soldiers required. As a result, a man could be legally compelled to carry the cross. Our Lord had referred to this law in Matthew 5:41, "And whosoever shall compel thee to go a mile, go with him twain." To refuse such a draft was very dangerous.

The place of execution was called Golgotha, or the place of a skull. We do not know why it was so called, although the guesses are interesting, if inconclusive.

There they crucified Him, He in the middle, with a revolutionary criminal on either side of Him (v. 18).

Pilate had been humiliated in being forced to decree a verdict of guilt. The religious leaders had finally come out with an "applicable" charge, namely, Jesus' assertion of His Kingship. Their preferred charge was blasphemy, but that offense had no legal standing before Pilate. They had been pushed into denouncing Jesus Christ's royal status and affirming, "We have no king but Caesar" (John 18:15). A more unpopular statement on their part is hard to imagine: it offended most Judaeans.

In v. 19, we are told how Pilate gained his revenge on the leaders. The charge against Jesus was placed on the cross in Hebrew, Greek, and Latin (v. 19). In a country of very high literacy, this statement was readable by virtually all. Although written by Pilate, it represented the legal ground of conviction on the charges filed by the religious leaders. This was profoundly embarrassing to them. It told everyone that Jesus was convicted as the Messiah, precisely what the leaders wanted to keep secret.

As a result, the chief priests protested to Pilate and demanded a revision: "Write not, The King of the Jews; but that he said, I am the King of the Jews" (v. 21). Make Him a false claimant, not the King. Having successfully used Pilate up to this point, they now expected further compliance, but Pilate refused to bend any more. He answered, "What I have written I have written" (v. 22).

It is significant that Jesus was crucified in the center position. H.A.W. Meyer noted, "Perhaps they scornfully assign to their 'King' the *place of honour.*"[1] This is quite likely, given the fact that two revolutionary brigands were placed on either side. In effect, Jesus was made the king of the lawless, surrounded by men who, like Him, were outlaws. Pilate, by refusing to alter the charges, made legitimate Jesus' Kingship. He in effect says, I find this man to be your legitimate King. The protest of the chief priest thus stemmed from an awareness of the fact that Pilate had convicted Jesus legally, because he recognized Jesus' claim to Kingship as valid and as a threat to Rome. Pilate was protecting himself and his verdict. Jesus was legally executed as the King of the Jews, as their Messiah. There is a grim irony in this decision. Isaiah 53:12 tells us, "He was numbered with the transgressors." The charge against Jesus by Pilate was also a charge against the nation, because Pilate would have been well informed on Jesus' great following. He was in effect saying that the nation was a rebellious one, and he had acted against that danger.

Crucifixion was the most painful form of execution known to the Romans. It originated in ancient Persia, where the condemned man was left for the vultures to pick his bones clean and white on the cross. The "sacred" earth would thus not be polluted by the criminal flesh. The Carthaginians borrowed crucifixion from the Persians, and the Romans borrowed it from the Carthaginians. No Roman citizen could be crucified, and it was normally used only in the provinces.[2] Scourging always preceded crucifixion, and the criminal was often compelled to go through as many streets as possible to publicize his crime. This latter march was perhaps omitted in Christ's case.

Golgotha, or Calvary, both meaning *skull*, was very close to the city in order to make executions as public as possible, stress Roman justice, and make the criminal offense a source of fear to others who might be like-minded.

[1.] H.A.W. Meyer: *Critical and Exegetical Handbook to the Gospel of John* (Peabody, MA: Hendrickson Publishers, 1883,1983), 510.
[2.] William Barclay: *The Gospel of John*, vol. 2 (Philadelphia, PA: Westminster Press, 1855, 1975), 250.

Without knowing it perhaps, Pilate's superscription for the cross was doubly insulting to the leaders because it read, "Jesus of Nazareth, The King of the Jews" (v. 19). For Judaeans to be ruled by a Galilean, or to have a Galilean called their king, was highly offensive.

Verse 20 tells us that Pilate's "title" was read by "many of the Jews," because Golgotha was close to the city, and thus easily accessible. Pilate was fully aware that this would create serious problems for the priestly rulers.

Raymond E. Brown rightly saw that the crucifixion, with Christ in the middle, and the charge of kingship, was a kind of enthronement.[3] John recognized that this was indeed part of Christ's enthronement. By the atonement, He destroyed the power of sin and death, and later ascended into heaven to reign forever as king over all. What had been done for other motives was a true enthronement after all, but the reality of what had taken place was lost on the depraved men who planned and executed it.

[3.] Raymond E. Brown: *The Gospel According to John (xiii-xxi)* (Garden City, NY: Doubleday, 1970), 919.

Chapter Sixty-Two
"It is Finished"
(John 19:23-30)

23. Then the soldiers, when they had crucified Jesus, took his garments, and made four parts, to every soldier a part; and also his coat: now the coat was without seam, woven from the top throughout.
24. They said therefore among themselves, Let us not rend it, but cast lots for it, whose it shall be: that the scripture might be fulfilled, which saith, They parted my raiment among them, and for my vesture they did cast lots. These things therefore the soldiers did.
25. Now there stood by the cross of Jesus his mother, and his mother's sister, Mary the wife of Cleophas, and Mary Magdalene.
26. When Jesus therefore saw his mother, and the disciple standing by, whom he loved, he saith unto his mother, Woman, behold thy son!
27. Then saith he to the disciple, Behold thy mother! And from that hour that disciple took her unto his own home.
28. After this, Jesus knowing that all things were now accomplished, that the scripture might be fulfilled, saith, I thirst.
29. Now there was set a vessel full of vinegar: and they filled a spunge with vinegar, and put it upon hyssop, and put it to his mouth.
30. When Jesus therefore had received the vinegar, he said, It is finished: and he bowed his head, and gave up the ghost.
(John 19:23-30)

In vv. 23-24, we see the soldiers dividing among themselves the clothing of the naked, crucified Christ. These were normally few in number, four or five items, counting the sandals. There was a difference in the value of the several items; in particular, in this case, the last was a seamless garment, woven as one piece, and therefore more valuable than such things as a belt or shoes. As a result, the soldiers cast lots. With each cast, the winner took his pick. The Scripture referred to is Psalm 22:18, a psalm of David, and it refers to the casting of lots for one's garment.

Among those near the cross were Mary, Jesus' mother, "and his mother's sister, Mary, the wife of Cleophas." The question commonly raised is this: does this refer to two women, the Virgin Mary's unnamed sister, and a woman named Mary who is the wife of Cleophas? Or was His mother's "sister" a cousin who was also named Mary? We cannot know for sure. The other woman is Mary Magdalene. These stood close by the cross (v. 25).

When Jesus saw His mother, He said to her, "Woman, behold thy son," and to John, "Behold thy mother." We are told that John thereafter took Mary into his own home (vv. 26-27).

In vv. 28-30, we have two of the seven last "words" or statements from the cross. These are:

1) "Father, forgive them; for they know not what they do" (Luke 23:34). He prays, Father, defer the charges against these soldiers for the time being, for they know not what they do. *Forgive* is a juridical term normally meaning *charges dropped*, here *charges deferred*, because the Roman soldiers were ignorant of what they were doing.

2) "Verily I say, Today shalt thou be with me in paradise," words spoken to one of the two malefactors crucified with Him. (Luke 23:43).

3) "Women, behold, thy son...Behold, thy mother" (John 19:26-27).

4) "My God, my God, why hast thou forsaken me?" (Matthew 27:46; Mark 15:34).

5) "I thirst" (John 19:28).

6) "It is finished" (John 19:30).

7) "Father, into thy hands I commend my spirit" (Luke 23:46).

Of these seven sayings, three are from John, three from Luke, and one is cited by both Matthew and Mark. The fifth phrase, "I thirst," comes with His knowledge, shortly before death, that He had fulfilled His calling to make atonement for our sins. He then gave thought to His desperate thirst, born of radical dehydration. A sponge was soaked in vinegar, meaning a sour, cheap wine, placed on a hyssop stalk, and held up for Him to take and suck on. A hyssop stalk could be two or three feet in length. Hyssop was used in Passover ceremonies (Ex. 12:22), and John may have called attention to hyssop to remind us that Jesus was the perfect Passover sacrifice.[1]

Then we have the sixth statement, "It is finished," followed at once with the seventh, "Father, into thy hands I commit my spirit." Together with "I thirst," these three sayings came shortly before His death. Speech was for a crucified man very difficult. "I thirst" was no doubt a call for something to drink to make speech possible. "It is finished" means "It is accomplished," my work is done. As Morgan stated it,

> It was not the voice of One defeated. It was the voice of the Victor. "It is finished." The Greek words mean far more than that something was over. It means that it was rounded out to perfection. Whatever He went to the cross to do was accomplished.[2]

The agony and horror of crucifixion cannot obscure this fact of victory. A new beginning in history was accomplished. The key to history would now be the fact of atonement, that sin was atoned for, man made a new creation in Christ: history would now see the beginning of a restored earth and God's Kingdom. In some respects, the battle against God and His

[1.] Leon Morris: *The Gospel According to John* (Grand Rapids, MI: Eerdmans, 1971, 1977.), 813 n., f.
[2.] G. Campbell Morgan: *The Gospel According to John* (New York, NY: Fleming H. Revell, n.d.), 297.

Christ would be waged more intensely and bitterly than ever before. The twentieth century is witness to that fact.

But victory was now in view, and the triumphant campaign was now under way. Because Christ's atoning sacrifice ended the power of sin and death over man, the resurrection was an inescapable consequence. Jesus Christ had destroyed the power of sin and death, and therefore death could not hold Him. His death on the cross and His time in the grave made clear the grim reality of sin and death, but His resurrection openly destroyed their power over Christ's new creation (1 Cor. 15:20-23).

The atonement is not often discussed in this context, because history is kept separate from theology. But is this possible? Can I be seen as a person, or known as one, if my sex, race, nationality, family, faith, and character are left out of the picture? Am I not then utterly stripped of my nature and being?

For a Christian, all life is theological: it has its meaning in terms of the triune God and His infallible word, and we can never be understood except as God's creation. To attempt to understand the death and resurrection of Jesus Christ apart from His incarnation and the atonement is to deny meaning. But the modern world does deny absolute meaning, in favor of an, at best, possible, tentative, and evolving meaning which may degenerate into no meaning at all.

Christian theology is not an abstraction about history, but rather a declaration of what history is, has been, and will be. It is what history *is*.

The atonement celebrates a new beginning. The power of sin and death is broken, so that, by Christ's regenerating power, man is made a new creation (2 Cor. 5:17). *History* is not limited to the physical fact of crucifixion: it also includes what that event accomplished. If man alone gives meaning to history, then it is only man's analysis and conclusions that count, but if God alone gives meaning to all things, then the meaning and the events are inseparable, because the ordination and accomplishment thereof are God's work. By separating history and theology in the Gospel narratives, the commentators have served the humanistic agenda.

Our Lord's statement, "It is finished," or, It is accomplished, is a theological statement. If we separate history and theology, we join the ranks of the "cultured despisers" of Christianity, and we separate ourselves from Jesus Christ.

William Barclay reminds us that Jesus, according to Matthew 27:50, Mark 15:37, and Luke 23:46, "died with a great shout on his lips," (no doubt His sixth and seventh words). "It is finished," Barclay says, "is one word in Greek — *tetelestai* — and Jesus died with a shout of triumph on His lips."[3]

[3.] William Barclay: *The Gospel of John*, vol. 2 (Philadelphia, PA: Westminster Press, 1955, 1975), 258.

We cannot report that cry, It is accomplished, apart from theology, because there are no brute facts, i.e., meaningless facts, or facts with no possible interpretation, in all creation. There are only God-created and God-interpreted facts.

Facts without meaning do not exist. If we are ignorant of the meaning of things, this does not mean that they have no meaning. There are many languages I do not understand, but this does not make them meaningless. As Cornelius Van Til pointed out so powerfully, there are no meaningless or brute facts.

In a television series of the 1960's, Detective Friday was given to saying, "Just the facts, ma'am." But to assume that facts do not exist in a context of God-given meaning is absurd. The woman reported to Detective Friday that she had been robbed. Her statement was totally governed by presuppositions. For example, it presupposed that robbing is morally and legally wrong, and that the man robbing her was a thief. Her statement assumed that the police had a duty to perform, and that they represented the law, and so on and so on. Men may refuse to believe in God, but their words are meaningless without the God-created context.

In hell, God and theology are rejected, and hence all facts are denied. There is only an unending destruction of meaning for those in hell.

Hell has meaning for Christians because for them there are no brute or meaningless facts, and hell is thus the futile rejection of meaning.

Chapter Sixty-Three
The Death and Burial of Jesus Christ
(*John 19:31-42*)

31. The Jews therefore, because it was the preparation, that the bodies should not remain upon the cross on the sabbath day, for that sabbath day was an high day, besought Pilate that their legs might be broken, and that they might be taken away.
32. Then came the soldiers, and brake the legs of the first, and of the other which was crucified with him.
33. But when they came to Jesus, and saw that he was dead already, they brake not his legs:
34. But one of the soldiers with a spear pierced his side, and forthwith came there out blood and water.
35. And he that saw it bare record, and his record is true: and he knoweth that he saith true, that ye might believe.
36. For these things were done, that the scripture should be fulfilled, A bone of him shall not be broken.
37. And again another scripture saith, They shall look on him whom they pierced.
38. And after this Joseph of Arimathaea, being a disciple of Jesus, but secretly for fear of the Jews, besought Pilate that he might take away the body of Jesus: and Pilate gave him leave. He came therefore, and took the body of Jesus.
39. And there came also Nicodemus, which at the first came to Jesus by night, and brought a mixture of myrrh and aloes, about an hundred pound weight.
40. Then took they the body of Jesus, and wound it in linen clothes with the spices, as the manner of the Jews is to bury.
41. Now in the place where he was crucified there was a garden; and in the garden a new sepulchre, wherein was never man yet laid.
42. There laid they Jesus therefore because of the Jews' preparation day; for the sepulchre was nigh at hand. (John 19:31-42)

It was the Roman custom to allow men to die on the cross and to leave their bodies to decay there. The sight of this would be a grim warning of Roman justice to all who passed by.

On this occasion, there was a problem. For the Jews, the next day being a Sabbath, it was not permitted that dead or dying men remain on the cross. Some men lasted three days before dying. Jesus, who had been severely beaten, probably to the point of exposing bones, was greatly weakened, and therefore died early.

Crucifixion was a death normally reserved for slaves, as was the breaking of bones to bring on death. Both were involved here, because the two malefactors crucified with Jesus were still alive. When Jesus' side was pierced with a spear to see if He were truly dead, blood and water both came out.

The screaming agony of the two malefactors when their leg bones were broken must have been intense. The Roman soldiers were used to this kind of horror and performed their duties routinely.

It is noteworthy that, while the three men were dying on their crosses, the Jewish religious leaders went to Pilate to ask that the condemned men's legs be broken. So far as they knew, this would apply to Jesus.

Jesus had twice declared to these religious leaders that God had plainly said, "I will have mercy, and not sacrifice" (Matt. 9:13; 12:7), but they were more interested in exercising vengeance against Jesus. To my knowledge, this kind of cruelty was still used as recently as World War I by Turks against Armenian prisoners, as a means of torture and execution.

At this point, in vv. 35-37, John interjects a passionate statement. He tells us that he was there and witnessed what he describes. He insists on the total accuracy of what he reports, and he calls upon us to believe him. Plummer's comment here is of interest:

> Why does S. John attest thus earnestly the trustworthiness of his narrative at this particular point? Four reasons may be assigned. This incident proved (1) the reality of Christ's *humanity* against Docetic views; and these verses therefore are conclusive evidence against the theory that the Fourth Gospel is the work of a Docetic Gnostic; (2) the reality of Christ's *Divinity*, against Ebionite views; while His human form was no mere phantom, but flesh and blood, yet He was not therefore a mere man, but the Son of God; (3) the reality of Christ's *death*, and therefore of His *Resurrection*, against Jewish insinuations of trickery (comp. Matt. xxvii. 13-15); (4) the clear and unexpected fulfillment of two Messianic prophecies.[1]

John cites two prophecies as here fulfilled. *First*, there is Psalm 34:20, "He keepeth all his bones: not one of them is broken." This echoes also Exodus 12:46 concerning the Passover Lamb, and Numbers 9:12. Jesus, says John, is our true Passover Lamb. *Second*, the citation about the piercing is from Psalm 22:16 and Zechariah 12:10. John refers to this verse again in Revelation 1:7. The origin of both citations is from David, and they tell us that David's experiences and concerns prefigure those of the Messiah.

In vv. 38-42, we have the burial of Jesus described. Joseph of Arimathea was a secret disciple. We are told about him in Matthew 27:57, Mark 15:43, and Luke 23:50. He was rich, and a member of the Sanhedrin, but we are also told that he was a good and just man. His fearfulness does not disbar him from his rightful place as a secondary disciple. The same was true of Nicodemus. These two men are named because we are to respect them.

---

[1] A. Plummer: *The Gospels According to St. John* (Cambridge, England: Cambridge University Press, 1880, 1906), 351.

Joseph of Arimathea had ownership of a new grave, and this was close by. He at once made it available for Jesus' body. Moreover, he went to Pilate to gain permission for the burial.

Nicodemus assisted him by providing a mixture of myrrh and aloes, about a one hundred pounds, or 1,200 ounces, to be packed around the body for its burial. This was established Jewish practice, although here a generous amount of embalming material is in evidence. As quickly as they could before sunset, the body was wrapped and buried. Apparently the final burial work was left for the women to take care of on the first day of the week. The tomb was not far from Golgotha. We are told specifically that the tomb was a new and unused one, not one designed for multiple bodies. This was to stress the total holiness of the Lord's body and the undefiled nature of His grave. To His followers, this was important. Though bewildered by the course of events, and finding it difficult to understand our Lord's predictions of His resurrection, they were still totally convinced of His perfect holiness.

The crucifixion, burial, and resurrection were for centuries common subjects of church art. Our more jaded era finds it less shattering a fact to imagine the death of God the Son in His incarnation; somehow, like the Gnostics, we have trouble seeing it as an actuality. Similarly, the resurrection is a problem for people now, because, in the modern era, death is seen as *final*, rather than as a *prelude* to heaven and hell, and to judgment. Modern man has a warped vision.

Before World War II, Dunne, a scientist, wrote a book on *An Experiment with Time*. He called attention to the fact that agnostics and atheists had predicted that, with a loss of belief in life after death, men would prize this brief life more and would behave more humanely. Instead, he saw a growing callousness towards life with the loss of faith in God and life after death.

We should not wonder at this. If life has no meaning, what value has it? And what then is morality but misguided behavior?

In recent years, the social importance of Good Friday and Resurrection Day has faded. Family funerals are less and less marked by family reunions and dinners. There are fewer tears at funerals and fewer family celebrations, and some treat funerals as a bad relic of a previous era. One group has advertised cremations and non-funeral dispositions of the dead. One writer of the late 1950's saw death as the new, coming "pornography," i.e., death would replace "dirty books" as the unspeakable and forbidden.

John, however, requires us to fix our attention on Christ's death and its grim nature because he sees it as central to the meaning of history and life. Believe me on this above all, he says, because here is life and redemption.

Chapter Sixty-Four

The Resurrection
(John 20:1-18)

1. The first day of the week cometh Mary Magdalene early, when it was yet dark, unto the sepulchre, and seeth the stone taken away from the sepulchre.
2. Then she runneth, and cometh to Simon Peter, and to the other disciple, whom Jesus loved, and saith unto them, They have taken away the Lord out of the sepulchre, and we know not where they have laid him.
3. Peter therefore went forth, and that other disciple, and came to the sepulchre.
4. So they ran both together: and the other disciple did outrun Peter, and came first to the sepulchre.
5. And he stooping down, and looking in, saw the linen clothes lying; yet went he not in.
6. Then cometh Simon Peter following him, and went into the sepulchre, and seeth the linen clothes lie,
7. And the napkin, that was about his head, not lying with the linen clothes, but wrapped together in a place by itself.
8. Then went in also that other disciple, which came first to the sepulchre, and he saw, and believed.
9. For as yet they knew not the scripture, that he must rise again from the dead.
10. Then the disciples went away again unto their own home.
11. But Mary stood without at the sepulchre weeping: and as she wept, she stooped down, and looked into the sepulchre,
12. And seeth two angels in white sitting, the one at the head, and the other at the feet, where the body of Jesus had lain.
13. And they say unto her, Woman, why weepest thou? She saith unto them, Because they have taken away my Lord, and I know not where they have laid him.
14. And when she had thus said, she turned herself back, and saw Jesus standing, and knew not that it was Jesus.
15. Jesus saith unto her, Woman, why weepest thou? whom seekest thou? She, supposing him to be the gardener, saith unto him, Sir, if thou have borne him hence, tell me where thou hast laid him, and I will take him away.
16. Jesus saith unto her, Mary. She turned herself, and saith unto him, Rabboni; which is to say, Master.
17. Jesus saith unto her, Touch me not; for I am not yet ascended to my Father: but go to my brethren, and say unto them, I ascend unto my Father, and your Father; and to my God, and your God.
18. Mary Magdalene came and told the disciples that she had seen the Lord, and that he had spoken these things unto her. (John 20:1-18)

The crucifixion had taken place on Friday; all remained inactive on the Sabbath, but early on Sunday, the women came to complete the preparation of the body for its permanent burial. Meanwhile, at the request

267

of the chief priests, Pilate granted permission for guards to be placed at the tomb, to prevent theft of the body and a claim of resurrection (Matt. 27:62 through 28:4). The chief priests remembered more of Christ's words at this point than did the disciples. The women apparently came singly, having agreed to meet at the tomb. At some point before dawn, an earthquake hit the area. While it was still quite dark, Mary Magdalene arrived. She was shocked to find the tomb open and ran at once to notify Peter and John (v. 2). She assumed that the authorities had transferred the body to another site.

Peter and John ran to the tomb, John arriving first (v. 3f.). Peter, however, entered first. They both saw the graveclothes neatly wrapped and placed to one side (vv. 5-7). In vv. 8-9, we are told that both John and Peter *believed*, but also that as yet they did not know the Scriptures which predicted the resurrection. They knew that something very remarkable had taken place, but its meaning escaped them. Their view of the future was still to Israel rather than to Jesus Christ, a failing very much with us today.

The disciples then left to return home. Jesus was apparently no longer among the dead, but the meaning of the resurrection for them was not yet evident.

Mary had returned, more slowly than Peter's and John's race to the tomb. She stood by the tomb, weeping. She looked into the sepulcher and saw two angels in white, one at the head of where Jesus had lain and the other at the foot (v. 12). She did not recognize them as angels. They said to her, "Woman, why weepest thou?" Her answer was, "Because they have taken away my Lord, and I know not where they have laid him" (v. 13). Quite plainly, she felt no fear and assumed that these two persons were no part of Pilate's or Caiaphas' entourage. She then turned back, not waiting to hear more, and she became aware of someone standing nearby. It was Jesus, who asked her, "Woman, why weepest thou? whom seekest thou?" She did not answer Him, but asked her own question, phrased as a statement: "Sir, if thou have borne him hence, tell me where thou hast laid him, and I will taken him away" (v. 15). Her assumption was that the authorities had reversed the permission to Joseph of Arimathea and had removed the body.

At this, Jesus simply said, "Mary," and she recognized Him at once, calling out, "Rabboni," my master (v. 16). She apparently tried to cling to His feet in joy, but He said, "Touch me not; for I am not yet ascended to my Father: but go to my brethren, and say unto them, I ascend unto my Father, and your Father; and to my God, and your God" (v. 19). The better rendering of "Touch me not" is *stop clinging to Me.* All relationships were now altered because all His followers had been given a task to cling to, a calling to fulfill, a world to conquer for Christ. Their relationship to Him was henceforth to be defined by service to His Kingdom, to one another, and to all peoples. Close ties with Him would be gained by doing His will, rather than through a personal presence.

"I ascend to my Father," or, "I am ascending to my Father," i.e., I am separating Myself from all of you physically because My task is now a different one. The promise of the Spirit or Strengthener is tied to this change.

Mary then reported these things to the disciples. Too many commentators give us a jaundiced view of the resurrection, because for them such a supernatural event is impossible. However, to deny an act of God is to deny the validity of all history, as indeed our scholars are busily doing. *Meaning* is seen by many as an artificial and man-made addition to events, and is thus subject to change or elimination. For others, the test of validity is repeatability. If something can be repeated under controlled conditions, it is then a natural and valid fact. The uniqueness of the resurrection makes it invalid to many.

Basic to many like views is the insistence that, *first*, reality is *natural*, and, *second*, that man is the final judge of the reality of things. By the *natural* is meant that which is part of our everyday experience and comprehensible within the physical universe as we know it. By definition, the acts of God are ruled out. Moreover, if man, a creature, is the final and authoritative definer of reality, then man can by simple definition render God and all His works non-existent.

The presupposition of the modern Biblical scholar is radically humanistic. In *The Death of God* school of religious thought, God is simply eliminated because he is not wanted. His existence is not denied; rather, God and His existence are held to be meaningless.

All meaning for John is God-ordained and God-centered. Jesus Christ, His birth, ministry, death, and resurrection, are more than episodes in history; they open up the meaning of all history, and of all creation.

In v. 17, our Lord twice refers to His coming ascension. His language indicated that in some sense He is already ascending. The ascension was to the right hand of God the Father, there to reign eternally (Mark 16:19). He is present there as the "first-fruits" of the new humanity and as the Head of the new creation. He is Lord over all creation as He reigns at the right hand of the Father. The ascension and enthronement are thus the logical conclusion of the atonement and resurrection. One cannot isolate the reign of the Son from His resurrection. To do so is to play the humanists' game and to reduce events to a non-theological meaning, or to meaninglessness.

Chapter Sixty-Five

Appearances to the Disciples
(*John 20:19-31*)

19. Then the same day at evening, being the first day of the week, when the doors were shut where the disciples were assembled for fear of the Jews, came Jesus and stood in the midst, and saith unto them, Peace be unto you.
20. And when he had so said, he shewed unto them his hands and his side. Then were the disciples glad, when they saw the Lord.
21. Then said Jesus to them again, Peace be unto you: as my Father hath sent me, even so send I you.
22. And when he had said this, he breathed on them, and saith unto them, Receive ye the Holy Ghost:
23. Whose soever sins ye remit, they are remitted unto them; and whose soever sins ye retain, they are retained.
24. But Thomas, one of the twelve, called Didymus, was not with them when Jesus came.
25. The other disciples therefore said unto him, We have seen the Lord. But he said unto them, Except I shall see in his hands the print of the nails, and put my finger into the print of the nails, and thrust my hand into his side, I will not believe.
26. And after eight days again his disciples were within, and Thomas with them: then came Jesus, the doors being shut, and stood in the midst, and said, Peace be unto you.
27. Then saith he to Thomas, Reach hither thy finger, and behold my hands; and reach hither thy hand, and thrust it into my side: and be not faithless, but believing.
28. And Thomas answered and said unto him, My Lord and my God.
29. Jesus saith unto him, Thomas, because thou hast seen me, thou hast believed: blessed are they that have not seen, and yet have believed.
30. And many other signs truly did Jesus in the presence of his disciples, which are not written in this book:
31. But these are written, that ye might believe that Jesus is the Christ, the Son of God; and that believing ye might have life through his name. (John 20:19-31)

In v. 19, we are told that on the day of the resurrection, in the evening, the fearful disciples were in a locked room together, all except Judas, now dead, and Thomas. They were afraid of the religious leaders. They had heard from Peter and John of Christ's apparent resurrection, but they were uncertain of its meaning. Suddenly, in this locked room, Jesus "stood in the midst, and saith unto them, Peace be with you."

Then Jesus at once showed them His hands and His side, the marks of His crucifixion and the soldier's spear thrust into His side. "Then were the disciples glad, when they saw the Lord" (v. 20). Up until now, they apparently believed that our Lord had appeared to Mary Magdalene in the

271

form of a ghost. By showing the disciples His very physical wounds, our Lord convinced them that it was indeed He. His appearance in a locked room heightened their belief that He was only a spirit, but the uncovering of His nail-pierced hands and His spear-pierced side convinced them it was Jesus in the flesh, and they were glad.

Then Jesus said, "Peace be unto you: as my Father hath sent me, even so send I you" (v. 21). Morgan called attention to the difference in the two words translated as *send* and *sent*. The Father's sending of the Son is *apostello*, from whence comes our word *apostle*. It means delegated authority. The Son sends the disciples, *pempo*, which is not delegated authority, but a dispatch under authority, by one who has the authority but does not delegate it. The church has no inherent authority. Christ, who sends out His messengers and commissions His church, surrenders no authority to them.[1]

This is very important in terms of what follows, because so much has been done to convert its meaning from a ministerial to a legislative one. A ministerial authority requires us to do only what we are commissioned to do, and no more. A legislative authority means the power to do what we think is right, irrespective of what we were told to do. In vv. 22-23, we are told,

> 22. When he had said this, he breathed on them, and saith unto them, Receive ye the Holy Ghost:
> 23. Whose soever sins ye retain, they are retained.

Verse 23 recalls two other similar statements in Matthew:

> And I will give unto thee the keys of the kingdom of heaven: and whatsoever thou shalt bind on earth shall be bound in heaven: and whatsoever thou shalt loose on earth shall be loosed in heaven. (Matthew 16:19)

> Verily I say unto you, Whatsoever ye shall bind on earth shall be bound in heaven: and whatsoever ye shall loose on earth shall be loosed in heaven. (Matthew 18:18)

All three verses have to do with *the keys of the Kingdom*. We have a reflection of the meaning of this expression in the Phi Beta Kappa key, an emblem of the ability to understand and interpret learning in a particular area. The keys of the kingdom referred to the power to understand and exegete Scripture, to explain its true meaning, not to create new ones. This is a ministerial, not a legislative task. Thus, the keys meant a knowledge and understanding of God's law-word and the faithful interpretation thereof. We can then tell men, *in terms of God's Word*, that their sins are remitted, or that they are retained or bound. No *independent* power is conferred

[1]. G. Campbell Morgan: *The Gospel According to John* (New York, NY: Fleming H. Revell, n.d.), 319.

upon the church, and to imagine so is to follow after the Pharisees, as the modern church has so often done.

Thomas, or Didymus, was not present that night (v. 24). When the others told Thomas of Christ's appearance, his response was, "Except I shall see in his hands the print of the nails...and thrust my hand into his side, I will not believe" (v. 25). Thomas has been much abused for this, and he is known as Doubting Thomas. But the other disciples were no different: our Lord had to show them His hands and His sides. To single Thomas out as a special case is nonsense. John tells this tale in order to illustrate how unready all of them were to believe.

Eight days later, when the disciples were again in a locked room, with Thomas present, Jesus again appeared miraculously, stood in their midst, and said, "Peace be unto you" (v. 26). Then He said to Thomas, "Reach hither thy finger, and behold my hands; and reach hither thy hand, and thrust it into my side; and be not faithless but believing" (v. 27). The purpose of this account is not to tell us what a doubter Thomas was, but to call to the disciples' attention the privileged status as witnesses that they all had. All the disciples are shown to be wanting.

Thomas' answer was, "My Lord and my God" (v. 28). Perhaps most quickly of all, Thomas acknowledged Jesus to be the incarnate God. Jesus told Thomas, "Thomas, because thou hast seen me, thou hast believed: blessed are they that have not seen, and yet have believed" (v. 29). This was also a blessing, a beatitude, pronounced on all of us who are in time remote to that day, but do believe.

Then vv. 30-31, like John 21:24-25, give us a concluding note which, in this case, tells us two things. *First*, many other *signs* did Jesus manifest in the presence of His disciples (v. 30). This gospel, like those of Matthew, Mark, and Luke is selective. These narratives stress the key miracles and words of Jesus. *Second*, John has recorded accurately the word and deeds of Jesus with this purpose, "that ye might believe that Jesus is the Christ, the Son of God: and that believing ye might have life through his name" (v. 31). Jesus, we are told, is the Christ, the Messiah of promise, *and* He is also the Son of God. The purpose of this revelation is that we might believe in Him and "have life through His name."

To separate what Jesus was and is, and His life and redemptive purpose, from "history," is to deny history by making it meaningless. We cannot describe the French or the Russian Revolution apart from the ideas and purposes of the revolutionaries. Even less can we understand Biblical history apart from the triune God. We do not have before us a series of naturalistic or meaningless events, but an account of things which are wholly the results of God's decree and which manifest God's sovereign purposes and acts. It is an exercise in unreason to attempt to empty the Gospels of their purpose. It rests on an implicit denial of history.

Chapter Sixty-Six
The Under-Shepherd and Duty
(John 21:1-17)

1. After these things Jesus shewed himself again to the disciples at the sea of Tiberias; and on this wise shewed he himself.

2. There were together Simon Peter, and Thomas called Didymus, and Nathanael of Cana in Galilee, and the sons of Zebedee, and two other of his disciples.

3. Simon Peter saith unto them, I go a fishing. They say unto him, We also go with thee. They went forth, and entered into a ship immediately; and that night they caught nothing.

4. But when the morning was now come, Jesus stood on the shore: but the disciples knew not that it was Jesus.

5. Then Jesus saith unto them, Children, have ye any meat? They answered him, No.

6. And he said unto them, Cast the net on the right side of the ship, and ye shall find. They cast therefore, and now they were not able to draw it for the multitude of fishes.

7. Therefore that disciple whom Jesus loved saith unto Peter, It is the Lord. Now when Simon Peter heard that it was the Lord, he girt his fisher's coat unto him, for he was naked, and did cast himself into the sea.

8. And the other disciples came in a little ship; they were not far from land, but as it were two hundred cubits, dragging the net with fishes.

9. As soon then as they were come to land, they saw a fire of coals there, and fish laid thereon, and bread.

10. Jesus saith unto them, Bring of the fish which ye have now caught.

11. Simon Peter went up, and drew the net to land full of great fishes, an hundred and fifty and three: and for all there were so many, yet was not the net broken.

12. Jesus saith unto them, Come and dine. And none of the disciples durst ask him, Who art thou? knowing that it was the Lord.

13. Jesus then cometh, and taketh bread, and giveth them, and fish likewise.

14. This is now the third time that Jesus shewed himself to his disciples, after that he was risen from the dead.

15. So when they had dined, Jesus saith to Simon Peter, Simon, son of Jonas, lovest thou me more than these? He saith unto him, Yea, Lord; thou knowest that I love thee. He saith unto him, Feed my lambs.

16. He saith to him again the second time, Simon, son of Jonas, lovest thou me? He saith unto him, Yea, Lord; thou knowest that I love thee. He saith unto him, Feed my sheep.

17. He saith unto him the third time, Simon, son of Jonas, lovest thou me? Peter was grieved because he said unto him the third time, Lovest thou me? And he said unto him, Lord, thou knowest all things; thou knowest that I love thee. Jesus saith unto him, Feed my sheep.
(John 21:1-17)

In v. 1, we are told that some time after the day of resurrection and before His ascension, Jesus appeared to His disciples at the Sea of Galilee, or Tiberius (v. 1). There were seven there, Simon Peter, John, Thomas, Nathaniel of Cana, James, and two other unnamed men (v. 2). Simon decided that they should go fishing, and the others agreed. This was commercial fishing. They fished all night and caught nothing (v. 3). Towards morning, Jesus appeared on the shore, but, because it was still somewhat dark, they did not recognize Him, although they were not far from shore (v. 4). Jesus called out to them and asked if they had caught anything, and the answer was no (v. 5). Jesus then told them to cast their nets on the right side of the boat, which they did, catching 153 fish without the net breaking (vv. 8, 11).

Peter now recognized Jesus, after John had observed, "It is the Lord." He belted on his outer garment and jumped into the water, heading for shore. They were close enough so that perhaps swimming was not required. They were only about 200 cubits from land, and instead of hauling in the fish, they dragged the heavy net to shore, to avoid damage to the net.

On landing, they saw that Jesus had a fire going, and bread and fish prepared for them. (v. 9). Jesus instructed them to bring their fish ashore, and He then fed them. (v. 10-12). The disciples held back, in timidity, and Jesus went forward, bringing the fish and bread to them (v. 13). This was His third appearance to them after the resurrection (v. 14).

After they had dined, Jesus asked a question of Peter, who perhaps had jumped into the water to ask Christ's mercy for his behavior, but had said nothing so far. "Simon, son of Jonas, lovest thou me more than these?" Peter answered, saying, "Yea, Lord, thou knowest that I love thee." Jesus' response was, "Feed my sheep" (v. 15). Again, a second time, Jesus asked the same question, but with a difference. The first time the word *lovest* translates *agapas*, a form of *agape*, and refers to God's grace-filled love. Did Peter have such love, and one greater than all the other disciples? Peter in his answer used the word *philo*, meaning a human love with all its frailties. Peter indicated that his love was real, but human, and not superior to the other disciples (v. 15). In His second question, our Lord drops the phrase, "more than these." He simply asks, Do you love me, *agapas*, with a holy, selfless love? Peter did not possess this perfect love, but he did insist that in his limited, human way, he did love, *philo*, his Lord (v. 16). Then, for the third time, Jesus repeated His question, lovest thou me?, this time using the word *phileis*, i.e., do you truly love even with a weak human love? This time, Peter was hurt and showed it, but, again, our Lord answered, "Feed my sheep" (v. 17). At the same time, our Lord's commands change, from the first instance when He says, "Feed my lambs," to, "Feed my sheep," or, better, "Feed my little sheep." Grace was being manifested to Peter *and to all the disciples* for their betrayal. A shepherd, providing a watchful eye, can allow the mature sheep to graze. Some of the lambs require special care, and the young sheep also. The Lord, having shown His patience with His disciples, now requires that Peter and the others be ever mindful of their sins and shortcomings, and that they be patient with the weak in Christ whom they must shepherd.

It is thus incorrect to limit these words to Peter. They were spoken to all under-shepherds of all time by our Lord, and this is why John records them. No more than Thomas was alone in his doubt, was Peter alone in betraying our Lord. John's purpose here was catholic or universal. Peter, meaning *the rock*, could only be a part of the Rock of Ages, Jesus Christ, if, with humility and a knowledge of his betrayal of the Lord, he could work patiently with Christ's sometimes very weak flock.

This is why the Donatist movement was so blasphemous: it required a fault-free faith; it insisted that those who, in fear of the Roman authorities, abjured Christ were forever anathema. This stance led to hypocrisy and Phariseeism. To require such perfection is to substitute pretense for growth. The Christian life is one of troubles that often find us wanting, but which increase our reliance on the Lord and stimulate our growth. Very early, as a student, I encountered the lines of James Russell Lowell in "Under the Willows," which read very plainly, describing us as "We, who by shipwreck only find the shores of divine wisdom." We who have grown in grace and in understanding are the veterans of many shipwrecks. We falsify the faith if we limit the frame of reference.

Thus John speaks here of the Lord's rebuke to all of them. All are called to be mindful of the weakness of Christ's young ones and new converts. It was Thomas Boston who, in his study of man in his fourfold estate, spoke of the fallacy of expecting to leap from Delilah's lap into Abraham's bosom.

John's purpose here is to teach us patience and understanding with others and with ourselves.

In what follows, our Lord makes very clear that He can expect everything of us, and we dare not deny Him; at the same time, He is all gracious.

Chapter Sixty-Seven
Predestination and Grace
(John 21:18-25)

18. Verily, verily, I say unto thee, When thou wast young, thou girdedst thyself, and walkedst whither thou wouldest: but when thou shalt be old, thou shalt stretch forth thy hands, and another shall gird thee, and carry thee whither thou wouldest not.
19. This spake he, signifying by what death he should glorify God. And when he had spoken this, he saith unto him, Follow me.
20. Then Peter, turning about, seeth the disciple whom Jesus loved following; which also leaned on his breast at supper, and said, Lord, which is he that betrayeth thee?
21. Peter seeing him saith to Jesus, Lord, and what shall this man do?
22. Jesus saith unto him, If I will that he tarry till I come, what is that to thee? follow thou me.
23. Then went this saying abroad among the brethren, that that disciple should not die: yet Jesus said not unto him, He shall not die; but, If I will that he tarry till I come, what is that to thee?
24. This is the disciple which testifieth of these things, and wrote these things: and we know that his testimony is true.
25. And there are also many other things which Jesus did, the which, if they should be written every one, I suppose that even the world itself could not contain the books that should be written. Amen. (John 21:18-25)

The conclusion to John's Gospel has not been justly expounded. It is a rather startling one. In v. 18, our Lord tells Peter, when you were young, you did very much as you pleased, but, in your old age, others will do with you what they will. There is a suggestion in Jesus' words of death, of execution at the hands of others. Peter certainly understood that some kind of arrest and execution was meant. This clearly came as a jolt to Peter. He looked at John, and then asked Jesus about John's future: What about this man? Jesus' answer was *very* blunt: "If I will that he tarry till I come, what is that to thee? follow thou me?" (v. 22).

Very obviously, our Lord's words presuppose predestination. It is He who ordains the lives of all men, and He has decreed the lives and deaths of His disciples. His statement is emphatic: "If I will." All depends on His sovereign will. Neither Peter nor any other disciple disputes this. His predestinational purpose differs from one person to another, so that no equality exists in His predestination. He *could* decree that John remain alive until the Second Coming, although He does not do so. His remark was construed by some as exempting John from death, a foolish misinterpretation. What He did say was that His will is sovereign, so that no man can complain about his portion. As Paul wrote in 1 Corinthians 4:7:

279

For who maketh thee to differ from another? And what hast thou that thou didst not receive? Now if thou didst receive it, why dost thou glory, as if thou hadst not received it?

What we are is as much a part of God's predestinating power as is what shall become of us later in time and in eternity. Hence our Lord's blunt statement: "What is that to thee?" God's purposes for us are determined by Him, not by us.

But this does not absolve us from our duty. Predestination does not mean that we are automatons; we are responsible creatures with a secondary responsibility and freedom. Therefore, our Lord tells Peter, "Follow thou me." This Peter can do, as can we. In the Greek, the order of the words is, "Thou — follow me." It is personal and intensive. We are not to look at God's treatment of others and then envy their blessings. We are all called to serve in a particular sphere and way, and we are also being prepared for our eternal calling.

But this is a problem, because ours is an age that stresses equality. Although we may be fully aware of the evils of equalitarianism, we are still so much the children of our times that we hunger for a leveling that will favor us. This tacit equalitarianism is anti-Christian. Our urge to say, "Why me, Lord?" is wrong.

Again, without predestination there is no grace. Predestination and grace are simply different aspects of God's sovereignty. If we remove God's election from the scene, we then have man's self-electing works, and no gospel at all.

John, throughout his Gospel, stresses God's sovereignty and predestination. At the conclusion, he records that Jesus confronted the disciples with this fact. *What He said to Peter applied to all.* John might not die in the hands of executioners, but his sufferings were no less than Peter's. The isle of Patmos (Rev. 1:9), where he was held as a prisoner, was a particularly brutal slave-labor site which few survived. Every disciple was to be used by men exactly as God ordained, because all were Christ's witnesses.

In vv. 24-25, John tells us that his account is attested as true. Again, as in 20:30, John tells us that more books could be written about Jesus than the world could contain. Certainly, if a daily journal had been kept by the disciples, we would have several large volumes of detailed accounts. But this does not seem to be what John meant. What his language in 20:30 and 21:25 tells us is that fully to describe and account for Jesus Christ is impossible: as the Word of God, God the Son, He is, like the Father and the Spirit, *inexhaustible.*

Fully to describe a man would be difficult, but, because man is a creature and limited, *theoretically* it can be done. Not so with God. How can one describe or comprehend One who is eternal, infinite, and invisible, as well as almighty, all-wise, most holy, most absolute, and most free in all His being? To comprehend God would require of us a mind equal to God. Although He is incomprehensible, we can still know Him truly through His revelation, because He is totally self-consistent in all His being.

It is this that John refers to, and that all his Gospel is about. Since John wrote his Gospel, the number of commentaries on the life of Jesus Christ, studies in the Gospels, theological works on the subject, and more, have been legion. Yet each generation sees afresh His total relevance, and no generation can exhaust His meaning. John writes, orthodox Christians have always held, under inspiration of the Holy Spirit in a unique way. As in all Scripture, in John we see the words which are God-given. In John more than in Matthew, Mark, and Luke, the deity of Jesus Christ is dealt with most plainly, but John's final word is that the subject is, like the Person, inexhaustible.

But John, in his prologue, gives us a summation (John 1:1-18) which rings out like music. John Calvin once wrote of the Apostles' Creed that it should be sung, because it is glorious music.

There is another curious fact about John's ending. Mark and Luke conclude with Christ's ascension. Matthew tells us that the disciples assembled at the mount of ascension, and although he concludes his account with the Great Commission, the ascension is implicit. John does not include the ascension. He tells us of our Lord's many references to it, but it is not recorded. His account of Jesus Christ presents Him as forever present and yet eternally on the throne of glory.

Twice John tells us that much remains untold about the *signs* Jesus "did... in the presence of his disciples" (John 20:30f; 21:24f). Why did John not make such a statement earlier in his Gospel? Why at the end, in connection with the account of the resurrection, and His appearances thereafter? The *signs* are miracles with a meaning that reveals the Gospel. Nothing more clearly reveals the Gospel than Christ's atoning death and His resurrection. They tell us that Jesus Christ has destroyed the power of sin and death. John therefore deliberately limits the number of miracles he reports in order to point to and concentrate on our Lord's death and resurrection. The Jesus of history is He who made atonement for us, died, and was resurrected. His life cannot be understood apart from this, nor can we know His history in any other light. This is why John's "testimony is true," and, while books filling the earth could not contain all that could be said, the testimony given by John is faithful.

9:13, 264
9:23-31, 149
10:3, 17, 195
10:24-25, 208
10:30, 48
10:40, 179
11:3, 16, 32
11:4-6, 32
11:9, 10
11:11, 10
11:14, 9
11:25, 124
12:7, 264
12:9-14, 116
12:10-13, 115
12:46-50, 21
13:57, 41
14:21, 56
14:22, 59
14:23-33, 59
14:26, 59
14:32, 60
16:15-23, 72
16:18, 23
16:19, 272
16:21-23, 16, 220
16:21-28, 124
17:1-9, 191
18:10, 18
18:12, 128
18:18, 272
19:10-12, 20
20:20, 187
20:20-28, 178
21:12-13, 23
21:23, 95
21:25, 95
21:31f., 91
22:23-33, 145
22:36, 80
23:38, 23
24:36, 16
26:6, 158

26:6-13, 148, 157
26:22, 182
26:42, 57
26:51, 240
26:61, 25
26:64, 18
27:3-10, 183
27:11, 245
27:13-15, 264
27:17, 249
27:19, 248
27:32, 255
27:46, 260
27:50, 261
27:57, 264
27:62, 268
27:62-66, 154
28:4, 268
28:18-20, 232
28:19, 31
7:29, 145

Mark
1:10, 14
1:21-26, 115
1:29-31, 115
2:23-28, 116
2:27, 116
3:18, 17, 195
4:28, 16
5:23-43, 149
6:4, 41
6:45, 59
6:47-52, 59
6:51f, 60
10:42-45, 174
11:40, 123
12:38-40, 87
14:3-9, 157
14:19, 182
14:47, 240
14:58, 25
15:1, 247
15:34, 225, 260

The Author

Rousas John Rushdoony is a well-known American scholar, writer, and author of over thirty books. He holds B.A. and M.A. degrees from the University of California and received his theological training at the Pacific School of Religion. An ordained minister, he has been a missionary among Paiute and Shoshone Indians as well as pastor of two California churches. He is founder of Chalcedon Foundation, an educational organization devoted to research, publishing, and cogent communication of a distinctively Christian scholarship to the world at large. His writing in the *Chalcedon Report* and his numerous books have spawned a generation of believers active in reconstructing the world to the glory of Jesus Christ. He resides in Vallecito, California and is currently engaged in research, lecturing, and assisting others in developing programs to put the Christian Faith into action.

The Ministry of Chalcedon

CHALCEDON (kal•see•don) is a Christian educational organization devoted exclusively to research, publishing, and cogent communication of a distinctively Christian scholarship to the world at large. It makes available a variety of services and programs, all geared to the needs of interested ministers, scholars, and laymen who understand the propositions that Jesus Christ speaks to the mind as well as the heart, and that His claims extend beyond the narrow confines of the various institutional churches. We exist in order to support the efforts of all orthodox denominations and churches. Chalcedon derives its name from the great ecclesiastical Council of Chalcedon (A.D. 451), which produced the crucial Christological definition: "Therefore, following the holy Fathers, we all with one accord teach men to acknowledge one and the same Son, our Lord Jesus Christ, at once complete in Godhead and complete in manhood, truly God and truly man...." This formula directly challenges every false claim of divinity by any human institution: state, church, cult, school, or human assembly. Christ alone is both God and man, the unique link between heaven and earth. All human power is therefore derivative: Christ alone can announce that "All power is given unto me in heaven and in earth" (Matthew 28:18). Historically, the Chalcedonian creed is therefore the foundation of Western liberty, for it sets limits on all authoritarian human institutions by acknowledging the validity of the claims of the One who is the source of true human freedom (Galatians 5:1).

The *Chalcedon Report* is published monthly and is sent to all who request it. All gifts to Chalcedon are tax deductible.

Chalcedon
Box 158
Vallecito, CA 95251 U.S.A.